BRIDGES TO FEMINISM

Bridges to Feminism

Marcelle Auclair, Marcelle Ségal, and Women's Magazines in Twentieth-Century France

Sarah Fishman

OXFORD
UNIVERSITY PRESS

OXFORD
UNIVERSITY PRESS

Oxford University Press is a department of the University of Oxford. It furthers the University's objective of excellence in research, scholarship, and education by publishing worldwide. Oxford is a registered trade mark of Oxford University Press in the UK and in certain other countries.

Published in the United States of America by Oxford University Press
198 Madison Avenue, New York, NY 10016, United States of America.

CIP data is on file at the Library of Congress.

ISBN 9780197791318 (hbk)
ISBN 9780197791325 (pbk)

DOI: 10.1093/9780197791356.001.0001

Printed by Integrated Books International, United States of America

FSC MIX Paper FSC® C183721

The manufacturer's authorized representative in the EU for product safety is Oxford University Press España S.A. of Parque Empresarial San Fernando de Henares, Avenida de Castilla, 2 – 28830 Madrid (www.oup.es/en or product.safety@oup.com). OUP España S.A. also acts as importer into Spain of products made by the manufacturer.

ACKNOWLEDGMENTS

It gives me great joy to acknowledge the people who have supported and helped me over the years, especially my husband Andy Boyd and my guiding lights Patrice Higonnet and Dominique Veillon. At Oxford University Press, Nancy Toff, in addition to being an amazing editor, has been an unerring guide. Anonymous reviewers' suggestions proved most helpful as I completed revisions. Susan Ferber's extremely valuable feedback and suggestions have made this a better book.

Thanks for being great colleagues and friends to Geneviève and Yves Dermenjian, Isabelle LeCoufle, Laurence Doubinsky, Irene Guenther, Adriana Wechsler, Pat Kelly, Sandy Ott, Annette Becker, Judy Coffin, Julie Fette, Anadeli Bencomo, Fabien Théofilakis, Paula Schwartz, Lou Roberts, Miranda Pollard, Ken Mouré, Alice Conklin, Steve Zdatny, Jonathyne Briggs, Shannon Fogg, Brian Newsome, Steve Harp, Ludivine Bantigny, Carolyn Eichner, Jean Pedersen, Rebecca McCoy, and Joelle Neulander. My deepest gratitude to Daniel Solomon for his invaluable research assistance in Paris when the pandemic prevented me from going.

I am extremely grateful to the University of Houston for continuing to support my research and for awarding me a John and Rebecca Moores Professorship. The History Department has been a wonderful home over the years, thanks to my excellent colleagues and to our amazingly diverse students who inspire both my teaching and research. Thanks especially to Nancy Beck Young, Karl Ittmann, Cathy Patterson, Hannah Decker, and Bailey Stone. A special thanks to graduate students Dmitrii Blyshko and Nicole McCarthy, who were always ready to help whenever I needed a hand.

Thank you, Rob Zaretsky. Not only is your work an inspiration, but you also gave me confidence in this project, read drafts, and provided many insightful suggestions.

In college and graduate school, women's magazines were my guilty pleasure. I would stock up on copies at the airport before a flight. It may not be a coincidence that my research has long relied on French women's magazines as a major source. This book allowed me to learn more about how they started and the remarkable women who animated them. Contributing enormously to that effort, both Jean-Victor Auclair Prévost, Marcelle Auclair's grandson, and Anne Brunswic, Marcelle Ségal's great niece, kindly spent time with me, sharing their memories and insights, answering questions, and helping me untangle some mysteries. They generously took time to meet with me and shared photographs for this book. Thank you also to Auclair's great niece Sandrine Servant for kindly helping me find the photograph of Auclair as a child.

For their friendship, and for letting me stay in their wonderful apartment walking distance to the BNF, many thanks to Ridgway Scott and Jan Englund.

I could not have figured out how to create and use still shots from old television broadcasts without the help of Brett Bowles, leading scholar of French film, and Sophie Bachman from the Institut National de l'Audiovisuel.

Thanks also to my three amazing, smart, talented, if sometimes pesky, sisters Becca, Liz, and Ellen; stepmom Sue, my sorely missed family, parents Erwin Fishman and Lois Lyman and big brother, Steve, who was much nicer to me growing up than I was to my little sisters. Always in the back of my mind while working on 'my' two Marcelles were my grandparents whose lives overlapped with theirs in several ways. David Samuel Lyman, an amazing, larger than life personality, immigrated, like Ségal's parents, from Imperial Russia. My loving, smart, and talented grandmother, Cora Geneva Lyman, born two years before Ségal, dropped out of college to marry but went back as a grandmother and finished her college degree.

Last but not least, I am so fortunate to have such an amazing family. Thanks and big hugs to Andy, Alex, Katy, and Ezra. I love you thiiiiiiiiiiis much!

CONTENTS

Introduction

The Advice Columnist

I've got a problem
I've got a problem
I'm ugly, stupid and mean
She's young, rich and beautiful
She's not married yet
About that I can bet
Should I marry her for her money?
Marcelle Ségal answer my letter
Please help me find my soul mate
Marcelle Ségal answer my letter
Without you happiness will wait
Jacques Dutronc, "The Advice Column"

When Jacques Dutronc, at the top of the charts in France in the late 1960s, begged Marcelle Ségal for help in this song, his listeners knew exactly why. By then Ségal and her competing columnist, Marcelle Auclair, had become part of the fabric of everyday life in France. Historian of private life Antoine Prost described Auclair and Ségal as "confessors to the nation. New moral authorities, they dispensed intimate advice to millions every week."[1]

Few Americans would recognize their names then or now. However, in the United States, similarly essential figures, known by their newspaper pen names Abigail Van Buren and Ann Landers, dispensed advice to millions of Americans in the 1950s and 1960s. While the printed newspaper advice column straggles on, these days readers also turn to websites, blogs, and podcasts, some with self-deprecating names like Aunt Acid and Miss Information. Amy Alcon's column, "Ask the Advice Goddess," started in the *New York Daily News* and is now syndicated in over one hundred newspapers. Until the US edition of *Elle* ended her contract in 2020 after she accused Donald Trump of sexual assault, E. Jean Carroll's "Ask E. Jean" column had been the longest running advice column in American publishing.[2] Carolyn Hax, whose *Washington Post* advice column is syndicated nationally, attributes the success of the modern advice column format to Abby and Ann. "The advice column was a backwater of the newspaper and now it is so woven into our cultural fabric. These columns are loved and widely read. . . . That couldn't have happened without them."[3]

In my youth, in the mid-1960s, I manifested the curiosity about other people's lives that ultimately led me to the study of history by reading both Ann Landers and Dear Abby avidly. Not a morning person, I made myself get up first to grab the papers before my pesky younger sisters awoke. Decades later when I began to explore similar columns in France, it occurred to me that I knew next to nothing about the women who wrote the advice columns I used to read, aside from seeing the blurry images of ladies with teased, 1950s hairdos. Although I was unsurprised to discover that they both wrote under pen names, everything else about them astounded me. They were sisters, twin sisters. Their parents, the Friedmans, Russian-Jewish immigrants, escaped anti-Semitic pogroms that swept across Lithuania, then part of the Russian Empire, and landed in Sioux City, Iowa, in 1905. They named their daughters, born on the 4th of July 1918, Esther and Pauline, nicknamed Eppie and Popo. They became known in Sioux City as the Friedman twins. Strangely highlighting the fact that they were identical twins, Esther's middle name was Pauline, and Pauline's middle name was Esther. Growing up they dressed alike, shared a bed, and took violin lessons together. As they reached adolescence they often dated together, sometimes double dates, sometimes with the same young man, always dressed in the same outfit. After high school, they both enrolled at Morningside College in Sioux City, where they collaborated on the school newspaper's gossip column, "Campus Rat." They both dropped out of college during their junior year to marry in a joint wedding ceremony; Esther and Pauline wore identical wedding gowns. Their husbands served in the same unit during World War II. A decade after the war, the two families moved to different cities, Esther to Chicago and Pauline to San Francisco.

In 1955, the *Chicago Sun-Times* advertised for someone to take over an extremely popular feature. A journalist writing under the name Ann Landers responded daily to readers' requests for advice. Esther applied, got the job, and kept the name Ann Landers. Without telling her sister, Pauline devised her own pen name, Abigail Van Buren, and pitched the idea of an advice column to the *San Francisco Chronicle*. When she found out about Pauline's move, Esther felt betrayed. For nearly ten years the sisters barely communicated. Pauline (Abby) insisted that they never completely broke off relations and that the press exaggerated their rift. Indeed, Paul O'Neal described their "fierce rivalry" in *Life* magazine, as "the most feverish female feud since Elizabeth sent Mary Queen of Scots to the chopping block." In this case nobody lost a head, and eventually the sisters reconciled. According to the journalist who covered their joint appearance at their high school's fiftieth class reunion, they had gone back to finishing each other's sentences.[4]

Pauline died in 2013, eleven years after her sister. In the entry for the *New York Times'* annual year-end issue, "The Lives They Lived," Suzanne Shapiro wrote the entry for Pauline/Abby and included her sister Esther/Ann Landers, who had died many years earlier. "The woman who was Dear Abby was defined as much by her twin as by her column." To Shapiro, Abby and Ann "helped transform the prim, lovelorn column into a vital interactive conversation on modern mores."[5]

Perhaps not surprisingly for a sister republic, France also boasted a pair of influential advice columnists, Marcelle Ségal and Marcelle Auclair who became equally renowned in France in the 1950s and 60s. Unlike Ann and Abby, they had no personal relationship with each other. Also, Ségal and Auclair wrote for the top two women's magazines in France, *Elle* and *Marie-Claire*, rather than daily newspapers.

Women's magazines reached their peak circulation in France in that era, giving Ségal and Auclair wide audiences.[6] Guides, counselors, and confidants, they dispensed intimate advice to millions of readers.[7] But aside from sharing a first name, overlapping for a brief period before World War II at *Marie-Claire*, and responding to their readers, I began to wonder, who were these women? Where did they come from? Why did they manage to attract so many followers? Were they, as some in the 1970s purported, perpetuators of conservative values and ideas about gender? Or did they contribute to changing ideas in France about women, gender, and family life taking place at the very same time their readership peaked, in the 1950s and 1960s?

A generation older than the Friedman twins, both Marcelles were born in the 1890s. Their childhoods reflected the geopolitical upheaval that shook their families' lives. They shared many of their life experiences with other members of their generation. French people born in the 1890s, particularly women, experienced the most rapid and profound transformations of any generation before or since and lived through the two deadliest conflicts in history. On the sartorial level, girls born in the 1890s would have worn long skirts and, as they matured, corsets. They wore long hair in elaborate styles and covered their heads with hats. By the time the two Marcelles reached their 20s, everything had changed. Loose shift or drop waist dresses or even pants, no corsets, and short hair, the "bob," defined how women dressed every morning and moved through the world. Those changes in self-presentation reflected broader, equally revolutionary changes in the technology of daily life. In their youth, they knew horse-drawn buggies, long-distance communication exclusively through the postal system, and intercontinental travel by ship. By their 20s, the automobile had replaced horses in the city, and the telephone in France began to replace telegraph for long-distance communication by 1909.[8] Radio Paris began broadcasting in 1922.[9] Silent films of the 1920s gave way to "talkies" by the 1930s. More changes would follow World War II, commercial aviation and then television, but new technology after 1945 represented extensions of what people knew, a less radical change than those the two Marcelles experienced in their early lives.

In addition, the 1890 generation lived through two world wars. Unlike earlier warfare, twentieth-century total wars required the mobilization of all economic and social resources in support of the war effort. During World War I, known in France as the Great War, combat in Western Europe took place almost entirely in northeastern France. Beyond that, the war touched every family. All young men served in the French army when they turned 20 and remained in the reserves until age 40. Production to support the war mobilized large numbers of women; working-class women moved into munitions factories from other sectors, and middle-class women joined the labor force, often for the first time, in clerical positions and as schoolteachers, bus drivers, and postal carriers. By 1918 France had lost 1.4 million men, a higher proportion of its population than anywhere else except Serbia. One in four French men who turned twenty in 1914 were dead by 1918. While traumatized by the huge loss of life, the French people recovered rapidly after 1918 and, owing to France's largely rural economy, avoided the depths of the Great Depression of the 1930s. While World War II cost France fewer lives, it had a much wider direct impact on people living in France. New military technology, tanks and aircraft, led to tactics that spread destruction across much of the country. Foreign occupation, massive population movements, the deliberate targeting of civilian populations, Nazi genocidal anti-Semitism, and combat across the land in 1940 and again in 1944–45 left no place safely behind the lines. Millions of civilians experienced dislocation, destruction, and death. This war killed more civilians than soldiers in France. After the war ended, rebuilding France's damaged infrastructure and housing stock took a decade.

Auclair and Ségal's lives vividly distill the tumult of the first half of the twentieth century and its impact on women: war and peace, collaboration and resistance, race and gender, marriage and divorce, parenting and loss. Along with the changes in external realities, ideas and assumptions about women, sex, and gender also changed dramatically over the century. Until 1944 French women did not have the right to vote. Married women fell under the legal authority of their husbands, who had total control over the family's financial resources. Contraception and abortion were illegal. Women's subordinate legal status rested on assumptions about the natural inferiority of women's intelligence and ability to think logically. Women's primary purpose was to marry, bear and raise children, and maintain their proper place in the home. By the end of the twentieth century all of those assumptions, along with women's political and legal status, had changed radically.

Rather than simply experiencing those changes, Auclair and Ségal, using their platforms at two of France's most popular women's magazines, *Elle* and *Marie-Claire*, encouraged women to think for themselves and take control of their lives, challenging assumptions about women and gender. According to historian Dominique Veillon, the two women "were at the same time a reflection of society (cf Marcelle Auclair's editorials and Marcelle Ségal's advice column) and they contributed to forging a certain image of women."[10] While they never rejected general assumptions about gender, marriage, and family life, and never identified themselves as feminists, both Auclair and Ségal encouraged women not to feel bound by traditional expectations. They downplayed the importance of physical appearance and encouraged women to look out for themselves. Ultimately, they played a critical role in changing attitudes about women, gender, and relationships.

Their personal lives help clarify why they saw beyond convention. Both women's childhoods were shaped by fathers who, by their presence or absence, left them with less conventional experiences of family life. Both experienced unusual childhoods. Their early lives gave them entrée to worlds and cultures beyond France. Through their platforms at *Elle* and *Marie-Claire*, they served as guides to living and loving through the three decades of breathtaking economic growth, material prosperity, and social upheaval that marked the postwar years in France.

Bridges to Feminism: Marcelle Auclair, Marcelle Ségal, and Women's Magazines in Twentieth-Century France.
Sarah Fishman, Oxford University Press.
DOI: 10.1093/9780197791356.003.0001

1

The Earth Moved

Growing Up as Outsiders

My parents packed their suitcases and left with their daughter for a country where there were no chimneys.

MARCELLE AUCLAIR, *A la grâce de Dieu* (1973)

We were different, "not like the others." At school the other students treated us like curious creatures.

MARCELLE SÉGAL, *Moi aussi, j'étais seule* (1971)

Growing up, both Marcelle Auclair and Marcelle Ségal felt different from other people in the community, encountered the unexpected, and were outsiders. They both adapted to new communities, became fluent in multiple languages, and learned to balance diverse cultures and expectations. While circumstances differed, the deaths of male family members led both Auclair and Ségal to question patriarchal assumptions about the family and to become more independent and personally ambitious.

From Lithuania to Roubaix

The Schereschewskys, the parents of Marcelle Ségal, arrived in France sometime in the 1880s. They joined a larger influx of Russian Jewish immigrants, some of whom were escaping persecution, others suffering from economic distress. The Schereschewsky family came from Lithuania, which had been part of Poland until 1795 when Russia took over the region, gaining territory, resources, and people, including a large Jewish population. Polish law had restricted Jews to fifteen provinces, designated as the "Pale of Settlement." When Russia took the territory, it retained the restriction on Jews who were "fenced in"—the origins of the word "Pale" being the Latin for fence stakes—and prohibited them from owning land and from practicing certain professions. Conditions changed little for Lithuanian Jews (Litvaks) with the Russian annexation until the mid-nineteenth century.

The Russian Empire's humiliating military defeat in the Crimean War, which ended in 1856, jolted the tsar, Alexander II, into bringing Russia into the modern age. In 1861, Alexander emancipated the serfs and loosened restrictions on Jews. However, his assassination in 1881 brought progressive reforms to an abrupt halt. Rumors held Jews responsible for the assassination, unleashing a wave of anti-Semitic pogroms, violent attacks by local non-Jewish populations against nearby shtetls (traditional Jewish villages) across the region that continued for several years. Violence temporarily subsided after the mid-1880s, but by then thousands of Jews had escaped Russia and emigrated to the West.[1] Because France had emancipated Jews in 1791 from all "adjournments, reservations, and exceptions," it became a safe haven for Jews.[2]

Anti-Semitism was hardly limited to the Russian Empire. Across Western Europe, older religious and xenophobic forms of anti-Semitism combined in the nineteenth century with new theories of race built on distortions of Charles Darwin's theory of evolution. A number of scientists applied the Darwinian notion of biological evolution through natural selection to humankind.

Intent on categorizing and ranking human races, anti-Semites asserted that Jews represented an alien, primitive race threatening to pollute Christian Europe. In France, rising discrimination against the Jewish race led to a surge in anti-Semitic propaganda, political movements, and newspapers in the 1890s.[3]

Nevertheless, the legal emancipation of Jews in France a century earlier had created a rooted Jewish population that lived peacefully in the country who were assimilated into French language and culture. They watched with some trepidation the arrival of thousands of Jews from the East, immigrants who did not speak French, dressed differently, practiced their religion openly, and, like most immigrant groups, tended to cluster in certain urban neighborhoods. The anti-Semitic press referred to the arrival of Eastern Europe Jews as a "Jewish invasion," although the total population of Jews in France numbered only around 70,000 including the new arrivals.[4] Tensions exploded in 1894 when Alfred Dreyfus, one of the first Jews to enter the French army's officer corps, was arrested, accused of selling French military secrets to Germany, and convicted by court martial, setting off the so-called Dreyfus Affair, a two-decade-long crisis.[5]

In spite of rising anti-Semitism on the right, French law did not discriminate against Jews, and France continued to attract Jewish refugees like Marcelle Schereschewsky's parents. The Schereschewskys left their town (Taurogen) in the 1880s for economic reasons, not to escape pogroms.[6] However, they joined the large-scale, pogrom-triggered movement of Jewish immigrants from Russia, and, like many other Russian Jewish emigres, they first settled in Daumesnil, in the 12th arrondissement of Paris. Marcelle commented that this neighborhood was home to so many Russian Jews that among themselves they called it Domenilovka.[7] At some point before Marcelle's birth in 1896, the family with their two older children moved to Roubaix, a city in northeastern France, where her father started a small textile business. The year after Marcelle was born, her father died.

Northeastern France, known for being Catholic and conservative, was an inauspicious place for a family of Eastern European Jewish immigrants. The Schereschewsky family also had the disadvantage of speaking what Marcelle referred to as German (probably Yiddish, a German dialect), hardly a neutral language in France. Relations between France and Germany remained tense. During the Franco-Prussian war of 1870, the Prussian army had invaded and then occupied that region of France. After its army was quickly overrun, France signed a harsh treaty in January 1871 under which it lost significant territory on its eastern border. Prussia continued to occupy the northeast until France paid off a heavy indemnity. Even worse, from France's perspective, the war led to the birth of Germany's II Empire, a newly unified nation with a large, powerful military and a booming, rapidly modernizing industrial sector. A power that had quickly vanquished the legendary French army, which under Napoleon I had conquered much of Europe, loomed along France's eastern border. Anti-German sentiment ran strong in the 1890s. In that atmosphere, "in a very Catholic city, in the midst of the Dreyfus Affair," Marcelle Schereschewsky imagined how alien her widowed Jewish mother, who hardly spoke French, must have felt.[8]

Marcelle described the other ways in which she and her family stood out. The local people in that region tended to be fair-skinned and blond. Her family had darker skin and brown, curly hair. In school, "pale Flemish kids with long, silky curls made faces" and called them names. Not only did her family speak German, but they also ate "Russian" dinners of herring, black bread, and cottage cheese rather than steak and fries with wine.

They knew nothing about the local food and habits. "We never sat outside on the terrace of a café."[9]

When Marcelle's older brother reached school age, their mother tried to send him to the local Catholic school for reasons unknown. After a few awkward exchanges between her son and his teachers, the nuns suggested to his mother that she send him instead to a "school without God." Even in the godless public schools, their fellow students at first viewed the Schereschewsky children as strange and foreign. Marcelle and her siblings, however wanted nothing more than to speak, act, and dress like everyone else. Ségal credits their ultimate success to that powerful desire to fit in.[10]

One other thing stood out about them to their fellow students and especially to their schoolmates' parents: all three Schereschewsky siblings did extremely well at school. They absorbed everything, the rule of three, the metric system, the *Fables of La Fontaine*, and local geography, like little sponges, Marcelle explains.[11] Apparently their schoolmates' parents grew frustrated hearing from their children about "the three Ski's" who always took first place on exams. With academic success held in high regard in French culture, the other families wanted to know more about them and began inviting them for afternoon snacks. Marcelle's mother reciprocated. Slowly the families became friends. The three Schereschewsky siblings, happy to have been adopted by their classmates' families, became "more and more French by the minute." Soon they refused to speak German at home, stopped eating herring for dinner, and, little by little, began to live like the locals.[12]

Her mother, without abandoning her Jewish faith, adopted French ways, learning from her new friends how to knit and to make gauffres, or waffles, a specialty of the region. Quickly, Marcelle explains, they no longer stood out. They even picked up the local accent when they spoke French. The elementary school they attended used the standard history textbook at that time. Written by Ernest Lavisse, the book opened by introducing "our" ancestors, the Gauls.[13] Marcelle absorbed that lesson, "We had descended from the Gauls, like everyone else!" She testified to the public school's success in its mission of creating a unified French people. The school "melted us down in its melting pot, shaped us in its mold. Without the least ostracism, the least racism, the school had welcomed three little Russian Jews and made them French." Like the rest of her compatriots, Marcelle admitted, "the Marseillaise brings a tear to my eye."[14]

Clearly, their academic success served the Schereschewsky children well. Marcelle also credited her mother's good will. Had they continued to live as if in a separate enclave, they would have remained outsiders. Marcelle noted the importance of that experience in shaping her responses as an advice columnist. She advised letter-writers who felt isolated living in a new place without friends or family to get to know their neighbors and adopt the local ways.[15]

Another aspect of her childhood that deviated from traditional family life also influenced her later interactions with readers. Marcelle explored the impact on her personality of having grown up without a father. She noted that she knew little about how fathers were supposed to behave and never experienced the conventional gendered division of labor in the family. There had never been a man to "protect" the family and, as a result, she explained, she never felt the need for a man's protection. In the end, she was unwilling to accept a man acting as her protector. Marcelle also resented her mother idolizing her older brother, the only son, who got preferential treatment. She began to dream about being a boy. She never played with dolls and hung out with boys. In the language of the time, she was an "unfulfilled boy" (un garçon manqué), a better reflection of her reality than the equivalent English term "tomboy."[16] Her account raises interesting issues regarding her gender identity, although she never went further in discussing that or her sexuality.

Normal life for the Schereschewsky family and their community ended abruptly with the start of the war in August 1914. The German army passed through the northeast within days of invading Belgium and occupied the region throughout the four years of the war. After fifteen months of living under German Occupation, the Schereschewsky family took what Marcelle describes as "an epic voyage." To reduce the number of people in need of food Germany offered French families in the German-occupied north willing to pay a sizeable fee the option of returning to France by way of neutral Switzerland.[17] Marcelle recalled that the family left "without a kopek." They spent four days in a sealed wagon, traveling in and out of war-ravaged areas in Belgium, Luxembourg, Germany, and Switzerland. When they finally made it to Paris, their extended family took them in.[18]

Once they had settled in in Paris, Marcelle's relatives offered to pay for her to continue her education. Already 20, she turned them down, explaining that she preferred to earn money like an adult. She had seen women figuring out how to survive while their husbands were away at war. She no longer wanted to live "like a parasite, in prolonged adolescence." Her mother was heartbroken by Marcelle's rejection of pursuing higher education, but Marcelle had no regrets.[19] She found a job in a women's clothing store and got to know the other sales clerks, learned their slang, heard about their romances, and laughed at their jokes. She took orders, sent bills, marked prices, and cleaned up the dressing rooms piled high with rejects. Her boss insisted that every sales clerk smile, greet clients by name, and ask about their families. Marcelle joked that she learned this way of interacting with customers "50 years before the Americans!" and kept up these habits long after she left that job. The experience taught her that everyone has their own rich and interesting stories. From then on, she started conversations everywhere and with everyone: the taxi driver, the concierge, the baker, her neighbors.[20]

The money she earned helped her feel like an adult. Reveling in her independence, she purchased a used bicycle, a means of transportation her mother had long denied her. The bicycle as much as the job gave her a sense of freedom, allowing her to explore the city and its outskirts on her own. Marcelle notes that she was part of a larger trend during the war of young women learning to take care of themselves rather than waiting for a husband to take charge. Her independence, the skills she developed, and her curiosity about other people shaped her ideas about women's lives and laid the foundation for her future career.

Although she loved her job, about a year after the Armistice ended the fighting, Marcelle quit work and married a military veteran. A member of the circle of Lithuanian Jews in Paris, her husband, Maurice Cherchewsky, a second cousin, ran a wholesale textile business in the garment district.

From Commentry to Santiago to Paris: The French-Chilean Connection

Marcelle Auclair began her life in Commentry, a small town in central France near Clermont-Ferrand, where her family owned a sawmill. Unlike Marcelle Schereschewsky, Marcelle Auclair found her life and outlook profoundly impacted by her father. Victor Auclair had trained to be a carpenter. At 18, he joined a venerable artisanal organization, the Brotherhood of the Duty of Liberty, under the name "Bourbonnais, Child of Progress." Six years later he left Commentry to study architecture at the Ecole des Beaux-Arts de l'Architecture in Paris and after graduation, he worked as an architect on the construction of the Gare du Nord train station in Paris. When Victor's father died in 1897, he returned to Commentry to take over the family business. There he met Marie-Eugénie Rateau, whom he married in 1899. That same year their first child, Marcelle, was born. Three years later their second child, a son, died in infancy.[21]

Although she was only three, her brother's death was an extremely painful loss and led Auclair to practice a personal form of spirituality. She regularly climbed up into the attic and sat under the skylight in a shaft of light where she communed with her brother. She found herself immersed in peaceful clarity, "without form, without shape, diffuse but glowing." She experienced "a complete internal clarity that I never could name." Her parents never knew about this, but she retained a vivid memory of her time in the attic under the skylight. From that point on she sought to repeat that mystical experience of "beautiful love."[22]

The loss shook the entire family. Two years later, in 1904, Victor closed the sawmill and moved the family to Montluçon to pursue his primary interest, architecture. In particular, he began working with a new building material, steel-reinforced concrete, which he proposed using to build military barracks in Montluçon.[23]

Victor Auclair's experiments with reinforced concrete proved auspicious. The year 1906 proved to be extraordinarily active, seismically, along the entire Pacific coast of the Americas, with four major earthquakes. On April 18, San Francisco experienced a devastating 7.7 magnitude earthquake resulting in enormous destruction intensified by fires, causing an estimated three thousand deaths.[24] Four months later two even more powerful earthquakes struck on the same day, August 17. An 8.35 magnitude earthquake hit the Aleutian Islands off Alaska, followed about

Marcelle Auclair at age 4 in Commentry. Photo courtesy of Jean Victor Prévost.

twenty minutes later by the most destructive and deadliest earthquake of the year. An 8.2 magnitude subduction earthquake hit the port city of Valparaiso, Chile, at about 8 p.m. local time.[25] In a December 1906 report, Dr. Curtiss, employed at the Mills Observatory in Santiago, described the experience, starting with two hard shocks. "The din was very great and all around could be heard the shrieks of the people." In addition to the massive destruction, the earthquake, which also shook Santiago, killed an estimated 3,800 people and injured another 20,000.[26]

Auclair's rural childhood too "was suddenly shaken by the shock waves from San Francisco and Valparaiso in 1906."[27] As it happened, one of the world's leading experts on earthquakes at the time was Fernand Montessus de Balore, a French aristocrat,

Caption, Postcard, Avenue Brasil, Valparaíso Chile after the 1906 earthquake, Ed Carlos Brandt. Public domain.

military officer, and graduate of the Ecole Polytechnique. In June 1906, after the San Francisco quake, Montessus gave a lecture at the Congress of French Architects. It is not clear whether Auclair attended that meeting, but Montessus de Balore knew of Auclair's work with the new steel-reinforced concrete building material.[28]

As Chile struggled to recover, Valentin Latelier, president of the University of Chile, lobbied the government to create an institution dedicated to the study and training of local experts in the science of seismology. In 1907, the government agreed and invited Montessus de Ballore to serve as Chile's first "state seismologist." Montessus created a series of seismological observatories to collect geological data about the frequency and intensity of earthquakes, while also advising the government on preparing for future earthquakes. In addition, he was tasked with training local professionals in earthquake-resistant building methods.[29] Since few locals were trained in the new methods, he contacted Victor Auclair and invited him to come to Chile. In 1907, Victor moved with his family to Santiago to assist with the massive task of reconstruction.[30]

Montessus and the Auclair family joined a French community of about 3,300 in Santiago. In his nearly two decades there, Victor, who eventually became president of the local Alliance Française, collaborated on all of the major construction projects using steel-reinforced concrete, both in Santiago and in Valparaiso, including multiple churches, a water tower, municipal buildings, bridge pillars, a train station, and a military aviation hangar.[31] Nearly everything Victor Auclair built has survived the earthquakes that have hit Chile since they were constructed.[32]

Meanwhile the rest of the family settled into their new lives abroad. Marcelle attended elementary school at a local Catholic school. She retained a vivid memory from her time there. One day she peeked into the chapel and saw two nuns kneeling in a prayer of perpetual adoration, which she found both beautiful and puzzling. When she turned ten, Marcelle's parents, worried that she might never develop reading and writing skills in French moved her to the only option for schooling in French, a private single-room school.[33] Marcelle found the teacher, from Lille, far more intimidating than the nuns. Tall, awkward, bewigged, and tending to spit when she spoke, this teacher believed in strict discipline, with frequent "washing out of the mouth with soap" and abundant use of the fear of eternal damnation for mental hygiene and character formation. The students nicknamed her Rumpelstiltskin. A stickler for ensuring that students followed her rules, the teacher regularly tested her "no talking" rule by leaving the students alone in the classroom, then bursting in to catch anyone talking. She encouraged denunciation and had several informants, whom the rest of the students referred to as Judases. Marcelle survived the disciplinary reign of terror for four years, eventually figuring out a way to minimize the pain. A few tears rolling down her cheek accompanied by abundant sniffles satisfied her teacher's need to be sure Marcelle felt adequately guilty and ended the teacher's tirade.[34]

Rather than instilling a hearty fear of God, the excessive zeal and injustice of the teacher's religious harangues about the students' sinfulness left Marcelle unmoved. She did learn French, however. She also developed a technique for appearing to concentrate during the teacher's endless prayers and monologues. She found a book, *L'Education de la pensée* (*The Education of Thought*), that recommended drawing a large black dot on an empty white piece of paper and then staring only at the black dot for as long as possible. Marcelle, who found concentrating on the black dot easier than paying attention to the teacher's lessons, ultimately mastered a meditation technique.[35]

Finally, after much begging and emphasizing the benefits of learning English, when she turned fourteen Marcelle's parents agreed to send her to an American boarding high school; she never reveals the exact location. Once she arrived, the principal recommended that she spend a year in a separate class to learn English before starting her high school classes. Marcelle, horrified at the idea of losing an entire year, insisted that she knew enough English to keep up with her classmates. She managed to negotiate a two-month trial period, after which the school would make a final decision. In those two months, she studied day and night, managing to do well enough to stay in the regular classes.

Compared to the Catholic teachers she had experienced in Chile, she described her Protestant American teachers as "nice ladies who enjoyed life!" They did not overreact to minor misbehavior and had no objection to the students having fun. Her Spanish literature teacher quickly discovered Marcelle's love of reading and got permission for Marcelle to spend her recess period in the library. There, she gorged herself reading "Poe, Keats, Shelley, Byron, the Brownings, and—last but not least—Shakespeare." During her summers back in Chile, her father added French poets to her reading list.[36]

Not only did Auclair pursue scholarly interests, but she also returned to the spiritual quest that started after her brother's death. The family was Catholic by heritage although, like many French families in that era, her father never attended Mass while her mother went daily. However, her mother cared little about doctrine, attracted instead to Christ's messages of love and forgiveness. Both parents opposed the Catholic Church's intervening in politics. Auclair described her family's orientation as "non-clericalism" rather than anti-clericalism. Marcelle had little interest in attending Mass, but when she turned 16 a friend of the family gave her a book with the writings of the mystic Saint Teresa of Avila, which she devoured.[37]

Not long after that, a friend passed along a book by American author William Atkinson, *Thought Vibration*.[38] Auclair hesitated to read it, having dismissed ideas like those of Emile Coué, a contemporary French psychologist/pharmacist who introduced a popular self-improvement technique using the sentence, "every day and in every way, I am becoming better and better." But Marcelle read Atkinson and loved his ideas. Atkinson asserted that thought, like light and sound, consisted of waves or vibrations that passed through the body. External events impacted a person by modifying or reorienting those thought vibrations, but people could also modify their internal state by reorienting their own thought vibrations. When she had finished Atkinson's book, she passed it along to her mother who had been suffering from what, in retrospect, Marcelle realized was depression. Her mother, who had been feeling ill and listless and lacking in energy, recovered after reading the book and trying the techniques. As Auclair explains, Atkinson never substituted in her mind for Christian spirituality. What she had wanted was "a method for inner life." Atkinson provided that method.[39]

While open to exploration, Auclair did not buy into all forms of alternate spirituality. What she labels mentalism was in vogue in Chile. Marcelle described Chile as rich soil for the hidden world of the occult, attributing the attraction to the air, the light, and the ground always vibrating. People lived with the constant threat of another earthquake.[40] One summer she and her mother accepted an invitation to a session with a visiting Tibetan yogi. During the session Marcelle noted with cynicism the yogi's system of having each guest put a gold coin on the table, to practice "letting go." Understanding that the yogi would collect the coins after they left, Marcelle was less than impressed. She found the experience salutary, however, in teaching her about the importance of staying lucid and not getting taken in by what she called "Merchants of Paradise." Nevertheless, interested in exploring the yogi's beliefs, she read the works of Karma Yogi and Raja Yogi. Growing up, Auclair constructed a spiritual worldview and techniques to attain it, an amalgamation of a spiritual, non-doctrinal Christianity with eastern religions and Atkinson's New Thought techniques from North America. Eventually, she published a series of books to share her techniques with her readers.

Marcelle spent the years 1914 to 1916 in North America, the bloody first years of World War I in Europe. The United States had not yet entered the war, and Auclair rarely mentions it in her autobiographical writings. While she and her family were well aware of what was happening in France, they did not share the years of mobilization, struggle, hardship, and loss that their compatriots experienced. By 1917, when the United States entered the war, Auclair had returned to Chile, further removed from the shadow of war.

Auclair was deeply shaped by her "childhood and adolescence out of the ordinary in Chile."[41] In addition, the loss of her younger brother left Marcelle the sole recipient of her father's attentions. She recognized that her father, who encouraged her intellectual and professional ambitions, had always spoken to her as if she were a boy. "I was both son and daughter for him." According to Marcelle, "the 'young lady' aspect of my upbringing always escaped him."[42]

With her father's encouragement, when she returned to Chile from America, she created an intellectual circle, the "Salon des Annales de Santiago," which held monthly meetings bringing together French and Chilean readers to discuss history and literature. In her teens she began giving presentations at conferences sponsored by Chile's National Library, one at age 14 on Romain Rolland's *Jean-Christophe,* another at 16 on Cuban-born French poet José Maria de Heredia.[43] Inspired by her engagement with literature and poetry, in 1919 Marcelle published a book of poetry in Spanish, *Transparence*. She persuaded a local paper, *El Mercurio*, to let her have a weekly page to write about French literature.[44]

By the early 1920s, in addition to writing, organizing study circles, and exploring spiritualism, Marcelle experienced several tumultuous relationships with young Chilean men, complete with fits of jealousy, break-ups, and reconciliations.[45] Her father found her crying in her bedroom after one break-up. He had worried about what he considered a bad relationship. Seeing her red-eyed, he hugged her and quietly offered to pay for her to travel to France and stay in Paris as long as she liked.[46] She turned down the offer and quickly found a new boyfriend. That young man proposed marriage and she accepted, but they quarreled continuously. Her parents announced that they would allow her to marry only after she and her fiancé had gone three months without a fight. They never lasted more than a few weeks.

One evening, sitting on a park bench in a public park in the center of Santiago, Marcelle and her boyfriend had a loud and bitter fight. The park was empty except for an older man in the distance, who turned out to be the President of Chile, Arturo Alessandri (nicknamed the Lion de Tarapaca), taking his daily walk. He recognized Victor Auclair's daughter and sat down to ask the two of them what was going on. Marcelle and her boyfriend commenced "unwrapping our grievances, each of us intent on interrupting the other, seeing who could mount the quickest and strongest attack." Alessandri listened and advised them that they needed time to reflect. "At the point of tension where you are, I truly believe you need to spend some time away from each other." Then he left, sending his regards to Marcelle's family. A few days later her fiancé was offered a job at the Chilean Consulate in

Buenos Aires, which he accepted. Within a few months, they simply stopped corresponding.[47]

Still, Marcelle hesitated to leave for Paris. She had recently published a novel in Spanish, *Toya,* and had enjoyed reveling in the glowing reviews across the Chilean press. Then a critical review appeared in the Chilean Communist Party's paper, shaking her self-satisfaction. The reviewer complimented her talent as a writer but insisted she would never succeed in writing great literature "if she doesn't escape the theatrical milieu where she lives."[48] Marcelle recognized that she had surrounded herself with a circle of praise and affirmation. She wondered if the isolation of Santiago, with its small, supportive, but somewhat incestuous French community, had made it all too easy for her. Rather than feeling hurt, Auclair decided in the end that her critic had been right. *Toya* was good but could have been better.[49] She determined that she needed to go somewhere where nobody knew who her father was and where she would have to make her own way, without relying on her father's connections. She and her parents had separately come to the same conclusion. She needed to go back to France.

As Marcelle prepared to leave, her father wrote letters of introduction to his many friends in Paris. Given her budding writing career, he included Emile Mâle, a writer he had known since they were children, and many other members of Paris literary circles. Many of their French friends in Santiago also passed along names and addresses. The Secretary of the French Legation in Santiago, Henri Hoppenot, mentioned his friendship with the conservative Catholic writer Paul Claudel and his ties to the editors of *La Nouvelle Revue Française,* a leading French literary journal. He explained that because he had found one decent poem in her book of poetry, *Transparence,* he would find and pass along the name of a friend who owned a bookstore in Paris.[50]

Marcelle carefully tucked all the letters of introduction away in her trunk. While she was waiting for the train to take her across the Andes for her transatlantic voyage, a messenger ran through the crowds and handed her Hoppenot's last, promised, letter of introduction. She tucked the letter behind the mirror of her toiletry bag and forgot about it.

Once on board the ocean liner *Lutetia*, Marcelle, determined to declare her independence, had a flash of inspiration. She opened her trunk and gathered together the letters of introduction she had packed in there. Standing on the deck, she ripped them all into tiny pieces, scattering them like confetti over the Atlantic. She wanted to make it on her own, not reliant on her father as she was in Santiago. After the ceremonial scattering of the ashes, "I was free." She forgot about Hoppenot's last letter, which never moved from her toiletry bag to the trunk.[51]

Bridges to Feminism: Marcelle Auclair, Marcelle Ségal, and Women's Magazines in Twentieth-Century France.
Sarah Fishman, Oxford University Press.
DOI: 10.1093/9780197791356.003.0002

2

From the Roaring Twenties to the Sober Thirties

Careers, Marriage, Children, Divorce

Our brand-new independence went to our heads... If you could have seen us... Flat shoes, flat chests, flat waist, short hair; drinking, smoking like crematories, swearing like legionnaires.

MARCELLE SÉGAL, *Moi aussi, j'étais seule* (1971)

I wanted to do it myself, get by on my own resources

MARCELLE AUCLAIR, *A la grâce de Dieu* (1973)

After four years of war and loss, the 1920s represented an era of recovery and prosperity for France. It was the jazz age, the era of the garçonne, the French version of the flapper, with young women freed from the strict constraints of the pre-war era. As children, both Marcelles had experienced being outsiders. As young women, both Schereschewsky and Auclair started down the conventional path. They also took part in their own ways in the new world open to them as young women. The 1920s and '30s proved decisive to their lives, forcing each woman to adapt and adjust to unexpected and painful turns of fate, experiences they drew on in crafting their empowering messages to their readers decades later.

Marcelle Schereschewsky and the Loveless Marriage

In her memoir, Schereschewsky wrote obliquely about her marriage to Maurice Cherchewsky, framing her comments as if she were responding to a "typical advice column letter."[1] Schereschewsky set herself up as both a generic correspondent and the advice giver. Starting as the correspondent, she described her problem. A man she did not love had proposed. What should she do? If she turned him down, she would cause him pain. Switching to the role of advice giver, Schereschewsky responded to her imaginary correspondent's query by asking a question of her own. "Wouldn't marrying a man you do not love also cause pain? You should have the courage to turn down the proposal." Her imaginary interlocutor then pointed out that her young man, a soldier leaving the next day for the war front, did not want to wait until after the war. The soldier threatened to get himself killed in battle if she refused his proposal or postponed her response. Advice-giver Marcelle responded with a warning. "Blackmail with the threat of suicide? Ouch! Be careful. A young man who uses that tactic will use it again at every opportunity, and, on the first whim, will abandon you without caring about your pain." Having set up the imagined exchange, Schereschewsky admitted to readers that she had personal reasons for warning her readers against giving in to that kind of emotional blackmail. That was exactly what had happened to her.[2]

Schereschewsky described her marriage as "my first serious defeat. And well deserved." As she explained it, she knew that she was not the right woman for her fiancé. She even hinted that she might not be the right woman for any man, but left the possible implications unspoken. Schereschewsky agreed to marry her suitor out of the goodness of her heart, hoping to spare a "war hero" additional suffering, thinking she would be able to make a man she did not love happy. Only twenty years old when he proposed in 1916, Marcelle felt in her family like the "unloved child." Her widowed mother had always lavished attention on her older brother Philippe, a graduate of the elite Ecole Polytechnique. Marcelle found herself unable to resist Maurice's repeated proposals, his threats of suicide, the heroic folklore surrounding him as a decorated war veteran, and her family's pressure to marry. Ultimately, having promised to marry him during the war, she felt powerless to renege after his return. Accordingly, one year after the war ended, Marcelle ceded to family pressure and married Maurice. A year later in August 1920 their daughter, Suzanne Benjamine, was born. At that point, Marcelle Schereschewsky Cherchewsky's life trajectory seemed fixed. She would be the wife of a Jewish businessman, raising their child in a tight-knit Jewish immigrant neighborhood of Paris, surrounded by her extended Jewish family and community.[3]

But things did not work out as expected. Before the end of the decade, her marriage had "gone the wrong way around very badly."[4] Schereschewsky omitted the details of the trauma, except that their daughter died six months before Mardi Gras of 1928. "I would have preferred to skip over this chapter of my life," she confessed.[5] Her memoir provided no details about her daughter, how old she was, or even her name. The death notice revealed that Suzanne was 7 years old. It did not list her cause of death, but a recent interview with her great niece revealed that she died of meningitis.[6]

In her account, Schereschewsky mentioned Mardi Gras to explain that she had been preparing crepes, the traditional French fare for this Catholic holiday. She finished the crepes and waited for her husband to come home from work that late February evening. After hours of waiting, a brief message arrived late that night, in the form of a "pneu"—Paris was then crisscrossed by a series of pneumatic tubes for sending messages—from her husband notifying her that he would not be coming home again, ever.[7] Stunned, she had no way of finding or communicating with him. She cried and ate her cold crepes all alone. In retrospect Schereschewsky recognized that Suzanne had been the only thing keeping them together.[8]

As Schereschewsky experienced her loveless marriage, child rearing, the loss of a child, and divorce, Auclair returned to France for the first time in nearly two decades.

Across the Street from Shakespeare and Company

Before she left Santiago in 1923, Auclair's father passed along some advice. Victor knew she desperately wanted to become a writer. She had also agreed to serve as a correspondent for Chile's largest daily, *El Mercurio*. Victor urged her not to start writing as soon as she arrived. Instead, he recommended that she take time to get acclimated to Paris, attend concerts and plays, visit museums and exhibitions, window shop, and spend time in cafés. "Each café," he explained, "is its own little universe."[9] Marcelle followed his advice. Having discarded the letters of introduction from her French community in Chile, she persuaded her grandmother, who had come to Paris to keep an eye on her, to return to Commentry. On her own at last, Marcelle enjoyed what Paris had to offer. She especially loved browsing the bookstores near her hotel on the rue de Vaugirard.

After several weeks of exploring, Auclair decided it was time to clean out and organize her trunk and suitcases. In her toiletries bag she came across the sole "letter [that] escaped the massacre on board the Lutetia," the one from Henri Hoppenot, introducing her to Adrienne Monnier, the owner of a bookstore, La Maison des Amis des Livres (The House of the Friends of Books).[10] The bookstore happened to be around the corner from Marcelle's hotel, just behind the Place de l'Odéon. Extending from that plaza, the short and narrow rue de l'Odéon overflowed with small shops and bookstores. This one, at 7 rue de l'Odéon, in addition to selling books, also served as a lending library and hosted literary events. Finding Hoppenot's letter inspired Marcelle to visit the store, figuring she might as well sign up to borrow books.

Many Americans know about another famous Paris bookstore of the 1920s and '30s founded by an American woman, Sylvia Beach, who had done volunteer work in France during the war. American tourists had begun returning in large numbers to Paris after the war ended in 1918, joined by a sizeable group of young American women, many recent college graduates, wanting to help France recover.[11] Beach had heard many English speakers lament their inability to find English-language books in Paris. As it happened, Beach's mother had given her three thousand dollars to use as seed money to start a business of her choosing. Beach decided to use the money to open Shakespeare and Company, an English-language book shop. Having become friends with Adrienne Monnier, Beach used Monnier's store, the Maison des Amis des Livres, as a model.

In 1923, Monnier informed Beach, whose store was on a nearby street, that a shop space had opened up on the rue de l'Odéon. Beach quickly moved her store to 12 rue de l'Odéon, directly across from the Maison des Amis des Livres. Throughout the 1920s, Shakespeare and Company served as the central headquarters for English-speaking authors in Paris, including the large group of American expats who moved to Paris after the war, such as Ernest Hemingway, F. Scott and Zelda Fitzgerald, and Gertrude Stein. Authors from England and Ireland, including James Joyce and Wyndham Lewis, mingled with the Americans. With Shakespeare and Company, Beach inserted herself into the center of the twentieth-century Anglo-American literary world.[12] Like the Maison des Amis des Livres, Shakespeare and Company, "the obligatory stop of all Anglophone writers," both sold and loaned out books.[13] Both stores also served as informal gathering places and hosted formal events. They invited artists to display their work, sponsored lectures about literature, put on concerts by new and exciting composers like Francis Poulenc, and invited musicians to perform, including Paul Robeson.[14] In July 1925, Shakespeare and Company hosted a reading by T. S. Eliot of "The Waste Land."[15]

Face to face at 7 and 12 rue de l'Odéon, these two bookstores/lending libraries/gathering places facilitated fruitful exchanges in an urban space that came to be known as "Odeonia."[16] Monnier and Beach not only provided space but also encouraged creativity, awakened talents, and engaged their patrons in exciting discussions, earning the nickname "literary godmothers." Monnier also earned her own nickname, a pun based on the word "mère" or mother; she was called the Emir (L'amer which sounds like la mere/the mother) of the Odeon River.[17] Shortly after Shakespeare and Company moved to the rue de l'Odéon, Beach and Monnier's relationship moved beyond friendship. Beach fell in love with Monnier and moved into her apartment on their shared street at 18 rue de l'Odéon.[18]

In addition to selling and lending books, Monnier created a new literary journal, *Le Navire d'argent* (*The Silver Ship*), a reference to the symbol of the city of Paris.[19] To serve as editor-in-chief, Monnier hired Jean Prévost, graduate of the prestigious Ecole Normale Supérieure, student of renowned philosopher, novelist, essayist, historian, and journalist Émile-Auguste Chartier, commonly known as Alain.[20] Filled with articles on the latest books, reviews of current literature, short stories, and poetry, *Le Navire* published both established and rising French writers and reviewed books written in various languages available in French translations. It commissioned and published translations of contemporary American writers, including Walt Whitman, Ernest Hemingway, E. E. Cummings, and William Carlos Williams.[21] Inside the back cover of the February 1926 issue of *Le Navire*, author Valery Larbaud promoted Shakespeare and Company as "the best, the most complete and the most modern Anglo-American bookstore and library in Paris." He went on to note that the owner, Miss Sylvia Beach, plays a role "as an editor and propagandist in France for the most recent English and American works" who brought together the best of young American, English, and Irish writers in Paris.[22] Adrienne Monnier played an equally critical role for French authors. Historian Laure Murat described Monnier's bookstore as a "fixed point of the literary world for forty-five years and for several generations."[23]

Marcelle Auclair, having rediscovered Hoppenot's letter of introduction to Monnier, visited the Maison des Amis des Livres and quickly found herself drawn in by the books, photographs, and especially the plain table where Monnier, "the chief justice," held court, surrounded by a few simple chairs and a cast-iron stove. In one of her early visits to the store Marcelle caught a glimpse of Paul Valéry and froze, afraid to speak until Monnier introduced them. Auclair compared Valéry's scintillating conversational style to that of André Gide, "who pontificated a bit."[24] The circle of authors at the Maison quickly adopted Marcelle, "the little provincial from Santiago Chile." Monnier wrote Henri Hoppenot back in Chile to thank him for his letter of introduction. "Marcelle Auclair is a person of the rarest quality, and I am very grateful to you for having sent her."[25]

Notwithstanding the high-flying status of its clientele, Marcelle found the Maison's atmosphere down-to-earth and cordial. Discussions of the latest books, paintings, and music could be "sharp, demanding," but they were "never hurtful… The intelligence there was cheerful." Valery Larbaud, who set two of his novels in Latin America, encouraged Auclair to try her hand at translating works from Spanish, which she did.[26] Larbaud also encouraged Marcelle to follow through on her desire to write another novel. Once she had started, Larbaud read and edited every chapter; suggested the title, *Changer d'étoile (Under a Different Star)*; and connected her to one of France's most prestigious publishers, Gallimard.

Marcelle Auclair in Paris in the 1920s. Berenice Abbott, *Portrait of Marcelle Auclair*, 1925–30, Clark Art Institute, Getty Images 2148871591, Photograph by Berenice Abbott.

Auclair pondered the fact that "one move—slipping a letter behind a mirror—had determined the rest of my life."[27] The Maison also brought Auclair together with Jean Prévost, the young, talented, and compelling editor of *Le Navire d'argent.* Prévost frequented both sides of the rue d'Odéon. Sylvia Beach described him as "rather erratic, temperamental, moody. He was a grammarian and of a philosophic turn of mind."[28] Unusual for someone in French intellectual circles, Jean Prévost was also athletic and active in a wide variety of sports, including canoeing, kayaking, and fencing.[29] He particularly loved boxing, which led to one of the more unusual Franco-American exchanges of the era. Having learned of Prévost's interest, Beach organized a boxing match between Prévost and Ernest Hemingway.[30] Monnier, Beach, and the others "were looking forward to quite a literary sporting event with everybody present," but the boxers preferred not to have spectators and went off on their own.[31] *Le Navire* summarized the match as a draw, "but Hemingway injured his right thumb on Prévost's skull."[32]

Auclair and Prévost fell in love and married in 1926. Many years later, Marcelle quoted Jean's letter to her father, Victor, asking for her hand in marriage. His letter clarifies that not just her father but also her husband would encourage and support her literary aspirations rather than stifling her ambition or trying to limit her to domesticity. Jean reassured Victor that "Marcelle wants to continue her own career in Paris. I hope to be able to help her . . . In our literary efforts we can provide each other continuous services, which we have already begun to exchange."[33] He apologized that his circumstances, "without relatives or protection or outside support," meant he could not offer her financial stability. But he assured Victor of his faith in Marcelle's career. With her father's blessing, they married in the Atlantic coast town of Hossegor, a favorite of Paris literary and artistic circles, with novelist François

Mauriac and literary critic Ramon Fernandez as their witnesses.[34] After marrying, they moved into an apartment in the loft above Monnier's bookstore. They had a sofa bed, one chest, and a tiny gas stove. A little over a year after they married, their first child, Michel, was born, followed quickly by Françoise in 1929 and Alain in 1931.[35]

Ségal, the Divorcee

As Auclair's married life got underway, Schereschewsky's came to an end, forcing her to figure out how to survive on her own. The day after her husband left, Schereschewsky took stock of her situation. She had just enough cash to buy a metro ticket to go see her mother. After much discussion, her mother and the rest of the family came to a decision: Marcelle should move back in with her mother. But Marcelle was determined not to take what she viewed as a step back and to figure out how to survive on her own. To pay her rent, she found a friend of a friend who needed a place to live, "a very nice gentleman," and took him in as a lodger in her spare bedroom. The very nice gentleman was the first of many renters she took in over the years, people of all ages, both sexes, married and unmarried. Some of the renters became good friends, others she describes as "des dingues" or nutcases—noting proudly that in her forty years of renting, she only had to call the police twice.[36] Marcelle loved the irony of being a single woman who never lived alone.

In addition to renting a room out, she also had to find a job. Although she had worked in a clothing store prior to the war, a decade later she had to start over again. Her ability to speak English was an asset. Marcelle also concluded that she must not have been too bad-looking because a fashion house looking for an agent hired her on the spot. By the 1920s, Paris had become a global fashion center for designers like Coco Chanel, Elsa Schiaparelli, and Jeanne Lanvin. The big houses inspired smaller start-up fashion houses all over Paris. In the years after the war, boatloads of wealthy Americans arrived in Paris every day. Schereschewsky got a job with a small fashion house reaching out to the arriving American women, well-to-do potential customers. Because newspapers included daily information on ship arrivals, Marcelle knew both when the Americans were docking and which hotel they were staying in. She started every day scanning the papers, writing down arriving passengers' names and corresponding hotels, and setting off with an armful of dresses. At each hotel, she inquired at the front desk about one of the women on the list for that hotel, as if she were delivering an order. When she arrived at her intended target's hotel room, she knocked on the door and tried to sell the dresses. After her first "client" either purchased or refused a dress, Marcelle then knocked on other doors, continuing to peddle the dresses.[37] Schereschewsky took on the challenge with her usual aplomb, amazed that none of the potential customers treated her rudely, even if they were not interested. She managed to sell a few dresses, partly because the Americans found her French accent "cute." But the job came to an end when the management at one of the hotels figured out what she was up to, chased her off the property, and told her never to return. Marcelle nonetheless showed up at the hotel the next day because she had made an appointment with one of the guests. Quickly escorted out, she returned the pile of dresses to the fashion house and quit her job. Luckily her employer paid her commission for the sales she made before she quit, giving her a small financial cushion of eight hundred francs.[38]

Amidst the booming stock market of the late 1920s, one of her friends knew of a banker needing a secretary and recommended that Marcelle apply. The banker agreed to meet with her, but the discussion ended quickly once he realized that Marcelle could neither type nor take dictation. The banker complained, "What the f. . . am I supposed to do with someone who's not good at anything?"[39] Having been rudely awakened to her need for new skills, Marcelle spotted a poster advertising secretarial training, with job placement guaranteed. She signed up for a year-long course in typing and dictation. In the meantime, she supplemented her fashion house commission nest egg by tutoring newly arrived Russian immigrants in French. Unlike Schereschewsky's cohort of Russian Jewish immigrants, the most recent immigrants included primarily "white" Russian elites escaping the Russian Revolution. Even before completing her year of secretarial training, Marcelle secured a secretarial position, mastering the remaining clerical skills "on the job."[40] Years later, the lesson she learned about the importance of employable skills regularly found its way into her responses to her readers.

Another bank job finally opened up. When she arrived for her interview, the employer apologized because the job was not, strictly speaking, secretarial. Rather than dictation and typing, she would be tasked with classifying and filing financial information. The pay was good, so Marcelle took the job and found it "not at all unpleasant."[41] She spent the day searching newspapers for articles about finance, gluing them onto sheets, and figuring out how to classify and file the articles for future reference. She found the task like piecing together a puzzle, a challenge she enjoyed. She also learned quite a bit about global financial markets. Marcelle marveled at the other secretaries who typed with remarkable speed and accuracy, even in English. To improve her skills in the hopes of moving up, Marcelle took a commercial English class during her lunch breaks and was able to advance to become secretary to one of Paris's top bankers. In that job, she continued documenting financial markets, which was what she was doing when the New York stock market crashed on October 29, 1929. On Black Tuesday, Marcelle struggled to keep pace with plummeting stock prices as losses piled up. By the end of the day the market had completely collapsed.[42]

Personal Life

During those years, Marcelle Schereschewsky lived "the roaring twenties." Single, earning a decent salary, and free of family obligations, she regularly stayed out all night long drinking and dancing at nightclubs. She signed up for a variety of night classes—Spanish, English, even a dance class. Her fellow students came from all walks of life, "an ex-consul, café waiters, hair stylists, lesbians... Oh, it was never boring." Often she found herself with just enough time to get back to her apartment, clean up, gulp down a strong cup of coffee, and run off to catch the metro for work. However, her days of burning the candle at both ends eventually came to an end. Late one night at a club, she explained that she, like Joan of Arc, heard a voice. In this case, rather than Saint Catherine, the voice she heard was "Saint Fatigue" urging her to go home and get some sleep.[43]

Her job offered something unusual at the time to its employees, a month of paid vacation. Putting away some of her earnings all year, Schereschewsky saved enough to travel to Spain, Germany, Austria, the Netherlands, and England. One year, she traveled to Palestine, interested in learning about the kibbutz system.[44] As she traveled, Marcelle noticed that both because she was French at a time when few residents traveled outside of France and because she was a woman traveling on her own, people found her either intriguing or scandalous. She discovered that hotel owners hated single female guests during high season for taking up a room and a table that could have been sold to two people but loved them in the off-season. The novelty of her status and tendency to travel off-season made it easy for her to strike up conversations and make friends. Locals regularly offered to show her attractions and to take her boating and hiking. Hungry for experiences, she accepted all offers. She described having seen Holland before the dykes and paved roads changed its relationship to the sea. She visited kibbutzim in their early, spartan manifestation.[45]

As Marcelle traveled, she began writing about the people and places she encountered. Hoping other readers might find her observations interesting, she tried to find a magazine or newspaper interested in publishing her essays. Although she sent samples to several editors, she got no responses. Marcelle's aunt encouraged her not to give up but to go in person to meet the editors. Marcelle pointed out that she could not afford to take time off from her full-time job to try and meet editors. Her aunt, an experienced salesperson, offered to go in her place and started by pitching Marcelle's essay on the kibbutzim in Palestine. One editor, intrigued, informed her aunt that, given Marcelle's talent, he would be willing to meet with her. When she arrived, the editor quickly disabused her of the idea that he might actually publish her article about Palestine. At that moment, the editor explained, nothing of interest was happening in Palestine, no wars, no revolutions, no earthquakes. "Journalism" he explained, "is the news." Having noted her talent as a writer, he advised her to read at least one newspaper every day, front to back, using colored pencils to highlight anything new. Then she should practice writing up brief summaries, a few lines at most, about those stories, to learn to pull out the essential elements. Doing that regularly would teach her what was considered "news" and how to write about it. Once she developed that skill, he assured her, she would be sure to get something published. While the meeting did not turn out as Marcelle had hoped, she did credit that editor with teaching her an essential aspect of journalism. The news, like a soufflé, had to be eaten hot or it would deflate.[46]

Much to Marcelle's surprise, her aunt's efforts paid off, as she managed to place two of Marcelle's articles. Although the pieces were edited down to three lines and appeared on the third page, Schereschewsky and her aunt rejoiced at her success and spent her entire paycheck on one celebratory meal. Marcelle learned a critical lesson: to have a chance at getting published, her articles had to touch the readers' emotions.

Schereschewsky noticed a new weekly magazine for women, the *Journal de la femme (The Woman's Journal)*, which first appeared in 1932. Her aunt submitted one of her articles to the journal's director, Raymonde Machard, who accepted it straight away. Machard, the author of a series of steamy romance novels with titles like *Possession, Seduction,* and *Two Kisses,* wanted to meet Schereschewsky.[47] Marcelle offered to quit her bank job and join the *Journal de la femme.* Although Machard declined her offer, she did publish Marcelle's very first full article, giving it an illustrated double page. The article, "Assembly-Line Meal," was listed as the first in a series called "In the margins of 'Modern Times.'" Her article described a new phenomenon in Paris: popular restaurants that served hundreds of meals between noon and 2:00 p.m. to working women with little time or money to spare. Schereschewsky knew about one such restaurant because she herself relied on it while working at the bank. She explained that, while it had not been conceived of as a form of Taylorism or rationalization, these restaurants had figured out how to quickly meet a large demand using a minimum of means.[48] From Marcelle's description, it was a cafeteria serving a variety of food and beverages for a modest flat price.

Happy with the response to that piece, Machard encouraged Schereschewsky to submit more articles but urged her to create a new name and identity. As she prepared to publish Marcelle's first article, Machard grew frustrated. "Scheu... Scheu... What the heck is that? You'll never go down in history with a name like that." Marcelle mentioned her mother's maiden name, Ségall, which Machard preferred, using Ségal without the last "l" as Marcelle's by-line for the article.[49] The *Journal* published two more of Marcelle's articles, including her piece on kibbutzim in Palestine, which appeared on the front page.[50] An illustrated article on the Netherlands took up a full page that extended to a second page.[51]

Unfortunately, Marcelle's run of articles in *Le Journal de la femme* came to an end when she landed unexpectedly in the hospital with a high fever, shortness of breath, and a rapid heart rate, passing in and out of consciousness. Aside from mentioning the episode, Ségal/Schereschewsky omitted all specific information about her illness in her memoirs, noting only that her near-death experience left her with an even more intense appreciation for life.[52] During her stay at the hospital, she received an exciting offer of a full-time job as an editor and contributor for a women's magazine that had recently started up, *Marie-Claire*.[53] The journalist who persuaded a publisher to start the new magazine was Marcelle Auclair.

Auclair: Personal Pain, Professional Success

Marcelle acknowledged that Jean never saw her as a rival or as less deserving of pursuing her writing career. He always supported her professional ambitions. For years after Marcelle and Jean married, their relationship thrived even as they struggled financially.

Some of the writers in their circle, André Gide, Jean Cocteau, André Maurois, and Valery Larbaud, lived off large personal fortunes. By contrast, both Auclair and Prévost came from middle-class families.[54] Like their colleagues of modest means Marcelle and Jean constantly took paid work, such as writing brochures for pharmaceutical products. Marcelle worked as an assistant for author Paul Morand. Jean wrote letters on behalf of a "society lady." One day, Auclair found two of their children, Françoise and Michel, repeating to each other "what are we going to do? How are we going to make it?" When Marcelle asked them what they were doing, Françoise explained that they were "playing mom and dad."[55] Marcelle and Jean also found more satisfying jobs. Together they undertook a number of important translations, notably of Federico Garcia-Lorca's poetry and his play *Blood Wedding (Bodas de Sangre)*.

At the time Prévost also served as a reader for the publisher Rieder (which in 1939 merged with another press to become the Presses Universitaires de France). One of the authors Jean had worked with at Rieder was moving and invited the couple to take over his apartment near the Seine River on the avenue de Versailles, in the tony 16th arrondissement. Jean spent hours walking along the banks of the Seine, getting to know the local mariners who worked on the barges, observing how they lived, worked, interacted, and spent their free time. From those exchanges, Prévost wrote his most successful novel, *Les frères Bouquinquant (The Bouquinquant Brothers)*, published in 1930, which won the Blumenthal Prize.[56]

Early in their marriage, Auclair struggled to manage full-time parenting and housework. She had never learned to cook, and her efforts did not meet with much success. Eventually her father offered to pay for a housekeeper/nanny, an offer Marcelle quickly accepted. While it may have seemed extravagant given their limited means, she decided that the entire family would benefit if she focused on writing rather than on cooking and laundry.[57] Marcelle knew of other women whose husbands insisted that they become full-time homemakers after marriage, but Jean fully supported her decision. In a conversation with her daughter many years later, Marcelle explained, "your father was more open-minded." She later drew on this experience with her readers, both on the limits of domesticity as a full-time occupation and on the importance of family support to maintain a professional life as a married woman with children. She also pointed out that, given her deep psychological need to work, if Jean had tried to limit her professional life she "would not have let it happen."[58]

In spite of their financial struggles, their early years together were happy. It was a time that, in retrospect, Auclair described to her daughter as "years without having to complain about your father."[59] Nonetheless, his manners at times were lacking. Auclair noted that rather than holding the door for her, he elbowed past her to go through first. But he was also "capable of so much tenderness, such kindness! He was so witty."[60] Jean introduced Marcelle to journalism circles in the city as he was a regular writer for *Marianne*, a left-wing literary weekly published by Gallimard.

One of *Marianne's* editors, Josette Clotis, invited Marcelle to lunch and unintentionally launched her journalism career.[61] As they finished their meal, Clotis apologized for having to leave before they could have coffee. She explained that the author Colette had agreed to write a weekly beauty column for *Marianne* but had never warmed to the assignment. Clotis constantly struggled to coax the weekly article out of her. When Colette refused, she had to scramble at the last minute to fill the empty space. The piece was due by 3:00 that afternoon, Clotis explained, but as of lunchtime it had not arrived, so she planned to rush over to Colette's place and badger her to get it done. Upon hearing the problem, Auclair proposed that Clotis stay and enjoy her coffee. She, Marcelle, would write something by the deadline, ensuring that Clotis would have something to substitute if Colette did not deliver. If Colette's piece arrived, Clotis could just discard Auclair's essay. Not surprisingly, Colette failed to deliver, and Auclair's piece appeared. When Colette saw Auclair's piece, she told Clotis, "She's not too bad, our little Auclair, on the topic of beauty... Couldn't you give her that rubric? It annoys me." The editor-in-chief, tired of the struggles with Colette, offered Auclair the column.[62]

Marcelle also began writing columns in another women's weekly, *Femme de France (Woman of France)*, becoming a regular contributor by 1931. Often, her articles focused on physical fitness with illustrations of exercises for women. Former businessman and press magnate Jean Prouvost noticed Auclair's column and decided he wanted something similar in his popular daily, *Paris-Soir (Paris-Evening)*. He offered Marcelle a "woman's page" where she could write under the moniker "Auntie Marcelle." Prouvost, having made his fortune in the textile business in the Nord, had become by the 1920s a highly influential figure in Paris press circles. In 1930, Prouvost purchased *Paris-Soir*, a daily that had started in 1923, and transformed it. Unlike many of the papers in France, *Paris-Soir* remained politically unaffiliated, promising to present the news objectively. However, Prouvost also developed and adopted new techniques to increase readership, using the attention-getting/sales-driving techniques of the tabloid press. Juicy sensational stories filled *Paris-Soir*'s front page, leading many intellectuals to refer to it contemptuously as "Pourri-Soir" (Rotten-Evening instead of Paris-Evening). Notwithstanding the scorn of elites, by the 1930s, *Paris-Soir* had a circulation of over two million, dwarfing all other Paris dailies. By the eve of World War II, its circulation had increased to 2.5 million.[63]

As Auntie Marcelle, Auclair wrote essays about topics of general interest to women and responded to readers' letters. The column proved to be a big hit. Auclair explained that the opportunity to interact with her readers taught her something important. Regardless of background, wealth, marital status, age, or education, women wanted "to be happy and make the people they love happy."[64]

On to *Marie-Claire*

Given the success of her woman's page, Auclair approached Prouvost with a proposal for a new magazine for women centered on "life's pleasures." Auclair assured Prouvost that this new magazine for women would differ from what was already on the market. *Femme de France* used a standard daily paper format, newsprint with black-and-white photos, as did the woman's paper Ségal wrote for, *Journal de la femme*. The era's illustrated weekly women's magazines focused entirely on high fashion for elite women. Marcelle envisioned a magazine accessible and appealing to all women, with ample illustrations, visual materials, tips for everyday living, recipes, reviews of books and films, and suggestions for activities. It would respond to readers' interests and invite their letters. Prouvost first responded in horror, "I will never publish a weekly!" Unfazed, Auclair contacted another publisher, Gallimard. The owners, Gaston and Raymond Gallimard, liked Auclair's idea and even came up with a title, *Anne-Marie*, the inverse of Marianne, symbol of the French Republic. When Prouvost heard about her meeting with the Gallimard brothers, he accused Auclair of betrayal. "You've cuckolded me! You're going to put out a magazine with Gallimard?"[65] Auclair pointed out that she had proposed the idea to him first, and he had rejected it.

At that point, Prouvost set up a meeting with Gaston and Raymond Gallimard, in theory to talk about plans, but actually hoping to scare them off. It worked. They turned the project over to Prouvost, who came up with the magazine's title: *Marie-Claire*. According to Vincent Soulier's study of women's magazines, Prouvost named the magazine after Marie-Claire Servan-Schreiber, daughter of fellow journalist Robert Servan-Schreiber, who "had the presence of mind to call Prouvost just as he was looking for a title for his new magazine."[66] However, Auclair's long-time collaborator, Jeanne Dodemann, had a simpler and more likely explanation. Prouvost adopted the name of the eponymous heroine of Marguerite Audoux's best-selling 1910 novel *Marie-Claire*, winner of the Prix Femina.[67] In this semi-autobiographical fiction, Marie-Claire, an orphan, suffered years of hardship. At a young age she went to work as a farmhand and then moved to Paris to work as a laundress. Eventually her hard work paid off, and she found success.[68] The name *Marie-Claire* signaled the magazine's outreach to women from all backgrounds with its message that every woman could find happiness and reach her potential.

In its first issue, Marcelle Auclair's editorial presented "What *Marie-Claire* Brings You." The team had a goal: "Give the French woman, in one magazine, every week, everything that could possibly interest her or be useful for her." They promised to keep the format both luxurious and practical. The pages dedicated to beauty and hygiene would allow the readers "to take care of themselves, protect their faces and their bodies without spending much and without taking too much time." As for fashion, they would include high fashion but also provide patterns that any woman could make and wear. They provided practical suggestions and advice "to make your life easier." Every issue included short stories and listed public lectures, entertainment, and activities. Their goal was "to understand the condition of women in modern life. We think of *Marie-Claire* as kind of a young girl or French woman, someone simple and elegant, enthusiastic and measured, courageous, selflessly committed to doing her daily tasks, but also very happy. All of you are a little bit *Marie-Claire*, and this magazine was designed for you."[69]

Marie-Claire launched in March 1937 and quickly took off. Soulier's study of women's magazines emphasized its importance for France. "*Marie Claire* brought to France the modern feel of the American woman's magazine." Beyond that, the magazine "had demanding editorial standards, thanks to the talented pens" it recruited.[70] By 1939 its circulation reached 900,000.[71] To Auclair, a sure sign of *Marie-Claire*'s success in reaching its readers was when a doctor told her that all of the female patients he visited in hospitals and clinics had copies of *Marie-Claire* on their bedside tables.[72]

The Slap that Ended a Marriage

Unlike her blossoming career, by the 1930s Auclair's marriage proved less validating, in spite of Jean Prévost's wholehearted support of her literary and journalistic endeavors. They had agreed from the start to be completely honest with each other. For Jean, that meant telling Marcelle about the extramarital affairs he started having after their third child was born. In his mind, he was not "cheating" on her because he never lied or tried to hide anything. For her part, Marcelle found his extramarital sexual behavior extremely painful but, out of bravado, she later explained, she never responded emotionally, determined not to cause a scene. She eventually started her own extramarital relationship with someone whose name she never revealed.[73] In conversation with her daughter forty years later, Auclair lamented her calm response to Jean's affairs. If only she had protested the very first time, if she had let Jean know how painful his affairs were for her, if she had manifested her love for him, perhaps he would have stopped. Her phony amour-propre meant that "I played fake cards."[74] Auclair, strong, successful, and contrarian, even blamed herself for her husband's philandering. Ironically, Jean Prévost also blamed Marcelle for the failure of their marriage. Marcelle had an intense fear of water and had never learned to swim. If she had only gone canoeing with him, Jean (unconvincingly) insisted, he would never have cheated on her.[75]

About a year after *Marie-Claire* launched, a couple invited Marcelle and Jean to a dinner party. Marcelle knew that Jean had been sleeping with the evening's hostess and had recently slept with another married guest. Still, she agreed to go and arranged to meet Jean at the Odéon Metro station after work so they could arrive together. At the end of a particularly hectic day, Auclair left the office much later than she had intended and rushed straight to the dinner party. Meanwhile Jean waited for her at the Odéon station. He finally arrived late, furious at having been stood up. When Marcelle realized what had happened, she apologized profusely. Jean, furious, slapped her and announced, "That doesn't change a thing about the beating you're going to get when we get home."[76] Marcelle never directly mentioned the fact that Jean slapped her; her daughter revealed that. Nevertheless Marcelle insisted that she had no doubt his promise of a beating was an empty threat.[77]

In a novel published nearly twenty years later, *Mauvais coeur* (*Evil Heart*), Auclair included a scene from the point of view of a fictional wife who had also mistakenly left her husband waiting. In the novel, which she later regretted as "too autobiographical," Auclair explored her emotions, expressing the profound sense of humiliation she had felt. Fiction provided an outlet for Auclair to write about her thoughts that night. In the novel, after the husband slapped her, the main character spent the rest of the evening pondering what it all meant, thinking back on her marriage as waves of emotion rolled over her. "Manifestations of anguish, of expectation, of despair, of disgust: the tension at the bottom of the stomach, the feeling of emptiness at the base of the spine, followed by skipped heart beats, pain in the chest bones, heaviness in the arms, legs, all of this threw her down onto a couch from which she immediately jumped up, driven by anguish as if she was on springs."[78]

Years later, Marcelle explained to her daughter that she understood that Jean had been "on his 'territory' " in front of two of his paramours. Having been stood up by his wife, Jean wanted to "be the rooster." Even after the slap and his public threat of a beating Marcelle made several attempts to talk to him out of earshot of the other guests. Jean coldly rejected her peace offerings. At that moment, Marcelle knew their marriage was over. She made it through the meal knowing what her next steps would be, then tried to slip out quietly, hoping to leave without notice. Just as she reached the doorway, she bumped into the host. She asked him not to say anything about her leaving, claiming that she was tired after a long day and telling him to let Jean know she had left if he asked. As she put on her right glove, she noticed Jean in the background closing in on the hostess, at which point the host, in a detached tone, asked Marcelle if her husband was "my wife's lover?" Marcelle responded by asking him, "Is your wife my husband's mistress?" She pulled on her left glove and walked out the door.[79]

Auclair returned home, packed her bags, and left that night. The divorce was finalized in 1939. In the end Jean and Marcelle parted on good terms and remained friends. Marcelle even agreed to separate the children. Except during his military service at the start of the war and after he joined the Resistance full-time in 1944, their two sons, Michel and Alain, lived with him, and their daughter, Françoise, lived with her. In a parallel to Ségal's experience, Jean had apparently threatened to kill himself if she "took" the boys from him.[80] Prévost's contradictory and overdramatic response to the divorce emerges in his personal papers. He journaled daily and wrote long letters to a wide variety of friends and lovers. At times he wrote at length about Montesquieu or Stendhal; other entries and letters include detailed accounts of day-to-day activities. In his journal he refers to Marcelle by her last name, "Auclair," as if she were just an acquaintance. Shortly after Marcelle moved out, Jean started a serious relationship with another woman, a doctor named Claude van Bièma. His letters to van Bièma included descriptions of his interactions with "Auclair." Notwithstanding his relationship with van Bièma, Jean reacted with dismay when Marcelle notified him that she had begun divorce proceedings, opening a note to van Bièma dramatically: "Disaster! Auclair wants a divorce."[81] Despite his distress, Prévost married van Bièma shortly after the divorce came through.

Convergence

By 1939, Marcelle Ségal and Marcelle Auclair had both experienced marriage, parenting, and loss. Their difficult marriages brutally awakened them to the messy reality of married life, disabusing them of any romanticized visions they might have had. Their painful divorces, at a time when divorce was rare, left them having to figure out how to make a living.[82] Although they did not develop a personal relationship with each other, they both found professional success working at *Marie-Claire*, Auclair as journalist and editorialist, Ségal as editor and contributor. They had already experienced a wide range of life events they drew on as journalists.

Bridges to Feminism: Marcelle Auclair, Marcelle Ségal, and Women's Magazines in Twentieth-Century France. Sarah Fishman, Oxford University Press.
DOI: 10.1093/9780197791356.003.0003

3

Surviving War and Occupation

It's hard to feel like a pariah in your own country.

MARCELLE SÉGAL, *Moi aussi, j'étais seule (1971)*

We didn't really feel like telling women "You can all be pretty!"

MARCELLE AUCLAIR AND FRANÇOISE PRÉVOST, *Mémoires à deux voix (1978)*

The onset of another war transformed both Ségal and Auclair's lives yet again. They shared the four years of upheaval, trauma, and grinding hardship with their compatriots. People in France often refer to the four years from the Battle of France in 1940 to the Liberation in 1944 as the "Dark Years." Ségal pointed out that people born after the war had "never gotten stuck on the roads, never counted their bread tickets, or their tickets for cooking oil, never felt like they were going to die of starvation, or from cold or fear, didn't spend four years of their lives waiting for the Allied landing while listening to Radio London."[1] Ségal and Auclair both were forced to draw on all their resources as they dealt with both daily hardships and long-term traumas. They developed new survival skills and experienced painful losses. In the end the struggles of the war years set the stage for their eventual successes.

From the beginning, nothing about the war followed people's expectations. On September 3, 1939, two days after Germany invaded Poland, France and England declared war on Germany and mobilized massive armies along the German border to ward off an expected German assault. Once deployed, instead of diverting German forces from Poland with an attack, French and British forces waited, nine months of inactivity that came to be known as the "Phony War."

From the Phony War to the Exodus

Throughout the Phony War both Auclair and Ségal were working at *Marie-Claire.* Along with its usual coverage of love, fashion, books, travel, and celebrities, the magazine included information and advice on war preparation. Early on much of that advice reflected what many of its editors and journalists expected based on their experiences during World War I. The first issue of *Marie-Claire* after the declaration of war in 1939 opened with "Take Precautions," an article that recommended that readers immediately prepare by locating the closest shelters, purchasing gas masks, and learning what to do in case of an alert. *Marie-Claire* also invited readers to donate items to send soldiers at the front and informed women about opportunities to contribute to the war effort. A photo spread included images of women bringing in the harvest, assisted by both Girl and Boy Scouts.[2]

Marie-Claire also called on its readers to be strong, not to panic, to have courage.[3] Auclair emphasized keeping up morale, displaying a good attitude, and keeping things in perspective. "Ever since the war started, I no longer allow myself the luxury of complaining about small details; of letting myself, from time to time, be in a bad mood all day . . . of getting angry or grumbling . . . . It just costs too much; it dries up ideas, imagination, all kinds of inner resources."[4] In December 1939, Auclair reported positively on her visit to troops at the front. She came away with an impression of force, order, and grandeur and passed along a message from soldiers: "Tell them behind the lines to do their jobs.... We'll do ours." Auclair urged her readers, "We must arm ourselves, like our soldiers, with patience, with stubborn determination, in good spirits, like them."[5]

The Phony War ended suddenly on May 10, 1940, at dawn when Germany attacked the Netherlands. *Marie-Claire* turned its next issue over to author Colette, starting with a full-page call to arms: "Young Women of Today, Colette Speaks to You." Colette observed that the "period of torpor" had exploded, "like a fruit spewing a thousand deadly seeds." The time for fun and games was over. Colette called on every woman to "stay at her post," whether that was a factory, a farm, or a home.[6] Marcelle Auclair echoed Colette's call for women to step up. Women needed to avoid conveying their anxieties to the soldiers. "Calm is the word of the day." Carry on, Auclair urged, without fear, with discipline and sang-froid. She noted that the war front, not just "over there," was "in each of us."[7]

The German army broke through the Allied defensive line by mid-May, setting off a massive movement of civilians leaving their homes in Belgium and northeastern France ahead of the advancing German army. As the German army approached Paris, the French government struggled to decide what to do. Chief editor at *Paris-Soir* Pierre Lazareff published a vivid account of those days. With his boss Jean Prouvost appointed Minister of Information, Lazareff had an insider perspective. He recounted the comings and goings, disarray and disagreements, and debates about whether to stay or go among French government leaders as the German army advanced. Lazareff watched Prouvost fluctuate between "highest enthusiasm and deepest despair."[8]

Then on June 3 the *United Press* reported, "Waves of German bombing planes raided Paris today.... Bombs fell in many parts of Paris.... Ninety-seven buildings were destroyed or severely damaged and 61 fires were set by the German raiders . . . A total of 1,060 bombs fell on the Paris area, 83 of them landing in Paris itself."[9] The raid, which hit both a school and a hospital, killed over 250 people, mostly civilians, and launched the massive, disorganized civilian evacuation of the city of Paris. By June 9, without attempting to lead any kind of an orderly evacuation of civilians from Paris, the French government simply packed up and moved to the city of Tours, 130 miles southwest.[10] To avoid additional air raids and prevent massive death and destruction, on June 13 General Maxime Weygand, Commander-in-Chief of Allied Forces, declared Paris an open city. By June 14, Auclair, Ségal, and two million other Parisians had left the city one way or another. The usual means of transportation fell apart as trains were packed to overflowing. Traffic along the roads, already crowded by six million refugees from Belgium and northeastern France, came to a standstill. The few lucky enough to have cars quickly discovered they could not refuel. The vast majority of those fleeing south left on bicycle or on foot, loaded down with luggage and push carts, accompanied by children of all ages. They sweltered in the June heat, unable to find food or water, sleeping in the fields and along roadsides. This few weeks of chaos and massive population movement came to be known as "the Exodus," indicating the sense that it was a disaster of Biblical proportions. In the end some eight million civilians took part in the Exodus, many of them women and children.

The Paris press joined in the Exodus. *Marie-Claire* published an issue on June 14, again calling on readers to volunteer. Then it went radio silent. Prouvost ordered *Paris-Soir* and *Marie-Claire* employees to make their way to Clermont-Ferrand, 215 miles from Paris. Then as the German army approached, he sent them on to Bordeaux. At that point, given the chaos and uncertainty, Prouvost temporarily laid everyone off, freeing them to make their own decisions about whether and where to go next.[11]

The "Exodus" of civilians fleeing the German Army, Alamy.

Three months prior to the start of the battle, fearing the worst, Auclair had sent her children out of the city to the Drôme, three hundred miles southeast of Paris. Following Jean Prouvost's orders, she and her mother left Paris to head south and found themselves "caught up in the gigantic lava flow of cars on the Exodus." They crossed a bridge near Bordeaux "swarming with cars with Paris license plates." As they traveled, at one point they heard air raid sirens and they took refuge in a convent. Auclair, in a panic, heard herself shouting Hail Marys. She and her mother made their way to the basement, where a group of nuns reciting psalms calmed her down.[12]

The French government moved operations southwest from Tours to Bordeaux. Then they moved again as the German army approached, finally landing in the small spa city of Vichy.[13] In the midst of the chaos and military collapse, French Prime Minister Paul Reynaud, who wanted to carry on the fight, was pushed out, replaced on June 17 by World War I hero Marshal Philippe Pétain, leader of a group in favor of ending the fighting. Pétain immediately requested Armistice terms from Germany and before it was more than a request, addressed the nation that same day over the radio, asserting that "the fighting must cease." The following day French General Charles de Gaulle broadcast a message to the people of France from London, disputing Pétain, denying that the war was over and calling on soldiers to join him in London. On June 22 France signed an Armistice with Germany, set to take effect on June 25, eight days after Pétain's first speech announcing that the fighting had to stop. In the confusion between Petain's announcement and the official start of the Armistice, nearly two million French soldiers were taken prisoner.[14]

Once the Armistice ended the fighting on June 25, millions of refugees struggled to get home. Some refugees from areas next to Germany were not allowed to return. While the intense trauma abated, most people living in France continued to experience harsh conditions. The German army occupied the northern two-thirds of France. The occupied and unoccupied zones were divided by a guarded demarcation line that required a special passport to cross.

By the fall of 1940 Prouvost, ready to restart operations, rehired and summoned his employees to Lyon, in the Unoccupied Zone. Ségal, Auclair, and their fellow Paris-based journalists faced a serious problem once they arrived: finding a place to live "in this city chock full of refugees."[15] Auclair had retrieved her children. She, her mother, and the three children crammed temporarily into a single room in an apartment, available only until its usual resident returned. For her part, Ségal discovered an address that had something extremely rare, rooms available for rent. It turned out to have been a brothel closed because of what she called the "Puritanism" that took hold after the defeat.[16] She and other enterprising members of the press crew took up residence in the vacant rooms. The bar became their restaurant. On the walls, huge portraits of Pétain covered up pictures of naked women. As Ségal explained, "they recycled everything, before recycling was a thing." The establishment's "former residents" became their waitresses. "Excellent girls, they sat on the edge of the table and called their clients 'my little one.' The ex-madame became the boss." Dislocated journalists who had not managed to grab a room at the former brothel lingered in bistros, looking for an empty side-room, and sleeping in closets or other obscure, dark, cold rooms. They traded "a room infested with mice for a room infested with fleas." The locals in Lyon did not look favorably on their new residents who, as Ségal pointed out, looked like bums in their shabby clothing, worn-out shoes, and other physical signs of their exodus and refugee-like existence.[17]

Shortly after *Marie-Claire* resumed publication from Lyon, the French government passed a law that would have huge repercussions on all Jews in France, including Ségal. At that time she worked at the "listening station," taking down information from foreign radio broadcasts and passing it along to the press's information services. The anti-democratic, ultra-conservative "French State" in Vichy passed a Jewish statute early in October 1940. In spite of its occupation of two-thirds of France, Germany played no role in Vichy's early moves against Jews. Rather, Vichy laws rested on long-standing French anti-Semitism that had grown stronger on the far right between the wars. The Vichy statute prohibited Jews from working in all public services and in leadership positions in cinema, theater, radio, and the press. It set quotas limiting Jewish lawyers, doctors, engineers, and professors.[18]

In June 1941 a more severe law superseded the October 1940 law, broadening the definition of the "Jewish race" and extending professional exclusion beyond leadership roles. Management of *Marie-Claire* did not act immediately after either law, but in November 1941 *Marie-Claire* fired Ségal. She recalled the pain of leaving the office that day, each step moving her further from the "noisy, crowded, warm world of the editorial team." Alone on the street that evening, without a job or money, having lost her only child, far from Paris, friends, and family, "I truly think I experienced the loneliest moment of my life."[19] Without thinking, she found herself heading toward the press cafeteria, now closed to her. She was suddenly aware she could not go in and worried about how former colleagues she might bump into would treat her. Then she heard a raspy voice inviting her to join him for a drink. Paul Gordeaux had been her section manager, a tough, hard-boiled boss. But as they sat over drinks, Ségal thought she saw a tear in the corner of his eye. The next day, Gordeaux found her another office job, though it could not have been with the press. "He really liked me, Gordeaux, in spite of my bad attitude." In the end, she concluded, "you are never completely alone."[20]

Choices: Three Paths Taken

While Auclair and Ségal faced very different circumstances, both had choices to make. One of the great debates about the years of the German Occupation and collaborationist ultra-right Vichy government centers on the question of choice. At a moment of extreme crisis, France's political leaders rejected Prime Minister Reynaud and others who held out in mid-June 1940 for carrying on the fight, either from London or from Algeria. France's large colonial empire and barely used navy gave it options. But Reynaud and elected representatives wanting to carry on the fight, some eighty of whom left on a ship for North Africa, were pushed out in favor of Pétain. The World War I "Victor of Verdun" favored accepting defeat and brought to power a group of extreme right wing, anti-Republican leaders who used the opportunity of their own nation's defeat to attempt to bring about radical changes to France's political, economic, social, and religious systems. Collaboration with Germany was just the start. On July 10, the last legislature of the III Republic voted to give Pétain full powers. The authoritarian French State, most often referred to by its location in the spa town Vichy, replaced the democratic Third Republic. Vichy, calling for a "National Revolution," disbanded political parties and labor unions, censored the press, prohibited access to certain professions and public spaces to Jews, empowered the Catholic Church, reshaped the public school curriculum, and encouraged women to leave the labor force, marry young, and have many babies.[21] In October 1940, along with the anti-Semitic statute, another Vichy law fired all married women working in the civil service, which included public schools.

While Vichy's reactionary conservatism had the support of a segment of the French population, many French citizens disagreed with Vichy's program. But what choices did the general public in France have, particularly just after the shattering defeat that left so many far from home? The day after Pétain's speech advocating an Armistice, Charles de Gaulle's broadcast called on French soldiers to join him in London to create a military force, the Free French, and carry on the fight. For decades after the war, those who wrote about the French people during the Occupation perpetuated the "Gaullist myth" that nearly all of France's 40 million people resisted the German Occupation from the start. Nearly thirty years later, in 1972 American historian Robert Paxton shredded this myth, describing collaboration not as a German demand imposed on reluctant French leaders but as French leaders' attempts to find favor with the Germans occupiers in the hope of gaining political and material advantages. Nor were the leaders at Vichy a small, isolated, and unpopular clique. In fact, Vichy leaders' ideology and programs, including its anti-Semitism, drew from long-standing French far right positions. While Paxton's argument offered a very limited definition of resistance that later scholars challenged as too restrictive, his seminal book put paid to the Gaullist myth.

Ironically, after Paxton's book, the pendulum of historical interpretation swung to the opposite extreme. Instead of 40 million resisters, France during the war was portrayed as a nation of 40 million collaborators. Debates about both myths created a paradigm applied to studying French society under the Occupation: everyone living in France between June 1940 and August 1944 either resisted or collaborated. However, most French people experienced a much more complicated reality. A wide variety of factors—location, social class, ethnic/religious background, gender, and age, to name a few—shaped each person's choices. Beyond that, people's ideas and responses to Vichy changed over time. Supporting Pétain in June 1940 did necessarily mean continuing to support him for the next four years. It might not even have meant approving of the foreign policy of collaboration. In his diary, André Gide railed at the start of the fighting against the stupidity and incoherence of his country between the wars, which he blamed for the disaster underway in June. In his journal entry for June 17, Gide approvingly quoted part of Pétain's speech calling for an Armistice, "Since the victory [of 1918], the spirit of pleasure took precedence over the spirit of sacrifice. We demanded more than we served. We wanted to spare ourselves trouble, today we meet with misfortune."[22] By June 24, just as the Armistice was about to take effect, Gide had heard enough. "Last night we listened to Pétain's latest speech. Could it be? Did Pétain really say those things? Of his own free will? . . . How could he have talked about France being 'intact' when more than half the country has been delivered to the enemy . . . How could he possibly not support Churchill? Not agree wholeheartedly with General de

Gaulle's declaration? Is it not enough that France was vanquished? Does it have to dishonor itself?"[23]

Most people in France paid less careful attention to Pétain's rhetoric as they slowly wended their way home from the Exodus. Some families returned to destruction, other evacuees came from zones they could not re-enter and had to find somewhere else to live. Even after the worst of the trauma faded, nearly everyone across France struggled to survive from day to day in difficult conditions that deteriorated over time. Almost immediately, given Germany's huge agricultural requisitions, food ran short in every city, leading to a rationing system that barely provided the minimum and quickly gave rise to a thriving black market.[24] Not only food but also clothing, shoes, heating fuel, gasoline, and car and bicycle tires became increasingly hard, if not impossible, to find. Allied air raids, starting in the summer of 1942, added new dangers to daily life for those in targeted areas. All semblance of normalcy ended again for most people in France in June 1944 with D-Day and renewed combat. When simply providing for a family took such extreme efforts, picturing ordinary people calmly deciding whether to resist or collaborate provides a misleading sense of how most in France experienced and responded to events.

Ségal, Auclair, and Auclair's ex-husband Jean Prévost illustrate just some of the choices people made, as well as how those choices changed over time. In mid-June 1940, Jean Prévost, mobilized at the declaration of war in 1939, followed military orders and moved with his unit from Le Havre, on the North Sea, to Cherbourg and eventually crossed the Mediterranean. He reached Casablanca by June 17, the day Pétain called for an Armistice. Prévost intentionally decided to return to France rather than join de Gaulle. However, his initial choice did not represent a refusal to resist. Prévost disliked Pétain's conservative ideas and did not condone

Queue of women outside a dairy shop in German-occupied Paris, June 28, 1940, Alamy.

collaboration, but he also considered de Gaulle too far to the right, too authoritarian. He particularly disliked de Gaulle's portrayal of himself as the incarnation of France in resistance.[25]

Vichy Anti-Semitism Targets Marcelle Ségal

Marcelle Ségal's options were limited early on by Vichy's anti-Semitic laws and eventually by Germany's attempt to round up and deport Jews in France. Ségal eventually worked with a resistance group, although she provides few details aside from her alias, Marie Salignat. Typical of her descriptions of other traumatic episodes in her life, Ségal refused to discuss her actions. "About my resistance work, I prefer not to talk about it. I did too little, way too little, our group having been decimated."[26] Instead she paid homage to her fellow resisters, Edmond Roze, who disappeared; Alfred Lelluch, who was tortured and executed; and Denise Clairouin, who died in deportation. She also mentioned "this unknown writer, hidden in the mountains, whose manuscript I typed. Its title was *Caligula*." The author was of course Albert Camus, who was not in fact "hiding" but taking a cure for his tuberculosis in Le Panelier, a small town in the Massif central highlands.[27]

Ségal crossed the demarcation line five times without the proper documentation, knowing the risks she faced, as a Jew, if she were caught. She only described in detail one of the crossings, the time she nearly got caught. Lost and hoping to get directions, Ségal wandered through an open gate. A young woman approached her. Ségal asked her how to get to the Unoccupied Zone. The woman shushed her and pointed to a sign indicating that she had entered a German guard station. Ségal ran so fast to get away that she fell into a ditch. Nearby a woman working in her garden saw her fall and went over to help Ségal out of the ditch. Rather than sending her on, the woman invited Ségal into her home, helped her clean up, offered her a meal, and then had her husband lead Ségal to a place where she could cross safely. "When pessimism takes hold of me, when I despair about the human race, I think about [that couple] and things get better right away."[28] In September 1943, Ségal crossed the line into the Northern Zone a final time and went to live with her mother in the small town in La Sarthe for the duration of the war.[29]

While Ségal could, by all rights, have despised German soldiers, she refused to dehumanize them. The tone of her writing about the war demonstrates her traits, downplaying herself and her actions, emphasizing the goodness of other people, and finding human connections, even with a German soldier. A stream of humor runs through her stories, from time to time swirling into pools of deeper emotions. She lived with her mother in a large boarding house that also lodged German soldiers. At times the French residents gathered to listen to Radio London's BBC French language broadcast: "The French speak to the French." Listening to Radio London violated German rules and could have landed them in trouble. One evening as they listened, the door opened, and a German soldier peeked in, then meekly asked if he could join them. Apparently he, too, avidly sought accurate information about the war since he no longer trusted accounts tainted by Nazi propaganda.[30]

During one air raid alert, the woman who owned the building hurried all the tenants down to the cellar, including a German officer and three German soldiers. Ségal described the situation:

> One of them, a boy—who couldn't have been more than sixteen—was sobbing in fear. The disgruntled German officer glared angrily at him. [The landlady] approached the unhappy soldier and reassured him in a motherly tone: "It's the English. They're bombing a train depot. It's far away from here and they aim pretty well. They won't do us any harm."

Ségal, astonished, emphasized her landlady's inclusive language: "Us, under the bombs, French and German. I will never forget her using the word '*us*.' "[31]

Auclair and *Marie-Claire* Carry On

Unlike Prévost and Ségal, Marcelle Auclair had minimal involvement with the Resistance during the war. She knew of her ex-husband's resistance activities and occasionally met him in Paris clandestinely. One night she took and hid documents for a friend involved in the Resistance who feared that the Germans planned to search his apartment. When she mentioned it to Prevost, he angrily insisted that she not get involved in resistance actions because she was responsible for their children; however, she would not have obeyed his directive had she wanted to be more active. But she did have food to find, rent to pay, and her children and her mother to care for, so she continued to work for and publish in *Marie-Claire* from the time it restarted in Lyon until it shut down again in August of 1944.

Did the life she led make her a collaborator? Historian Philippe Burin proposed a different term for the behavior of people like Auclair, "accommodation," which better reflected the realities of ordinary people going about their daily lives trying to survive the upheaval and hardships.[32] As the vast majority of French people went about their lives, only a few, mostly extreme fascists, were happy about the German Occupation; a few more than that may have, at least in the first two years, supported Philippe Pétain and the Vichy government's program. But even among people initially positive about Pétain, over time the majority of people in France shifted away from supporting Vichy, especially after 1942 and the public round-ups of Jews. Still, to survive from day to day, keep their farms or businesses going, and raise their children, most people in France lived and worked within the parameters Vichy and the German authorities set. As for journalists, Vichy occasionally required the press to cover particular policies or speeches and kept a close eye on the media, as did the German Occupation authorities, making direct criticism of Vichy or the Germans impossible in the officially sanctioned press.

Annoyed by the responses in one of France's literary magazines to the question, "Was it acceptable to publish during the Occupation?" Michel Prévost, the eldest son of Marcelle Auclair and Jean Prévost, took up the issue in the 1990s. Michel challenged the editor of a major weekly and host of cultural programming on television, who had argued that "no one should have allowed their work to be published or performed during the Occupation: the only people who showed any dignity were those who did not let themselves make any concessions in that area." Michel firmly disagreed with that kind of absolutist thinking. Many journalists, including his father, lived entirely off their writing. Authors from wealthy backgrounds could afford to retire somewhere obscure; neither of his parents had that option. At times Michel and his younger brother Alain lived with their father and his second wife, Claude van Bièma, prohibited from working as a doctor because she was Jewish. His sister lived with his mother Marcelle, who also had no family fortune to fall back on.[33] Furthermore, prior to his 1944 departure to join resistance groups hiding in the mountains, often referred to as the maquis, Jean Prévost lived in Lyon, completed his dissertation, and published a book on Stendhal in 1942 and articles in the provincial editions of *Paris-Soir*.[34] Rather than debate whether or not authors, journalists, and playwrights should have published during the Occupation, Michel insisted the real issue was "the content of the writing." Had an article published in a particular journal condoned "unacceptable" points of view?[35]

As the Occupation began in the summer of 1940, the German authorities in Paris without Prouvost's consent restarted a version of *Paris-Soir* under their control. The Paris edition looked exactly the same as it had before the war but became a vehicle for pro-German propaganda. The content was virulently pro-Nazi and anti-Semitic. However, in the Unoccupied Zone, Prouvost re-started and published entirely different versions of *Paris-Soir* in three cities, Lyon, Clermont-Ferrand, and Marseilles. A careful comparison of the various versions revealed that the content of the provincial editions of *Paris-Soir* bore no resemblance at all to the content of the German-controlled Paris edition. Prouvost's provincial *Paris-Soir* reported the news, global developments of the war, local events, and human interest stories, without explicitly promoting collaboration or supporting Vichy leaders or programs.

In response to the Allied invasion of North Africa on November 8, 1942, the German army invaded France's Unoccupied Zone and by November 26, Germany occupied the formerly "Unoccupied Zone" of France, renamed the "Southern Zone." At that point, owner Jean Prouvost announced, "*Paris-Soir* will no longer appear in the region." Angered by his announcement, German authorities threatened to cut off the paper supply for *Marie-Claire* and another of his periodicals, *7 Jours (7 Days)*. Adding to the pressure, Vichy Prime Minister Pierre Laval demanded that *Paris-Soir* resume. Prouvost complied, according to a former editor, worried that the editors, journalists and staff of his other periodicals would find themselves unemployed. However, six months later, on May 24, 1943, Prouvost closed down all three provincial editions of *Paris-Soir*.[36] *Marie-Claire* continued to appear up until the Liberation in August 1944.

Prior to *Paris-Soir*'s shutdown, Jean Prévost continued publishing articles in the Lyon edition, including a true crime series about a young man's attempted murder of his former employer's wife with whom he had had an affair, the crime that formed the basis of Stendhal's novel *The Red and the Black*.[37] Surely, Prévost's son Michel pointed out, having eventually died fighting with the Resistance, his father was beyond reproach.[38]

In addition to the practical necessity of earning a living, Michel argued that, had all authors opposed to Vichy's politics and collaboration refused to publish during the war, it would have "deprived French people, France, during the Occupation, of any kind of intellectual life save that offered by Vichy and collaborators."[39] The only option would have been the clandestine resistance press, which offered a strongly dissenting point of view. However, clandestine resistance papers could not be publicly distributed, making them difficult to find. Furthermore, getting caught distributing, or even reading, a resistance paper had serious, potentially deadly, repercussions. Michel argued that careful readers could discern in many articles that not everyone shared the values of Nazism or Vichy's National Revolution. A teenager during the war, Michel recalled his feelings of relief when he read anything that echoed his thoughts, reassured that not everyone agreed with writers like notorious racist, fascist collaborators Lucien Rebatet and Drieu la Rochelle. Drawing the line between right and wrong at whether or not a person published anything at all during the Occupation in effect rendered his father and Aragon equivalent to Drieu and Rebatet. Michel Prévost argued that writers like his parents did their best, under surveillance and censorship, to keep alive a culture that refused to follow Vichy in lock step.[40]

Prioritizing the content, what kinds of articles appeared in *Marie-Claire* during the Occupation? *Marie-Claire* regularly published unsigned editorials. Auclair published articles, short stories, and editorials under her own name. She also responded anonymously to "*Marie-Claire*'s Mail." What was the general tone and point of view expressed in *Marie-Claire*'s articles, features, reviews, unsigned notices, and editorials? What point of view did Auclair convey in her pieces?

In the first issue to appear after the June 1940 Exodus, Auclair, via the "*Marie-Claire*'s Mail" feature, apologized for not having been able to respond to mail over the previous difficult months. She reassured readers that they could again count on *Marie-Claire* to convey critical information and pass along "all the advice that can help make their lives easier."[41] Helping its readers cope with the circumstances that complicated everyone's lives became a constant theme of the magazine throughout the war.

In the first few months after resuming, a few articles in *Marie-Claire* echoed Vichy's conservative ideology. The editorial most favorable to Vichy appeared in the very first post-defeat issue of November 16. "A New Life is Beginning for Us" described the fall of France in June 1940 as "the defeat of our illusions." To start over, "we will search more deeply, in ourselves and in life, for sources of happiness." Similar to Vichy rhetoric that blamed France's prewar degenerate, hedonistic, and self-serving lifestyle for the defeat, *Marie-Claire* called for the end of "small egoisms and great cowardice, poverty of the heart and of the spirit." A reversed version of Vichy's motto, Work, Family, Fatherland, appeared at the end of the editorial. *Marie-Claire* promised to speak to its readers, "with an open heart about all that makes the true beauty of life: fatherland, family, work."[42]

The editorial was the product of the magazine, not Marcelle Auclair personally. While she was not an editor, Auclair played a role in the magazine's overall direction and published about ten signed editorials in its pages during the Occupation. As to the content, without directly contesting Vichy ideology, Auclair embedded in her editorials a different set of values, ones that emphasized women's strength and independence. Applying her philosophy to the war context, Auclair used articles to help women find peace, and even happiness, amidst difficult and painful circumstances. Trust in your intuition, she urged women, using as an example a mother who, as the German army approached Paris in June 1940, insisted on sending her children to stay with relatives in Normandy rather than sending them south. Facing down the dismay of her husband and family, this mother had faith in her intuition, according to Auclair, and prevented her children from experiencing the nightmare of the Exodus.

Auclair's advice regularly instructed women to look for the good and not to lose hope.[43] In November 1940, while many people were still reeling from the summer's events, Auclair published a short story, "Never Give Up," set in a train car. The lights were off in the car, leaving the passengers sitting in the dark. Then a new passenger arrived and decided to do something none of the other passengers had thought to try. He flipped the light switch. The lights turned on. Auclair's lesson: sometimes the solution to a problem is right in front of your eyes if you look carefully and dare to try.[44]

In the first December after the Battle of France, Auclair addressed a topic of great concern to conservatives at Vichy: women in the labor force. The title, "Working Women are a Problem," clearly echoed Vichy rhetoric. Auclair repeated Vichy's complaint. Before the defeat women had 'invaded' men's jobs and prioritized advancing their professional ambition over their families. The start of the editorial seemed poised to rehearse again the evils of women's paid work, but Auclair quickly changed course. Many a woman, Auclair pointed out, took paid work to avoid the "intolerable humiliation of having to beg a cranky husband every time she needed 100 francs" just to keep the household going. Vichy passed a law in October 1940 requiring public agencies to fire married women, partly to force women back into the home and partly in response to the spike in unemployment that followed the demobilization of the army after the Armistice. Auclair understood that letting married women go in a time of high unemployment of men might seem reasonable, but she insisted that women had gained the right to work outside the home, "by force of will." Women had proven their energy and competence; they played an important role in the economy. During the war, women had been "perfectly dignified and courageous." If the government intended to leave married women financially dependent and at the mercy of their husbands, then the law needed to provide them with financial assistance. Some husbands were worthy, but others treated their wives like "their employee and their maid." Nodding to Vichy, she lauded the idea of allowing women to leave the labor force to return home and focus on domestic tasks, "the sweetest of jobs." Auclair's intense personal dislike of domestic work makes this statement more than a little ironic. However, even after paying lip service to Vichy's celebration of domesticity for women, Auclair insisted that leaving the labor force and returning to the domestic sphere must not leave married women "completely disarmed."[45]

Then, on the page directly after Auclair's editorial, an illustrated article asked, "Young Women, have you Considered these Careers?" Countering the idea that young women should think only of marriage and children, the article listed and illustrated a variety of potential careers, including journalism, photography, teaching, library work, and dispensing in a pharmacy.[46] In a later issue, Auclair published an article on careers and encouraged young women to "Follow your Heart's Desire."[47]

A few articles about Philippe Pétain, head of state in Vichy, appeared in *Marie-Claire.* Generally complimentary, articles about Pétain all appeared in the first nine months after publication resumed, and only in features on children or youth. In February 1941, *Marie-Claire* ran an illustrated, two-page spread: "All the little children in France send letters that say, 'I love you Marshall!' " They included a child's letter to Pétain that closed, "I embrace you with all of my little heart."[48] Through the summer of 1941, two articles on the topic of children fell in line with Vichy's rhetoric, although not without criticism. In July 1941, a year after the Battle of France, an unsigned editorial used one of Pétain's statements as its title: "Too few children, that's one of the causes of our defeat." However, after that brief nod to Pétain, the editorial complained, based on numerous letters from mothers or expectant mothers, about the extreme difficulty of obtaining supplies needed to care for newborns. One expectant mother pointed out that the one hundred francs she had eked out of her husband's salary would pay for exactly four diapers and one outfit for their baby.[49] Emphasizing the difficulty of procuring fundamental items implicitly criticized a government that pushed families to have more children while unable to ensure the provisioning of necessary supplies.

A week later, in August 1941, *Marie-Claire* shifted back to the celebratory tone with a three-page illustrated spread on Vichy's Chantiers de la Jeunesse (Youth Worksites). To substitute for military service, compulsory prior to but forbidden under the Armistice, young men when they turned twenty spent six months in the Chantiers de la Jeunesse living in rural camps. In addition to wearing uniforms, marching, and singing patriotic songs, the men provided community service like clearing land and building roads.[50] The article, "New Uniforms, New Men," described the young men as the "Radiant dawn of a regenerated France."[51] The issue also reported on the Compagnons de la Jeunesse (Youth Companions), another Vichy youth movement that provided an optional boy-scout like experience for boys ages 15–19.[52]

For the first year after the creation of Vichy, *Marie-Claire* articles that touched on Vichy and Pétain were mostly positive, promoting admiration of Pétain but at times critical of Vichy's ideology and failure to live up to its promises about family and youth. However, after the August 1941 issue covering the Chantiers and the Compagnons, *Marie-Claire* never again mentioned those or any other Vichy organizations by name. The magazine, which appeared once a week through 1941, then every ten days until August 1944, provided readers with a form of escapism through its usual features on fashion, recipes, books, films, movie stars, travel, sports, and leisure. Its articles on the contemporary situation focused on raising morale, inspiring readers to help others. Increasingly over the years *Marie-Claire* offered practical advice on coping with the ever-worsening restrictions and shortages. "Good cooking even with hardly any butter, oil, or fat." Another article, "The Art of Saving from A to Z," explained how to preserve the food that was available.[53]

Marie-Claire had been clear about what it considered its mission from the start. When announcing to its readers in December 1943 that it would only appear twice a month, an editorial, "Faithfully yours," described how much the magazine had changed. No longer the lavish sixty-page prewar magazine on glossy paper, by 1943 the magazine more practically promised readers to "help them stay elegant" in spite of the restrictions, prepare delicious meals without key ingredients, and keep themselves healthy and in good shape. *Marie-Claire* understood its readers' problems and

Marie Claire Magazine Cover, 1941, Alamy.

challenges and reassured them, "*Marie-Claire* is and will always be your faithful friend, a friend who knows how to smile, but also who knows how to understand and console."[54] By 1944, *Marie-Claire* focused heavily on matters such as food shortages and helping women find substitutes for ingredients.[55]

Although not explicitly political, a number of *Marie-Claire* articles contradicted Vichy's insistence that all women should dedicate themselves only to family and children. Here Michel Prévost's insight proves useful. These pieces highlighted successful women deeply engaged in a profession or a sport; they informed young women about opportunities and training for careers; and they extolled women's accomplishments outside the domestic realm. A two-page spread in January 1941 celebrated the adventures of young downhill ski racer Cécile Agnel, "Latin professor, team captain, ski champion." She trained for downhill ski races in Chamonix while also studying for a diploma in Law and Letters. Agnel's group of twelve "young, studious, artistic, athletic" female skiers were all "undertaking both advanced studies and rigorous athletic training." *Marie Claire* described them as the kind of women France needed.[56]

A later issue featured a law student who, once she passed the bar, would become the youngest person of either sex at the bar. An article celebrated a woman who worked as a nurse by day and as an acrobat by night.[57] Given its similarity to a passage in Ségal's memoir about finding a job after her divorce, she may have written one unsigned piece titled "Let's Talk About it as Friends . . ." Even as large numbers of men and women searched for jobs, Let's Talk pointed out that those hiring complained that they could not find people with the needed secretarial, accounting, and other skills. "Let's Talk" assured readers that, if they acquired the needed skills, they would find jobs. This and similar articles may not have been an open declaration of war against Vichy's National

Revolution, but ideologues at Vichy wanted young women not to take up higher education, law, accounting, competitive sports, or acrobatics, but to marry young and have lots of babies.[58]

By 1942, not only had *Marie-Claire* ceased mentioning Pétain but several editorials also explicitly criticized Vichy. That year Jérome Tharaud, member of the Academy, and his brother and co-author Jean complained about Vichy's constantly blaming the selfishness, egoism, and hedonism of French people for the disastrous defeat in 1940. Their article, "It's Time for Enthusiasm," disputed the assertion that before the defeat, "courage, endurance, sacrifice, eagerness to work, confidence in destiny...had disappeared from France's soil." Instead of criticism, people in France deserved praise, particularly "the French woman" whose two key virtues, "enthusiasm and common sense," had always saved France. The Tharauds pointed out that in France, a woman represented "the highest expression of our national soul," a thinly veiled reference to Marianne, a symbol of the French Republic Vichy leaders despised and removed from government buildings.[59] Léon-Paul Fargue, a poet, also paid homage to the "extraordinarily subtle and courageous attitude of women who were 'ahead of men' when it came to adapting to new situations." He concluded that women in France, "from humble to chic...seem to be saving the world from ruin and deceit."[60]

In general, the magazine embedded challenges to Vichy orthodoxy in issues filled with the usual practical advice and tips like recipes for cooking with only 20 grams of butter and one egg, reports on fashion, features on life in Paris, and exercises to improve legs, shoulders, and bust.[61] As for Auclair's messages about Vichy, after her initial article that seemed to support but really contested Vichy's law restricting married women's paid work, few of her pieces either directly supported or contradicted Vichy. Rather, she offered readers the personal philosophy she had developed during her youth in Chile and America. She bolstered the courage of women whose husbands remained in German POW camps as the holidays approached again, for the third time, in 1942.[62] In another editorial, Auclair returned to the theme of not giving up before trying. In "A Seat Up Front?" Auclair described arriving for a performance and finding the theatre packed, jammed with people standing in the aisles and in the rear. Rather than assuming there were no seats left and joining them, Auclair walked up to the front of the theater where she discovered plenty of empty seats. Failure to look carefully, fear of doing something wrong, and assuming a simple solution would not work left too many people uncomfortably, and unnecessarily standing.[63]

Auclair explored the relationship between husband and wife in a light-hearted exchange with fellow journalist Pierre Bost titled: "Men are perfect Pierre Bost affirms. Do you agree madam?" Writing tongue in cheek, Bost instructed women to accept their men as they were and stop demanding that they change. Men were perfect, he insisted. Only women's lack of perfection rendered them blind to men's perfection. Bost followed with advice on getting along with their "perfect" spouses, including knowing when not to bring things up, not constantly complaining about how hard it was to find food, not dragging their husbands shopping, never criticizing them in public, and most of all, always being ready on time. Auclair responded to the question in the title, do you agree that men are perfect, in a separate inset "Oh! No! Marcelle Auclair Responds." Bost had picked up on precisely the thing that most exasperated women. Recognizing Bost's sarcasm, Auclair worried that some of the men who read the magazine might actually believe him. She proposed a different way of thinking about the relationship between husbands, wives, and perfection. Every woman, Auclair explained, thinks that the man she loves is perfect "deep down," in spite of his multiple surface imperfections, irritating ticks, socks left on the floor, egoism, and other less than perfect traits. Men may be perfect, Auclair conceded, but only "deep down," not in real life.[64]

Auclair occasionally published short stories in *Marie Claire*, another way she conveyed her ideas about how to live. Auclair's story "The Hat and the Architect" played on an old trope. Underneath the nerdy, professional woman a beauty queen waits to emerge. In this story, an architect, furious at having been passed over for a promotion unfairly given to her male colleague, fumed about the injustice. She went home, where she discovered a box that had been delivered to her apartment. She had not ordered anything, but opened the box to find a fancy hat, the kind of thing she never wore. She had always favored practical clothing, plain hair, flats, and no make-up. She had not ordered the hat, but out of curiosity, she tried it on. To her surprise, seeing herself in the mirror, she discovered how attractive she looked. The anger she had been feeling lifted. Happy in the new hat, she decided to go for a walk. Several men flirted with her. Then, accidentally, she bumped into her ex-husband, who did not recognize her at first because of the hat. They talked and decided to meet for dinner and shortly thereafter ended up reconciling. No doubt the message reinforces the importance of appearance and of making an effort to look attractive to men, even for a skilled professional woman, if she wanted to have a man in her life. But this kind of message was hardly new or unique to the Vichy years. It was the kind of story that appeared before and would appear after the war. One point however remains. The story never even hinted that the newly attractive, remarried heroine should leave her professional life as an architect behind.[65]

Auclair, like *Marie-Claire* in general, evolved from a tone of guarded support for some of Vichy's ideals to ever-greater distance from its desired goals. The content in *Marie-Claire,* after the three early pieces in late 1940/early 1941 lauding Pétain and the new youth movements, was not expressly pro-Vichy. Even from the start, some of its messages directly contested conservative dogma and policies. A simple comparison of the tone and content of truly collaborationist publications makes that clear. Given the Vichy government's active censoring of the press, it is hardly surprising that *Marie Claire* avoided the significant and traumatic events of the Occupation, the anti-Semitic laws and round-ups of Jews, the execution of hostages following an attack on a German soldier, and the imposition of forced labor for young French men in 1943. *Marie-Claire* and Auclair stuck with helping readers manage the rationing, restrictions, and shortages that resulted from the Occupation. Marcelle Auclair, divorced mother of three, earned her living at *Marie-Claire*. Should she have left? Stopped publishing? Joined the Resistance? Could she have prevented the firing of Ségal? There are no easy answers, but her wartime writing did not promote collaboration and by 1941 pushed back gently against Vichy's conservative agenda for women.

Even many people who eventually resisted accommodated the reality at the start. Auclair's ex-husband, Jean Prévost, continued to publish through 1941 in the Lyon edition of *Paris-Soir*. He continued publishing essays and books up to the day he went fully underground in 1944. Their son Michel, who eventually joined his father in the maquis, reported that his father practically ordered his mother not to get mixed up in the Resistance for their children's sake, not that she had ever let him tell her what to do. But she had valid reasons to keep working and avoid trouble with the authorities, as did the majority of ordinary people living France. Mostly Marcelle ignored Vichy rhetoric and sometimes she thwarted it. She kept the family together.

Marcelle Ségal and Marcelle Auclair started down the same path just after the Armistice, faced radically different circumstances, and made different choices. Auclair continued as she had before the war, while Ségal faced discrimination and persecution as a Jew. Denied the option of continuing her career, she chose to lend her skills to the Resistance. Both women survived the war, Auclair's positive orientation and Ségal's humanism and humor intact.

Choosing to Resist: Jean Prévost

The clearest rejection of Vichy collaborationism was going underground into the Resistance. Jean Prévost ultimately sacrificed himself in the struggle to liberate France. While he and Auclair were no longer married, until his death their lives remained connected through their children.[66]

In spite of his ultimate decision to resist, Jean Prévost's life, intellectual positioning, and choices had always been complicated. Like his mentor Alain, Prévost was a contrarian. Back in 1933, in response to Hitler's coming to power in Germany, Prévost published an essay in a literary journal, *Pamphlet*, titled "Neither Fear nor Hatred." He opened his article with a shocking assertion, "I still love the German people." Prévost insisted that the Nazis did not represent all German people. Besides, the world had much to thank the German people for: Beethoven, Nietsche, Bach. Prévost speculated that a person who voted for Hitler may have been suffering and "must have found in Hitler and his excessive nationalism the remedy to his misery." France's mistreatment of Germany after 1918 was in part to blame for what happened. Prévost insisted he wrote not as an apostle of nonviolence.

But until such time as he was called to arms, he insisted on remaining "as wise and fair as I can be."[67]

In 1939 when war came Prévost was indeed ready to take up arms. He had witnessed in horror the reality of Nazism. After the fighting ended in 1940, he returned to France, wary from the start of the leaders at Vichy. He rejected Pétain's ideology and policies. Yet, as his son pointed out, once demobilized Jean had to make a living and returned, as did Albert Camus, to work at *Paris-Soir* from Lyon. Prévost edited and published serialized features in *Paris-Soir*, an article on medicine and industry, and practical articles like those in *Marie-Claire*. He reported in detail on British, and eventually American, war efforts. According to journalist Jérôme Garçin, "In 1941 we see the journalist Prévost working to divert, to instruct, but also to encourage."[68] In other words, what he wrote resembled *Marie-Claire*'s content. *Paris-Soir* became "his platform, his country schoolhouse."[69]

At the same time, Prévost began his double life, supporting the Resistance in the shadows. Michel Prévost, annoyed after the war about being asked when his father "joined the Resistance," noted that it was hardly a matter of filling out a membership card. Given the need for secrecy, people like his father did what they could, first searching cautiously to find fellow travelers they could trust, then attempting tasks like writing and distributing tracts, and passing messages between groups who could not use the postal system to communicate. Prévost went on several missions to Paris, often meeting Marcelle when they were both in town. Louis Aragon told Michel after the war that his father had been one of the first members of a group of prominent authors who, in February 1942, formed the "National Writers Committee," a resistance group that put out a clandestine paper, *Les Etoiles* (*The Stars*).[70]

In March of 1941, while doing research for his dissertation in Grenoble, Prévost bumped into a prewar friend, Pierre Dalloz, who confided in him about a resistance group beginning to take shape in the Vercors, a mountain range in eastern France.[71] Dalloz later told Prévost about a plan to organize a "military unit in the mountains" that would distract the German army during the anticipated future Allied landing. That idea formed the basis of the "Mountaineer Plan" developed early in 1943 under General Delestraint of the Secret Army, a military Resistance movement. Prévost remained in Lyon but spent time with the maquis. Many of the young men in the maquis had first gone into hiding to avoid forced labor in Germany. Once underground, many of them joined resistance groups. Because these young men had not experienced the military service compulsory before 1940 for all men when they turned 20, they needed basic military training. Prévost offered both academic classes and instruction in weapons handling. Back home in Lyon, Michel completed his Baccalaureate in the spring of 1944. His father never talked to Michel or his other children about his clandestine life, knowledge of which would have put the entire family in danger.[72]

In April 1944, sensing that the war had reached a critical point, Jean left Lyon for the Vercors mountains to join the maquis full time. Under the alias Captain Goderville, he led a unit of the maquis awaiting the Allied landing. On June 8, two days after D-Day, a BBC broadcast called on the Vercors maquis to implement the Mountaineer Plan. The following day, Michel left home to join his father, then in Saint-Nizier, a plateau in the mountains. There, about 3500 members of the maquis formed five companies, with Prévost/Goderville leading a unit of three hundred fighters. When Michel appeared, rather than telling him he was too young and sending him home, his father embraced him, joking that it was "odd to have one's son as a brother-in-arms." Michel, certified in first aid, became the unit's medic.[73]

The original plan rested on the assumption that after D-Day, the Allies would land a team in the mountains bringing weapons and ammunition. That never happened, leaving Prévost's group with one British short cannon and a few light machine guns. Nevertheless, after the BBC's call, the full Vercors maquis launched an attack on German troops in the area and forced them to retreat to Grenoble. Determined to crush the resistance in the Vercors, the German army regrouped, assembled fifteen thousand soldiers, and counter-attacked in July. Without any help from the Allies, maquis fighters engaged in guerilla warfare but could not stop the advancing German army. Michel left his father's unit to care for wounded soldiers in a different unit. His father's group found itself in Gillets, the outlet of a road to Grenoble. Meanwhile, the German army surrounded the entire plateau and counterattacked the maquis on three fronts. Facing a much larger and better armed force, orders went out to the maquis to disperse.

Prévost and a few of his men took refuge in the woods.[74] They hid for a full week near the town of Sassenage, in a cave called "the Fairies' Grotto," where they had access to water and some food. Prévost, convinced he would die, let drop his anonymity, an essential element in the Resistance. Giving away his real identity freed him to discuss his work as an author.[75] After a week, with food running out, the cave was close enough to the town of Sassenage that at dawn on August 1, Prévost and four companions decided to try and make a run for it. All five were killed by German fire as they reached a bridge 50 meters from the relative safety of the village. Jean had attempted to escape the bullets by jumping off the bridge; locals eventually recovered his body. Only Simon Nora, who had stayed in the cave, escaped the ambush. As they retook control of the area, German forces killed some six hundred maquis fighters and two hundred civilians.[76] Prévost scholar Jérôme Garcin highlights Prévost's uncanny prediction from the end of his 1933 essay "I still love the Germans" that Germans might very well kill him someday.[77]

The Liberation

Three months after D-Day, in August 1944, the Allies landed in the south of France, forcing the Germans to retreat from most of France. At that time, the Resistance launched a popular uprising in Paris. The Allied Supreme Commander, US General Eisenhower had decided to by-pass the city of Paris, but General Leclerc insisted on going in. On August 26, Leclerc and de Gaulle celebrated the Liberation of Paris with a parade. Most of France had been liberated by the end of August 1944, although pockets of German forces remained in cities and towns along the Atlantic coast. Germany packed up the remaining Vichy government leaders and sent them to a castle in Sigmaringen, Germany. That winter, the German army attempted a final counterattack in eastern France, the Battle of the Bulge.

In the chaos and confusion of the final liberation of Paris, one minor incident of note to this story took place in mid-August 1944. On the rue d'Odéon, Adrienne Monnier had kept her bookstore, La Maison des amis des livres, open. Sylvia Beach, however, closed Shakespeare and Company in 1941, in defiance of a German commander. He had entered the store and tried to purchase Beach's last copy of *Finnegan's Wake*. When she refused to sell him the book he stormed out. Expecting him to return and confiscate the book, that night Beach simply made the bookstore disappear. She packed up the entire store, stashed everything upstairs and painted over the shop's sign. After the United States entered the war, Beach, an American citizen, was arrested and sent to a camp for foreign nationals.[78] Released six months later, Beach returned to Paris but laid low at a nearby student hostel, stopping by to visit Monnier at her store from time to time. On August 19, 1944, Monnier and Beach watched an American jeep drive slowly down the street, "liberating" the rue d'Odéon. The jeep rolled to a stop and Ernest Hemingway got out to greet his old friends.[79]

As France was liberated, in many cities and towns across France a wave of reprisals against notorious collaborators followed. Having heard rumors of a price on his head, Jean Prouvost, publisher of *Paris-Soir* and *Marie-Claire,* went into hiding. Ségal and Auclair were both alive and ready to restart. They had managed to keep going under extreme circumstances, motivated by racism for Ségal, sexism for both women. Ségal, targeted by Vichy anti-Semitism, also recalled the good people who went out of their way to help her. Auclair kept things going for her three children, at the start and end without her ex-husband's support. She bristled at Vichy's limited vision of women and in her own backhanded way published articles that pushed back against that vision. Both Auclair and Ségal were eager to restart their careers as journalists, but the group Prouvost had hired at *Paris-Soir* and *Marie-Claire* would never be reassembled.

Bridges to Feminism: Marcelle Auclair, Marcelle Ségal, and Women's Magazines in Twentieth-Century France. Sarah Fishman, Oxford University Press.
DOI: 10.1093/9780197791356.003.0004

4

Starting All Over Again

The Long Postwar Recovery

The bloody years of the war and Occupation gave way to the gloomy, mucky years of the long period that followed the Liberation. Jean's death left me with three children to raise . . . and not a penny to my name.

MARCELLE AUCLAIR, *Mémoires à deux voix*

It was September 6 [1944]. I had to start all over again from scratch.

MARCELLE SÉGAL, *Moi aussi, j'étais seule*

Marcelle Ségal describes the return to Paris in September 1944 as the Exodus in reverse. Everyone who had abandoned the city in 1940 was desperate to get back as soon as possible, in any way possible. Ségal hitched a ride in an uncovered military truck in the sweltering heat and rain. Only after she arrived in the city at 3:00 a.m. did it dawn on her that she had nowhere to stay. She wandered the streets aimlessly until a cop finally picked her up and took her to the local police station. She spent her first night back in Paris on a bench next to a body covered with a black sheet. "We got along great, the two of us," she quipped. At 6:00 a.m., the police kicked her out. She had an old handbag that contained all her worldly possessions. Wearing espadrilles punctured with holes, she was hungry, unemployed, and homeless.[1] She had to start all over again, again.

In history books, wars have an end date, the day one party capitulates, May 8, 1945, in the case of Germany. But nothing about what the United States dubbed World War II followed previous trajectories. For one thing, while the fighting in Europe ended with Germany's unconditional surrender, the treaty on the final settlement with Germany was not signed until 1990. The Cold War prevented the formerly allied powers from agreeing on a definitive territorial or political settlement as Europe broke into two hostile camps. Having established separate occupation zones prior to Germany's defeat, the Soviet Union in its eastern zone and the United States, England, and France in the west meant territorial boundaries were simply established based on the facts on the ground.

Similarly, France itself had no "liberation" date to celebrate. The Nazis left Paris on August 25, 1944, but retained areas of France through the spring of 1945. The Battle of the Bulge finally expelled German forces from eastern France at the end of March 1945, and pockets of German soldiers remained in bases on the Atlantic or North Sea coast in Dunkerque, Lorient, Saint-Nazaire, La Rochelle, Royan, and Pointe de Grave.[2] The French commemorate several key dates connected to the war: June 18, 1940, when de Gaulle called for resistance; June 6, 1944, D-Day; August 25, 1944, the Liberation of Paris; and May 8, 1945, Victory in Europe Day.

The absence of a clear end date to the war and German Occupation of France is just one sign that expelling the Nazis represented only the start of a long process of liberation. Particularly given the disaster of June 1940, the contested decision to seek an Armistice in 1940, and the Vichy regime's collaboration with Nazi Germany, the end of hostilities hardly ended France's internal strife. From the national to the personal level, people faced or evaded the consequences of the choices they had made during the war.[3]

Given the complexities of those choices, which changed for some people over the four years of occupation, France's liberation did not represent a simple return to peace and harmony. Immediate reprisals, summary executions, and other violence, including public shaming by shaving the heads of women accused of collaboration and sleeping with the enemy, were eventually channeled into a legal process that lasted through the end of the decade and continued to have repercussions through the end of the century.[4]

After the Liberation, the press' wartime operations also resulted in unclear consequences. Although some newspapers shut themselves down after June 1940, the press in general continued to function throughout the Occupation. Some publications put out by extreme right political groups like the Action Française had rejoiced in the fall of the Republic and creation of the authoritarian, collaborationist, anti-Semitic government. Other papers were less explicitly pro-Vichy. Women's magazines in general shied away from politics. After the Liberation, France's Provisional Government purged the media. The law of September 30, 1944, shut down all publications that continued to appear during the German Occupation, for the Northern Zone counting from two weeks after the June 25, 1940, start of the German Occupation, and for the Southern Zone counting from Germany's November 26, 1942, occupation of that zone. Publications that continued after those deadlines had their business assets sequestered while awaiting either a judgment or dismissal of charges. In 1945, the Provisional Government authorized publications that had shut down before the wartime deadlines to restart. In 1946, it turned the sequestered physical assets of suspended publications over to a new organization, the National Society of Press Entrepreneurs, which rented the equipment either to journals that originated as clandestine resistance papers or to new titles born after the war. The closure of several mass circulation dailies like *Paris-Soir* opened the door for new daily newspapers, like *Le Monde* and *France-Soir*. Many prewar press groups disappeared, their property transferred to new owners. A corresponding purge of journalists targeted fascists and ardent collaborationists. Three of them, Jean Luchaire, Georges Suarez, and Robert Brasillach, were tried, convicted, and executed for their wartime activities.[5] Other ultra-collaborationist or fascist journalists spent time in prison or went into exile.

Reversal of Fortunes: Ségal and *Elle*

Despite being Jewish and active in the Resistance, Marcelle Ségal had survived the war and Occupation, her humor and self-deprecation intact. What she would do with her life after the war, however, remained an open question. *Marie-Claire* had closed even if Ségal would have considered working there again after having been fired. Her prewar apartment had been rented out. While waiting to get it back, the concierge allowed Marcelle to stay in the studio apartment owned by a cousin who had been deported to Germany. Daily life continued to pose serious hardships for everyone in the city. Long after the Liberation, food and clothing, still in short supply, continued to be rationed. Electricity and heat only operated sporadically. The black market continued to flourish. According to Ségal, "You couldn't get anything without scheming."[6] Still, she described herself as "crazy happy" to be back in Paris, reconnecting with friends and family, free to live and work without fear. Ségal loved the atmosphere in Paris in the winter of 1944–45, people dancing to American swing, smoking American cigarettes, and discovering American inventions like instant coffee and ballpoint pens. She enjoyed listening to "the boogie woogie" even though she considered herself too old at that point to dance to it. To her delight, her aunt, who handled advertising for a magazine called *Jazz Hot,* got her tickets to see musicians including Louis Armstrong, Duke Ellington, and Dizzy Gillespie. Ségal knew from the "Yankee go home" graffiti that not everyone in Paris appreciated the presence of so many Americans. She quickly found a job with one of the many new dailies that appeared after the war. To celebrate, she purchased herself a new outfit, happy that she could finally find shoes with leather, not wooden, soles, something unobtainable during the Occupation.[7]

By the end of 1944, the war had mostly ended in France. As the Allies pushed into Germany from both sides, nearly two million French nationals remained in Germany as prisoners of war, deportees, and forced laborers. The German army, rather than leaving foreign prisoners behind as they retreated, marched them with German troops toward the center of Germany. Air raids, forced marches, and extreme hunger compounded years of captivity in conditions ranging from harsh to deadly.[8] As the Allies liberated various camps starting in April and May 1945, train loads of French nationals began returning to France: many of the returning POWs and forced laborers weak and in poor health and concentration camp survivors shockingly emaciated and in even worse health. The loss of contact between French nationals held by Germany and their families after France's liberation meant that few families knew if or when their returnee would arrive in Paris. On the other side, some returnees had no family to greet them, their family members having died fighting in the Resistance, in air raids, or in other areas of combat. Volunteers quickly organized to greet and help orient French nationals returning from Germany.

Ségal volunteered her services at the Gare de l'Est, the train station where most of the returnees arrived. She had in part hoped to find her cousin. He never returned. She described her shock when one returning Jewish concentration camp survivor responded to being asked her name by reciting the number tattooed on her arm, "43178 Neuengamme." While at the station, Ségal spontaneously found her friends, Pierre and Hélène Gordon-Lazareff, who had also worked before the war for Jean Prouvost.[9] The Jewish couple had spent the war in the United States. The three of them were thrilled to see each other. As Ségal reflected, "At that time, still being alive seemed like a minor miracle."[10]

After the war, Pierre and Hélène Gordon-Lazareff established themselves at the center of Paris journalism. Pierre had been editor-in-chief for *Paris-Soir* in the 1930s. At that time, Hélène Gordon, a student of ethnography at the Sorbonne, worked with a team of anthropologists at the Musée de l'Homme, including such luminaries as Georges-Henri Rivière and Michel Leiris. She had traveled with Marcel Griaule to Africa to study the masks of the Dogons. Like Ségal, Gordon wanted to publish articles about her experiences.[11] Rivière, her mentor and Assistant Director of the Musée de l'Homme, recommended her to his friend Pierre Lazareff, who hired Gordon to help with a new children's page. Lazareff sent Gordon to the United States twice in the 1930s, once in 1937 for a special edition on motherhood in America and again in July 1939 for a special edition on the New York World's Fair.[12] In between those trips, Lazareff divorced his first wife and married Gordon. Gordon's American connections proved extremely useful during the war, which started a month after she returned from reporting on the World's Fair in 1939.[13]

During the Phony War and Battle of France, Pierre Lazareff's experiences destroyed his trust in his boss, Jean Prouvost, who wobbled from implacable foe of the Germans, opposed to any compromise, to supporting negotiations for an Armistice. Two days after Pétain's June 17 announcement that he had requested an Armistice, Prouvost accepted a position in Pétain's government as High Commissioner for Propaganda. Lazareff concluded that Prouvost lacked "strength of character." To him, Prouvost primarily wanted "to tag along," following whatever direction public opinion took.[14] Lazareff kept his distance from Prouvost after the war even though Prouvost had in fact been responsible for the couple getting out of France in June 1940. As the Germans advanced toward Paris, in one of his wobbles, Prouvost decided to make plans to go into exile. He instructed Pierre and Hélène to go to Lisbon and wait for him. When they arrived at the border, French border authorities informed them they could not leave France without explicit permission from their employer. In the midst of the chaos, they managed to send word back to Prouvost and then they waited for a response. At the last minute, Prouvost's official permission to leave arrived. The couple made it to Lisbon and from there to Canada. By November 1940, Pierre learned that he had been deprived of his citizenship and that the Vichy government had confiscated their property. Pierre and Hélène moved to the United States, where they were "most cordially and hospitably received," and resumed their work as journalists. Hélène, fluent in English, tapped into her prewar journalism contacts and ended up writing for *Harper's Bazaar* and the *New York Times*. Pierre went to work for the US Office of War Information.[15]

After the Liberation, Pierre and Hélène returned to Paris to discover another family living in their apartment and their possessions gone. Like Ségal, they too had to start over. They also volunteered to greet French nationals returning from captivity. Prouvost was in hiding and *Paris-Soir* had been closed, though it is unlikely Lazareff would have wanted to work for Prouvost after the war. Instead, Lazareff and another prewar *Paris-Soir* editor, Marcelle Ségal's former boss Paul Gordeaux, joined a former resistance paper, *Défense de la France,* to create a new daily, *France Soir-Défense de la France*. By 1949, with Lazareff as its General Director, the paper, by then simply *France-Soir,* had become

France's top daily. *Marie-Claire* also shut down, leaving Hélène Gordon-Lazareff to contemplate a new woman's magazine. Inspired by her time in America, she envisioned a weekly magazine with a luxurious style and color photographs.[16]

When Ségal ran into Pierre and Hélène Gordon-Lazareff at the train station, these publications had yet to emerge. But Ségal knew something would happen. She described the couple as "journalists from head to toe. To the tips of their fingernails. It was their function, their nature. They produced magazines like an apple tree produces apples." As a train with returning prisoners and deportees approached the station, Ségal had just enough time to yell to her friend Hélène, "if you start a women's magazine, keep me in mind."[17] A few months later, Hélène did just that. When she launched *Elle* in November 1945, she hired Marcelle Ségal to cover film and literature. In addition to her unsigned feature near the front of the magazine with brief reviews of plays, films, and books, Ségal regularly translated serialized fiction from English and occasionally published her own short stories.[18]

A year later, in 1946, as *Elle* struggled to increase its circulation, Hélène decided that the magazine needed to build a more personal relationship with its readers.[19] What better way to establish an ongoing dialogue with its readers than soliciting readers' letters and publishing responses? As they discussed plans, the editorial staff decided to divide readers' letters into categories matching the magazines' various rubrics. Letters about "beauty" would fall naturally to the editor of *Elle*'s beauty beat, the same for fashion, home decoration, and so on. Ségal, in charge of film and literature, waited. Someone asked who would respond to letters from readers asking for advice about love. None of the editors volunteered. Ségal was sure no one wanted the "vulgar role of ridiculous auntie and, to be honest, the bad taste of reading tea leaves for good luck." But by the time the idea came up, all the other editors had been assigned their categories. Ségal, realizing she was the last one standing, responded with horror. "Me? Answer the . . . the . . . letters from the heart?" At that instant, she had created a name for her rubric. The rest of the editors laughed, but Hélène, completely serious, took her response as an affirmation. "Letters from the heart? Perfect. That's what we'll call it." Ségal knew resistance, in this instance, would have been futile.[20]

To generate reader mail, a new feature appeared in July 1946, "Thank you for writing to us." That title headed a box with three columns, side by side, under the rubrics Heart, Home, and Cuisine. Each column included short excerpts of letters and brief, unsigned responses.[21] When the feature first appeared however, Ségal discovered she had a serious problem. Letters with questions about home and cuisine poured in, but few readers wrote for advice about their personal lives. Without letters to answer, Ségal primed the pump by writing them herself, drumming up ideas at first from prewar issues of *Paris-Soir*, where Marcelle Auclair had responded to those kinds of questions. Ségal also adapted situations she knew about from her friends' lives and disguised their identities, until one of her friends recognized her situation and complained.[22]

Fortunately for Ségal, letters asking for advice on relationships began trickling in. By mid-December 1946, *Elle* expanded Ségal's advice section, giving it a separate column with the full title "Letters from the Heart." Ségal's name appeared in the column the following week along with the instruction, "for letters about relationships write to Marcelle Ségal."[23] The number of letters quickly increased and before long, as Ségal described it, the trickle turned into a raging river. From then on, Ségal insisted, all the extracts of letters that appeared in Letters from the Heart were "rigorously authentic."[24] She corrected only the spelling but left the wording as is, she explained, to give readers a sense of the "letter's flavor," which revealed as much about the writer as the question she (or he) posed. In fact, to make clear that the letters came from both women and men, in the late 1940s, the column had a subsection, "Guys Write to Us Too." Nevertheless, doubts about the source of the letters persisted for decades. Nearly forty years later, in 1982, *Le Monde* journalist Anne Gallois admitted that at age 14 she and her friends had sent phony letters, hoping to "trip up Marcelle Ségal and make her waste her time." But they found, "no phony letter could withstand her [Ségal's] eye, trained by 36 years of practice." They gave up.[25] By the time Ségal published a book about her career as an advice columnist, she described having to avoid being buried by the avalanche of mail. Although she received some twenty letters a day, according to several interviews, she responded personally, and at some length, to every letter whose sender included a return address, not just the letters that were printed in *Elle*.[26]

The rubric provided Ségal with what would become a powerful mouthpiece, as she attracted questions from every kind of reader and engaged in public and private dialogue with her readers. As she began to craft her responses, she slowly developed her voice. Initially she offered somewhat conventional advice. For example, she often recommended that women having marital problems try counseling to maintain their marriages. However, from the start Ségal's advice did not entirely conform to upholding traditional values. Nor did Ségal extol romantic notions of love. Instead, she pointed out the benefits of sticking with the devil you know. She explained that once a woman left a boring husband to marry an exciting lover, the lover quickly became the boring husband. To her mind, the best solution would minimize the pain and the expense for all parties, including children. She advised women to be realistic about husbands rather than seeking the perfect husband, since such a thing did not exist. "The best is the enemy of the good enough!"[27] On the more conventional side, Ségal counseled women that rather than complaining about a husband's various provocations, including infidelity, to maintain their equilibrium and create a warm, welcoming, and happy home that might inspire their husbands to behave.

While she generally advised married women to stay in their marriages, from early on Ségal regularly exhorted unmarried women not to exaggerate the importance of marrying. Often she received letters from young women obsessed with finding a husband as soon as possible. One writer whose boyfriend had recently broken up with her bemoaned, "I'm afraid I'll never get married. What should I do to get married–quick quick?" Ségal pushed back, asking her, "Why quick quick? Take your time." Ségal advised young women that worrying about finding husbands was the wrong approach. In this case, she urged Quick Quick to make friends, take up an activity, join a sports club or an art group, and be kind and helpful to her friends, rather than worrying about finding a husband. Eventually, Ségal assured her readers that, rather than focusing on finding a husband, they should build a circle of friends since getting involved in outside activities and groups created the most favorable conditions for meeting potential husbands. If her young female readers did that, she insisted, a boyfriend and eventually a husband would follow naturally.[28]

Ségal offered similar advice to correspondents who worried about their personalities or their appearance. In a June 27, 1949, essay Ségal informed correspondents who felt insecure about themselves that they were overlooking an important reality: other people were too busy worrying about their own flaws to be judging those of their friends. Rather than wasting time worrying about themselves, Ségal urged her readers to focus on filling their lives with study, work, and friends.[29] Ségal also wove her wry humor into the column. Weary Heart complained that Ségal would probably "tell me I'm young, but I can't get used to this idea because I really want to be 2 years older." Ségal had a solution. "You want to be two years older? Here's a trick that cannot fail... Wait two years!"[30]

Concerned about some of her correspondents' more serious situations, Ségal regularly invited letter writers to come visit her in her office at *Elle* instead of publishing their letters in her column. Early on she also asked specific correspondents to write back once the situation resolved to let her know what had happened. She reassured correspondents worried that somebody else might see their letters that their secrets were "well guarded." She respected their privacy and destroyed the letters on a regular

Marcelle Ségal in her office at Elle. Photo courtesy of Anne Brunswic.

basis. She also was careful not to include in her column details about her correspondents, such as where they were living. "Lady Discretion keeps an eye on me like a guardian angel as I write my responses."[31]

Parenthood Round Two

Just as she started her career at *Elle*, Ségal finally acted on an idea she had been considering since before the war. In 1946, she adopted Harold, a 10-year-old boy. Three years later, Ségal published a full, two-page article in *Elle* about her adoption experience. According to her great-niece, his Jewish parents had been deported and died in the camps.[32] Ségal not only never mentioned that aspect of his past, but in the article she also referred to him as Christian, not Harold, a pseudonym that further protected his privacy.[33]

Ségal wrote about her experience in the hope of encouraging her readers to consider adoption. She straightforwardly addressed concerns she had often heard.[34] She acknowledged that adoption had altered her lifestyle, putting an end to late nights out with friends, but she emphasized that from the moment she met her son, none of that mattered. She described the first time she saw him. He had been living in a small town outside of Paris. He was standing in the front yard as she drove up. She parked, walked over, and asked if he was Christian. Rather than answering, he smiled. At that moment, she found, "I was won over. I still am."[35]

She addressed some of the challenges of raising an older child. She had to learn to stifle her urge to try and correct all his flaws, poor grammar, and table manners such as holding his fork like a pitchfork and shoveling food into his mouth. Doing so might have killed his appetite and certainly would have inhibited him from talking to her. Although he was a quiet and sensitive boy, he figured her out quickly. Rather than defying her head on, he eluded her. She described their parent-child struggles as "a bulldog versus a cloud." She also pointed out that, while she was sold from the start on adopting him, it took longer for him to adopt her. She mostly regretted not having another child to make Christian feel less alone. In the article, Ségal does not mention something she wrote about in a later book. After adopting Harold, she fostered another boy of similar age and raised the two boys together.

Ségal took exception to friends complimenting her for the sacrifice she had made, insisting "I sacrificed nothing." On the contrary, she insisted that adoption helped her. Rather than worrying about her wrinkles and fading good looks, "I rejoice in seeing every day my son's qualities flourish." He doubled her happiness, she concluded, closing the article simply, "Thank you Christian."[36] Ségal clearly hoped to encourage others, not just married couples but single women like herself, to adopt. While she did not write about it in *Elle*, a decade later, as she entered her 60s, Ségal adopted a second boy, also an older child, and fostered another boy his age.[37] She would write more about both of her postwar rounds of parenting, its joys and challenges, in her memoir.[38]

Marie-Claire Is Dead, Long Live *Marie-Claire*

Ségal launched her dream job with her friends at *Elle* magazine, which quickly became a global phenomenon. In the meantime, Marcelle Auclair had a bumpier professional landing after the Liberation. Her ex-husband had been killed in the fighting. Because *Marie-Clare* had continued to publish after Germany occupied all of France in November 1942, the Provisional Government closed it down under its 1944 law, throwing her out of a job. Targeted by the Resistance at the Liberation, her boss at *Marie-Claire*, Jean Prouvost, had gone into hiding. The post-Liberation charges against Prouvost rested on his initial support for the Armistice of June 1940, his three weeks as Propaganda Commissioner in Pétain's first cabinet, and a "bitterly anti-British speech" he gave in response to the British attacking the French fleet at Mers-el-Kebir shortly after the Armistice.

Disputing Prouvost's perfidy, Marcel Haedrich, the wartime editor of the *Paris-Soir* Lyons edition who eventually went into the Resistance, claimed that several months prior to France's liberation, Prouvost sent the Resistance Finance Minister a sum of 18 million francs to support the Resistance's embryonic Provisional Government.[39] Haedrich also revealed that, after shutting down *Paris-Soir* in May 1943, Prouvost continued to pay Haedrich's salary. Not having to find a new job made it possible for Haedrich to go into the Resistance full-time.[40]

Nevertheless, in 1944 the BBC announced that the Resistance "had condemned Prouvost to death." The French Revolutionary Committee for the Fight against Terrorism charged Prouvost with providing intelligence to the enemy, condemned him to death, and put him on its blacklist, which signaled that their followers could execute him on sight. In January 1944 a photo of Prouvost appeared in *Libres*, a wanted poster of sorts. Haedrich, shocked, again pointed out that he had been only able to resist "thanks to Prouvost." Was Prouvost really "a traitor?" Haedrich asked, "To be shot?" To avoid summary execution, Prouvost went into hiding and changed locations a dozen times. As he put it, "For three years I was a wandering outcast."[41]

While Prouvost was hiding, the authorities in Lyons raided the offices of *Marie-Claire*, arresting everyone there, including the secretaries. Prosecutors in Lyons prepared a case against the Lyons edition of *Paris-Soir*, at the same time as Paris prosecutors targeted the Paris version.[42] Minister of Justice François de Menthon ultimately decided that the dossier assembled against Prouvost "didn't have much in it." Finally, in July 1947, the courts dropped all charges against Prouvost, although his business property, given to a former Resistance paper in 1944, would not be returned.[43] Like Ségal and Auclair, Prouvost found himself starting over.

In the meantime, in August 1945, Auclair launched a new magazine, *Votre amie* (*Your Friend*), a title that exactly expressed Auclair's vision of the purpose of women's magazines.[44] Stylistically reminiscent of *Marie-Claire* and less lavish than *Elle*, *Votre amie* printed sketched illustrations and black-and-white photos. In March 1947, *Votre amie* merged with another postwar woman's magazine, *Marie-France*, to become *Votre amie Marie-France*.[45] The merged magazine continued to appear until 1956.[46]

By the early 1950s, Auclair's attention and efforts had shifted. Concerned about a new kind of magazine that she thought gave all women's magazines a bad name, she joined an organization called the Committee for the Dignity of Women's Magazines, which she became president of in 1953. The Committee worked to warn the public about a specific set of periodicals, so-called romance magazines or "la presse du coeur," which they differentiated from women's magazines (la presse féminine) owing to its nearly exclusive focus on romance, its highly sexualized images, and its inclusion of lowbrow features like horoscopes. In 1953 the Committee published a newsletter, *Le vrai visage de la presse du coeur* (*The True Face of Romance Magazines*) inviting French men and women to join with them in the struggle against romance magazines. While the Committee referred to romance magazines in the plural, it primarily targeted one magazine, *Nous Deux* (The Two of Us) considered the worst offender. First appearing in

1947, *Nous Deux* was published by Italian press magnate Pacifico (Cino) Del Duca.

The Committee for the Dignity of Women's Magazines never gained the same traction as a similar group created in 1949 that set its sights on protecting minors. The Committee for the Oversight and Control of Publications for Children and Adolescents primarily targeted *Tarzan,* the American comic book series Del Duca brought to France. Children and youth were easy to portray as vulnerable, impressionable, and in need of protection. In contrast *Nous Deux,* despite its visual resemblance to children's comic books, was aimed at adult women. Its covers featured a vivid illustration of a woman and a man engaged in an activity like skiing, cooking, or boating. Both the man and the woman were modestly attired, their bodies covered, but the images were highly sexualized, the woman's breasts pointy; the couple exchanged suggestive looks. Many images included barely disguised Freudian suggestions of penetration or ejaculation. Inside the front cover, *Nous Deux* featured a postwar novelty, the photo-story. Like a comic strip, the photo-story narrated a story in visual panels with captioned dialogue and text balloons, but each panel was an actual photograph rather than a drawing. *Nous Deux* proved extremely popular. From a circulation of 326,000, it rose to 1.4 million by 1955, and by 1957 it was the top-selling magazine in France.[47]

Why was there such a strong objection to *Nous Deux*? With its visual storytelling and simple text, *Nous Deux* targeted working-class women such as factory, sales, and clerical workers. The Committee for the Dignity of Women's Magazines worried that young working-class women were not sufficiently educated to decipher the false messages the magazine sold. The Committee, with Marcelle Auclair presiding, included an impressive range of public figures—journalists, judges, Christian activists, Communist women, educational leaders, lawyers, a rabbi, and a representative of the CGT, France's largest labor union. In fact, the Communist Party had created the Committee in 1952 because it viewed popular magazines as critical in shaping "feminine representations and imaginaries."[48] The Communist Party's influence can clearly be seen in the Committee's newsletter, *Vrai visage,* which denounced the ideological content of the magazines, their so-called servitude to the United States, and their equating of happiness with evasion rather than work, which all had the effect of corrupting women.

Auclair could have broadened the Committee's appeal. In 1954 she gave a talk, "The Romance Press Challenges Reason," broadcast over the national radio station. According to Auclair, "From these journals emerge pestilent, poisonous fumes."[49] Romance magazines presented their stories as real life, a bit like today's reality television, making it all the more dangerous for susceptible readers. The Committee warned that working-class women, struggling with low wages and the hardships of daily life, had a need for distraction, which made them particularly ripe for exploitation by "unscrupulous entrepreneurs." Rather than practical information and appropriate distraction, *Vrai visage* insisted that romance magazines offered them "real poison."[50]

In its first issue in 1953, *Vrai visage* explained, "everything pushes the reader towards hoping for personal success based on luck." In its second issue, an editorial complained that *Nous Deux* presented sex as "a fate that no one can escape."[51] Stories in *Nous Deux* focused only "on romantic adventure." It featured characters involved in "multiple liaisons, abandonment, divorce." The stories, embedded in an atmosphere of hatred and jealousy even within families, included prostitution, debauchery, swindling, spying, and crime. The settings evoked a "fake exoticism that favors the development of racial prejudice." *Vrai visage* cited the concerns of high school teachers, lawyers, and even a prominent juvenile court judge, Jean Chazal, who testified to the role these magazines played in cases of child abandonment, crimes of passion, and even suicides. By turning its readers away from social problems, focusing on success via chance rather than hard work, romance magazines favored "the subjugation of the women [they] pretend to distract."[52] Beyond the damage caused by the romanticized portrayal of debauchery, sex, and betrayal, particularly galling to the Committee's Communist women, "this press undermines the honor of work." Rather than helping women deal with the difficulties of their daily lives, lack of housing, and low salaries, romance magazines painted a picture of "easy luxury," suggesting that luck, and sex, were the only ways to get ahead. The inclusion of horoscopes only reinforced superstitious ideas about luck. Together, these factors diverted young women "from honest work," leading them down the path of adventure, venality, and even prostitution.[53]

The Committee further objected to the vulgarity of *Nous Deux*, its lack of literary quality, and the regular inclusion of translations of what it considered foreign junk. Often the same magazine appeared in multiple languages in different countries, depriving French authors and artists of work, damaging French cultural traditions, and turning women away from worthy French authors. *Vrai visage* warned that all of this lowered the intellectual and moral level of readers, "annihilating their will, their conscience, their sense of duty," and teaching young women that only individual success and success in love mattered. *Vrai visage* described romance magazines as "shrill, vulgar and ugly." In all caps, the Committee warned, "THIS PRESS UNDERMINES MORALE AND BREAKS UP FAMILIES."[54]

The ultimate target of the campaigns relating both to children and to women was the man who published both *Tarzan* and *Nous*

Deux, Cino del Duca. In response to the accusations, in 1953 Del Duca sent a letter to the Committee, which it published in *Vrai visage* without commentary. Del Duca complained that the Committee's June bulletin accused him of having published in Italy, "papers inspired by Mussolini entirely made up of comic strips drawn by foreigners." Del Duca vigorously denied the allegation. "Anti-fascist and a resister, I took no inspiration from Mussolini against whom on the contrary I had fought with all my power, which earned me several stays in prison."[55]

Cino del Duca's statement was only partially true. Born in Italy, after World War I, Cino did in fact join a local socialist party in the town of Ancona. A rail worker, Cino became the local leader of the Young Socialists. When fascists took over the city of Ancona in 1922, a police raid turned up a list of Communist Youth Federation members that included Cino del Duca's brother Dino. Consequently both he and Dino were arrested. Cino claimed to have spent time in prison after his arrest, though this is uncorroborated. In any case, Cino lost his job working for the Italian railroad system but quickly found a job working for a publisher selling popular novels, "gruesome true crime stories, in the Fantoma style."[56] Cino also brought comic books to Italy, importing *Tarzan, Dick Tracy,* and *Flash Gordon.* In 1928, he and two brothers joined forces to create their own publishing house, Casa Moderne, and in 1935, they launched their own comic book series, *Intrepido.*[57] In spite of their early brush with fascist authorities, the Del Duca brothers prospered under Mussolini's rule. Casa Moderne's comic books and magazines easily accommodated fascist heroes, with patriotic adventures that readily lined up with "fascist principles."[58] Del Duca rejected that charge, insisting that his comic books were not meant to be political persuasion but were meant to provide entertainment and to sell.[59]

As a result of a falling out with his brother, Cino moved to France in 1932. When France declared war in September 1939, the French government sent Italians living in France, including Del Duca, to a camp. After it took over the Vichy government released him in July 1940. Del Duca, determined to restart his press and publications in the Unoccupied Zone, set up publishing operations in the city of Nice. However, in mid-1942, facing a critical shortage of paper, the Vichy government shut down all children's comics including those of Del Duca.[60]

Like Ségal, Auclair, and Prouvost, Del Duca started over after the war. By the 1950s he had again become a leading press magnate. Evidence about his past clarifies that the Committee for the Dignity of Women's Magazines had grounds to question his political sympathies. Del Duca's letter asserting his anti-fascist bona fides may have been partially accurate, but it hardly presented a full picture of Del Duca's political position in relation to fascism.[61] In the end the Committee objected to the style and content of *Nous Deux* more than his questionable past. At the height of its activities in the early 1950s, the Committee for the Dignity of Women's Magazines spawned a number of regional affiliates and organized conferences and galas. In Paris, in 1952 the Committee sponsored the production of Auclair's translation of *Dona Rosita,* a play by Federico Garcia Lorca, Spanish playwright killed by Franco's forces during the Spanish Civil War.[62] The following December the Committee convened a national Congress.[63] Eventually however internal differences, heightened by the Communist Party's desire to tighten the reins, pulled the Committee apart.[64] The Committee ceased publishing *Vrai visage* in 1955.

Auclair and the Return of *Marie-Claire*

In 1954, a full decade after the Liberation, a law finally settled the status of publications that had continued to appear during the German Occupation.[65] Publishers whose cases had been dismissed were free to restart, although they would not get back property confiscated after the war. They would have to restart with new resources.[66]

Since charges against Jean Prouvost and his wartime publications had been dismissed, he was finally free to relaunch his prewar periodicals. However Prouvost had no interest in reviving *Paris-Soir.* Once he emerged from hiding in 1949, he had figured out a way around the rules. Shortly before the war, in 1938, he had taken over a daily sports newspaper called *Match.* It shut down in 1940 and never restarted during the war, meaning it escaped the prohibition directed at papers that continued to appear during the war. In 1949, he relaunched it as *Paris-Match* and converted it from a sports-oriented monthly into an illustrated weekly newsmagazine. Thus the family tree of *Paris-Soir* included two rival postwar offspring, *Paris-Match* and *France-Soir,* each of which inherited a group of journalists from the parent company. Prouvost was keen however to revive *Marie-Claire,* putting his longtime collaborator Marcel Haedrich in charge. *Marie-Claire's* first issue appeared in October 1954. By the second issue circulation reached 600,000; by the third issue it was up to 800,000.[67]

The restart of *Marie-Claire* without Auclair made clear the strength of her connection with her audience. Haedrich quickly discovered the loyalty Marcelle Auclair had built with her readers over the previous decades. No sooner had the magazine reappeared than Haedrich began receiving letters, in large numbers, asking for Auclair, dubbed by Haedrich the "female pope of *Marie-Claire.*" Prouvost, on the other hand, described Auclair as "a pain in the ass." He had no desire to bring her back and denied Haedrich's request to rehire her. But letters demanding Auclair's return continued to pour in, so Haedrich decided to approach her directly, despite Prouvost's rejecting her return. By then, Auclair was making good money from a series of biographies that, according to Haedrich, "sold by the wheelbarrow." She lived in a comfortable house in the countryside with her mother. When they met, Auclair expressed ambivalence about returning to the Paris publishing world. Finally, Haedrich persuaded Prouvost to make Auclair an offer. Sensing their panic, she turned it down and asked for more. Prouvost, annoyed, complained, "With her, you never see the end of it."[68] Haedrich, under continuing pressure from *Marie Claire's* readers, pressed Prouvost.

Instead of making another offer, Prouvost set up a tryout of sorts for Auclair, without letting her know that it was a test. He convened a group of *Marie-Claire*'s writers and asked each of them to devise a test for their readers, by then a popular magazine feature. In order to engage their readers, magazines devised tests and quizzes that, based on the score, revealed something about the readers' lives or personalities. Prouvost proposed as the topic: how do you know if you have a good husband? Each journalist in turn suggested a question for readers to answer that would determine if they had a good husband. They came up with unsurprising questions. "Does he bring you flowers on your birthday?" "Does he take you out to dinner?" "Does he remember your anniversary?" Prouvost, not impressed, sent Haedrich to visit Auclair and get her suggestion. Her question? "Does he squeeze the toothpaste from the end or the middle of the tube?" When Haedrich reported Auclair's suggested question, Prouvost, delighted, responded, "Now that's journalism!" Finally, they reached a deal to bring Auclair back to *Marie-Claire*. Haedrich, who arranged for Auclair to meet with Prouvost at his office, described the scene. Haedrich and Auclair entered Prouvost's office together. Prouvost, already standing, approached Auclair. "My dearest Marcelle! – she's in his arms, 'Dear boss, my dearest boss.'"[69]

The flood of readers' letters demanding Auclair's return and the popularity of *Elle* testify to the wide reach of both Auclair and

Ségal. By 1954, both had established and extremely popular public voices, at each of the two largest women's magazines in France. After decades of struggle, they finally had stable lives and financial security. Through their positions at *Elle* and *Marie-Claire*, they nurtured a relationship and created and sustained a powerful dialogue with their readers. Given their personal struggles, both were determined not simply to entertain the women who read their columns but to encourage them to take care of their personal needs, to ensure their ability to support themselves, and to have confidence in themselves and their ability to manage difficult situations.

Bridges to Feminism: Marcelle Auclair, Marcelle Ségal, and Women's Magazines in Twentieth-Century France.
Sarah Fishman, Oxford University Press.
DOI: 10.1093/9780197791356.003.0005

5

Superstars

Women's Magazines and Advice Columnists' Messages of Empowerment

"[Auclair] is back. She's come back to the spot we left open, waiting for her. Many of you have asked about her .... "When will she take up her dialogue with us again?" So here she is, with as big a smile as ever, with her inexhaustible resource of clear-sighted goodness. Truly your friend, your confidant, the one to whom you can confess everything that weighs on your heart." Marie-Claire (February 1955)

In 1964, New Wave filmmaker Jean-Luc Godard released his eighth film, *La femme mariée (The Married Woman)*. The story centers on a love triangle, a married woman having an affair who discovers she is pregnant but does not know whether her husband or her lover is the father. In the film, the heroine writes to Marcelle Ségal for advice. In fact, while he was making the film, Godard sent Ségal a letter written by the actress playing the heroine. To an interviewer, Godard explained, "The end of my film will depend on [Ségal's] actual response."[1]

Godard's statement is a testament to the centrality of Marcelle Ségal in popular culture and public discussions of love, marriage, and family. The blurb on the back of Ségal's second book, *Moi aussi, j'étais seule* (*I Was Alone Too*), may not have been hyperbole. "Marcelle Ségal's name is known by nearly every woman. Around the world, it evokes a memory, it's synonymous with common sense, humor, joy, but also and especially with understanding."[2] As for Marcelle Auclair, *Marie-Claire* readers insistently demanded her return. When she appeared on a television talk show in 1960, the host felt she was so widely known that she needed no introduction, describing her as "a kind of director of our modern conscience . . . she's a professor of life, a professor of existence."[3]

Clearly important voices, Auclair and Ségal interacted in various ways with women and men from a wide range of backgrounds through their immensely popular columns. When giving advice about love, marriage, family, and children, they did not directly contest the broad contours of the era's gender expectations, in particular the assumption that most women expected and wanted to marry and have children, a consistent theme in the letters they received. Still, they highlighted women who followed other paths. In his book about women's magazines, French scholar Vincent Soulier found in reading Ségal's responses to readers in the 1950s, "I wasn't really struck by her conformity."[4] Both journalists felt their complicated and at times painful personal experiences prepared them to help women figure out how to solve their problems. Both Ségal and Auclair urged women—married, divorced, never married, young, and old—to take control of their lives. They discouraged young women from focusing only on finding a husband, stressed the importance of being able to live independently, and downplayed the importance of physical appearance. Their advice promoted an approach to women's personal lives that pointed to feminism. Rather than using a judgmental tone or invoking guilt, they tried to help women manage their situations and encouraged them to take care of themselves.

Both women reached a pinnacle of renown and influence in the thirty years after World War II. That era, a time of rapid economic growth, urbanization, and modernization, has come to be called the "Thirty Glorious Years," after the title of Jean Fourastié's book about France's postwar recovery.[5] The immediate postwar years, however, felt less than glorious for most people. Daily life continued to be a struggle through the late 1940s as the French government focused on repairing the widespread damage to its transportation and production infrastructure. The destruction of housing left many families unable to find a place to live. Food rationing continued through the end of the decade. Although the war in Europe had ended, the late 1940s marked the beginning of nearly two decades of decolonization wars that brought French colonization to a close in Indochina in 1954 and Algeria in 1962.[6]

After a decade of shortages and other hardships, the benefits of France's postwar economic boom finally began to trickle down to most residents of France by the mid-1950s. The government shifted from infrastructure to building housing, including low-rent apartments for working-class families, while factories began producing consumer goods, such as refrigerators, washing machines, televisions, and cars, that an increasing number of families could afford. With full employment, rising wages, a generous welfare state, and rapid urbanization, France was finally on the road to becoming an affluent society.

Their Platforms: *La presse féminine* (*Women's Magazines*)

Consumerism created a perfect market for the expansion of the popular press, particularly women's magazines. In the 1950s and 1960s, *Marie-Claire* and *Elle* reached peak circulation and readership, providing highly visible platforms for Auclair and Ségal. From 110,000 copies at its creation in 1945, *Elle's* weekly circulation reached 727,161 by 1963. When it reappeared in 1954,

Marie-Claire's first print run of 500,000 copies sold out on the first day. The print run for the second issue was 900,000 copies, and by 1962 *Marie-Claire* had reached a monthly circulation of 1,069,785. In the early 1960s, both magazines' circulation exceeded that of *Constellation,* a popular monthly similar to *Reader's Digest,* circulation 600,000, and dwarfed that of *L'Express,* a weekly newsmagazine with a circulation of 146,000 in 1963.[7] While they were not devoid of politics, women's magazines did not aim to provide the same coverage of current events, elections, or foreign policy as daily newspapers or weekly newsmagazines. They covered political leaders, cultural figures, economic issues, and events from an angle considered relevant to women.[8]

Marie-Claire, Elle, and other women's magazines have been criticized by academics for perpetuating conservative attitudes toward gender. However, features on figures like media personality Menie Grégoire, renowned psychoanalyst Françoise Dolto, and feminist sociologist Evelyne Sullerot went against the grain of traditional housewives.[9] Equally important, many members of *Elle*'s editorial board were women; most of the journalists were women; and issues highlighted books by women and featured fashion designed by women. The magazine responded to a letter in 1950 from "Miss D" who complained about an article that led her to conclude that "*Elle,* the magazine for women, is not feminist." The editorial board, in no uncertain terms, asserted, "Yes we are feminists." Miss D's criticism "hit us where it hurts," because, they insisted, they never stopped being feminists or "defending women's interests."[10]

That clash of perspectives raises questions about the nature of feminism in postwar France. Because women in France did not gain the right to vote after World War I, French feminists continued to focus on women's suffrage. Silenced and vilified by the ultra-conservative Vichy regime during the German Occupation of World War II, feminists resumed their activism after the

Elle magazine cover, 1957, Alamy.

Liberation in 1944, the year French women finally gained the right to vote. In 1946, the foreword to the new French Constitution guaranteed women "in every domain, equal rights with man," and a law stipulated equal pay for equal work. With feminist political activities less visible than they had been during the fight for suffrage, some observers describe the 1950s as a period without feminism.[11] Others contend that rather than disappearing, feminism redirected its efforts. The Ligue Française pour le droit des femmes (French League for the Rights of Women), the group that had led the struggle for the vote, continued their activities after the war, shifting their attention to marriage law and women's reproductive rights. And their advocacy work for the most part took place from inside or in alignment with political parties rather than as a gender bloc.[12]

In that era, women's magazines represented an important voice advocating feminist demands.[13] Having insisted on its feminism in 1950, *Elle* regularly featured articles on issues relating to women. An article in 1950 complained about the lack of women in the Prime Minister's new cabinet, proposing an alternative, all-female cabinet with a list of women they recommended for each ministry.[14] In 1956, the magazine surveyed five hundred women who worked outside the home about "their solutions to the major female problem of the 20th century, 'Career-Home,'" about how to balance job duties with domestic responsibilities.[15] Jean Duché, one of the few male columnists at *Elle*, regularly addressed women's struggles for equality. In his 1959 review of Celia Bertin's book on women in the labor force, *Le Temps des femmes* (*The Time for Women*), Duché celebrated the increasing number of women in management positions but deplored the fact that women still remained far from the "levers of command."[16] A few years later, he cited at length a letter he received from a female executive at a textile factory. She described her male colleagues as "distrustful or hostile." They often took credit for her ideas and regularly, in her words, tried to "dominate her sensually." She closed with a question. "Is it possible to hope that in the future, a race of perfectly virile men will accept a woman as more than just her sex?" Duché encouraged her. "I think that Madame Director can hope:

boys today already seem very capable of seeing a woman as 'a being in her own right.' "[17]

Duché's editorials are just one example of the dialogue between columnist and readers, a format in which women's magazines addressed women's lives, concerns, and expectations.[18] Ségal and Auclair were central figures in those conversations. For over thirty years they engaged directly with their readers, responding to their intimate questions and comments. For the most part, they did not instruct readers, even those asking for advice, simply to follow social expectations. Instead, their exchanges worked to empower women and urged them to solve their own problems without being constrained by rigid expectations.

Over time readers developed a strong attachment to both Auclair and Ségal. Every week for forty years, from 1947 to 1987, Ségal responded to her readers' letters in the pages of the magazine and, according to her accounts, privately answered all letters that included a return address. She regularly invited correspondents to meet with her in her office at *Elle*. She also appeared occasionally on the radio and later on television. Although less frequently than Ségal, Auclair, in her column "Your Problems," responded to issues her readers raised and to specific letters under the occasional rubric "Reader's Mail."[19] In what may have been a backhanded dig at Ségal, someone she never wrote about directly, Auclair claimed to have brought the advice column format back to France after discovering it during a visit to the United States in 1935. After the war she decided against reviving a formula that had become "an ineffective kind of exhibitionism." She had found that many letter writers were more interested in seeing their letters in print than in finding solutions. Instead, concerns that came up regularly in the letters she received determined the topics Auclair wrote about in *Marie-Claire*. In a televised interview Auclair remarked that, rather than a regular advice column, she responded to readers privately and met with some of them face-to-face.[20] Shortly after she returned to the magazine, *Marie-Claire* informed readers in 1956 that Auclair was available by appointment on the first Tuesday of every month for in-person meetings at her office.[21]

Auclair and Ségal did not consider themselves guardians, promoters, or upholders of a specific, "traditional" vision of womanhood. Their personal lives hardly followed a standard script. Although both women married and raised children, they went through painful divorces, and neither of them remarried. For different reasons they were forced to survive independently. Rather than reinforcing idealized visions of marriage and family life, their personal lives countered traditional stereotype. Because of their outlets, women wrote them regularly around their personal lives, love and marriage, parenting and family life, sex and infidelity as well as beauty and body image. Education and professional life came up less often in these periodicals. To better understand their interactions with readers, both Auclair and Ségal addressed head-on why their correspondents wrote to them for guidance.

Why Ask a Stranger for Help?

Why would a person write to someone she doesn't know for advice? Ségal and Auclair both contended that not being personally known by a letter writer enhanced their legitimacy. Ségal, when asked why people wrote to a stranger, responded, "Because she's someone they don't know!"[22] On a television broadcast, Auclair agreed. Some people found it easier to reveal their problems to a stranger. They hoped that an advisor with no personal stake in the matter would have a broader perspective and be less judgmental.[23] As the letters demanding Auclair's return to *Marie-Claire* demonstrate, readers had clearly developed a connection to her over the years. They felt something of a personal bond, but it was their public personas responding to an everywoman more than the concerns of specific letter writers. Ségal and Auclair wrote in ways that were both specific and intended for a broader audience. In an interview Ségal explained she chose letters for the magazine "based on the interest of the topic, the universality of the situation and especially on its urgency," while admitting "I always prioritize the most dramatic letters."[24] It was journalism after all!

I Feel Pretty!

A frequent topic of letters, women's anxiety about their physical appearance, illustrates the fundamental messages Ségal and Auclair conveyed as they buttressed women's self-esteem. While Auclair found it "normal" for a woman to want to be pretty, her response articulated a key aspect of her outlook on life and happiness in general: "thought plays a paramount role in creating reality." Nothing was less objective than a woman's judgment of her own appearance, and nothing influenced her destiny more than how she saw herself. In her years at *Marie-Claire* Auclair found that nine times out of ten, "a woman becomes what she believes she is." She cited a young woman who worked at the magazine. Shy, unhappy, and ashamed, she thought she was ugly, "but she was gorgeous." To Auclair, the cure was not a makeover but restoring the woman's self-confidence by "compelling her to work in order to occupy her with something other than herself." Over several weeks on the job, the woman's self-confidence grew and she stopped worrying about her appearance.[25] Auclair then gave a counter example of a plain-looking young woman, "full of life, of good cheer, grace and charm." Young men lined up to date her.

One young man got angry and sarcastically asked her if she thought she was pretty. She responded, "What does it matter since everything happens as if I were?" To Auclair, the key was for a woman "not to waste hours in front of a magnifying mirror, counting her blackheads or her developing wrinkles." Rather than worrying about appearance, Auclair recommended exercise and a healthy diet. To be beautiful, "it's important . . . to have beautiful and good thoughts, to love beautiful things, to contemplate them."[26]

Women should not spend time worrying about their appearance, Ségal agreed, but she also enjoyed pointing out the ever-changing nature of beauty standards. She cited the letter from a young woman convinced she would never find love because she was too tall. Ségal insisted the problem was not her height; "the problem is on the inside." Being 1 meter 72 (5′8″) might not be such a bad thing, she pointed out. "Look at Ingrid Bergman and her 1 meter 80."[27] Ségal received a letter from a young woman who described her ugliness; she was fat and had skin like a toad. She had no friends, no boyfriend, and no job. The one time she worked to make herself attractive, men mistook her for a prostitute. In response, Ségal insisted she could not be as ugly as she thought she was. Try again, make an effort, and with a little fine-tuning, she would be pretty, Ségal recommended. But Ségal emphasized that what most needed fine-tuning was her attitude, not her appearance. Inviting her to visit, Ségal reassured her, "my ugliness will comfort you."[28]

In the same issue, Ségal made a similar point by responding to two letters from women with opposite concerns about their size. 'Maryse' complained that she had "enormous hips that make me look ridiculous." "Fil de fer" (iron wire) on the other had described herself as "frightfully thin." To Maryse, who asked about skirts that would hide her horrifying hips, Ségal recommended that, once her hips were camouflaged, "All that's left is to forget about them while waiting for the day when big hips are the thing." To Fil de fer, Ségal pointed out "mannequins and stars are more string beans than feather quilts." If her big sister and friends continued to tease her about being skinny, "learn to laugh first."[29] Ségal reassured another writer claiming to be hideously fat that beauty standards in the past had celebrated ample breasts and hips as attractive and recommended that she not be so thin-skinned.[30] Women tormented themselves. Their interminable discussions, preoccupation with their bodies, weight, diet, beauty products, and aging, all of it represented to Ségal a "feminine evil."[31] In the 1930s, she noted, fed up with women's magazines that "that only talked about beauty" she had published, "for my personal satisfaction," an article in a Belgian magazine titled "The Joyous Words of an Ugly Woman."[32]

Marriage: Don't Rush In!

Neither Auclair nor Ségal were revolutionaries; they never identified themselves as feminists. They met their readers where they were, gaining their trust and building credibility. Ségal, in an essay about the contemporary French woman published in 1961, explained that only ten of the 200,000 letters she had received over the years "show evidence of the modern woman's supposed disaffection towards marriage."[33] From this she surmised, "Girls want to marry. Women want to keep their husbands." Ségal gathered from her letters, the majority of which were about marriage, that most young women expected and wanted to wed other heterosexuals and have children.

While she never questioned young women's expressed desire to marry, Ségal encouraged women not to rush this stage. In part Ségal here reflected on her personal trajectory. A young woman wrote that she was "haunted by the thought that I'll become an old maid," which was "becoming an obsession." "Don't panic," Ségal reassured her.[34] She advised another writer, only 18, not to submit to pressure to drop out of school to marry. She needed to take time to live, Ségal explained, to experience life, and especially to finish her education and establish her own career, even if she might give it up in the future to marry and raise children. She encouraged the young woman to "take advantage of your youth." Not only that, Ségal warned, in dropping out of school, "you disregard your security and your independence."[35] Ségal responded to another 17-year-old writer confused about her feelings for an older suitor. The young woman's hesitation suggested to Ségal that she was not in love. So, Ségal asked, "why marry at 17?"[36] She gave similar advice in 1957 to Desperate Catherine who had been talking about marriage with her boyfriend of three years when he suddenly left on vacation with his friends, saying he needed "to think about it." Desperate Catherine took that as a sign that he did not want to marry her. She was 25 years old. All her friends were already married. Having counted on marrying this young man, if he abandoned her, she closed, "I lose everything, my life is finished. I think I'll never find the Happiness I'm in the midst of losing." Ségal countered, "You may find a better life," especially since she had fooled herself about her boyfriend in the first place. If her young man needed time to think things through, Ségal recommended that Desperate Catherine do the same. Instead of despairing, she should rethink the relationship, and talk to her married friends. They would let her know that being single has great advantages over being "badly married." Her boyfriend's behavior had led her to discover the painful reality. "Better it should happen before the wedding than after. At age 25, life is not over."[37]

Auclair shared Ségal's point of view about the obsession with marriage. In 1961 she published *Qui épousez-vous?* (*Whom Will*

You Marry?). Aimed at young single men and women, Auclair's book, rather than feeding romantic myths about falling in love, warned young readers to give the question serious consideration. A sales clerk in a furniture store, having interacted regularly with engaged couples buying furnishings for their new homes, told Auclair that many of the couples, "poorly tuned," clearly spent more time choosing furniture than they had building their relationship. When one young woman cancelled the furniture she and her fiancé had ordered, the relieved salesclerk thought to herself, "good, she's come to her senses!" Auclair included the salesclerk's story to encourage young couples considering marriage to think at least as seriously about their relationship as they did about purchases for their home. Possibly reflecting on her own experience with her former fiancé in Chile, Auclair included a set of questions for each partner to answer about the other. If they could not respond positively to at least half the questions, she recommended that they call off the wedding.[38]

Auclair advised readers against feeling compelled to marry. She echoed Ségal's warning to young women not to leave themselves vulnerable, stressing the importance of being able to support themselves financially, married or not. Auclair pointed out that women who had a profession and could support themselves would have less reason to tolerate husbands' bad behavior. In a 1957 article celebrating *Marie-Claire*'s twentieth anniversary, Auclair lamented the serious limits on autonomy the French legal code imposed on married women. Married women lost control over their financial resources, their paid work, and even decisions about their children. Auclair exhorted women to use the vote their foremothers had struggled to win to change their legal status.[39]

Auclair cited a letter from a woman who wrote "I'm afraid of causing my husband shame." She suffered from a serious complex because her husband was well educated, whereas she had little formal education, having been obliged to leave school for work at a young age. She felt intelligent and was interested in current events but had a hard time "correctly expressing my ideas." Often when with their friends she wanted to express her opinion but "I don't dare take the risk." Instead, she simply responded yes or no without engaging in discussion because she feared sounding ridiculous. Afraid her husband might tire of her, she asked Auclair to suggest advice books. Auclair started by reassuring her, "your letter is very well written, which proves that your problem is not nearly as serious as you think it is." Her shyness and admiration for her husband had given her a complex, but she already had the remedy. "As always, be natural, simple, direct and you will never come across as maladroit or unoriginal." She did share one "trick" the actress Arletty used whenever she found herself "[f]acing a fancy lady trying to intimidate her. She wouldn't utter a word but would stare hard at the lady's hands. Try it!"[40]

Domestic Violence

Some of the problems married women faced could be more painful and dangerous than the usual marital misunderstandings. Auclair's only discussion of domestic violence pertained to her personal experience when her then-husband Jean Prévost slapped and threatened her at a dinner party. That is the only reference I found, and only in two of her books, to physical abuse. Clearly embarrassed enough to avoid openly describing the slap and her emotional response except in a work of fiction, Auclair downplayed the threat in her case, insisting that her ex-husband had never done anything like that before and that she knew his threat about future mistreatment was empty. Regardless, this behavior had been the final straw for her. Auclair left him that night.

While not a direct recommendation, her unwillingness to tolerate Prévost's behavior and immediate decision to leave the marriage conveyed a clear message to her readers.

Ségal addressed the issue in an early column. In 1947, "Chagrin" (Pain) wrote that her husband not only insulted and hit her but also objected to, screamed at, and terrified his stepdaughter who often ended up clinging to her legs. Ségal responded,

> Life has cruelly tested you and I understand your desire to get back to your life with your little "sunshine." If you determine that you have serious enough grievances against your husband and feel you have the strength to support your needs and those of your child on your own, go see a lawyer. But remember it can take even more courage to get yourself out of a tough situation than it does to submit to it. Much optimism too. Be brave. Sending my best wishes from the bottom of my heart for good luck for you and your little girl.[41]

The issue came up again the following year when Ségal used her entire Letters from the Heart page in *Elle* for a group of letters on topics that regularly appeared in her mailbox. She chose the letters "because each one includes one of the constant dramas whose echoes I find in so many calls for help." Although specifics may have varied, Ségal hoped the letters and her responses would speak to other women in similar situations. Alongside letters about a lover who dumped a wife after she had left her husband for him and a young woman complaining about young men only interested in sex, the first letter she included, from Suzanne, under the heading "I'm afraid he's going to kill me," presented the most serious and painful situation, a husband who physically and emotionally abused his wife. Suzanne's letter was direct and blunt. "I have been married for two years, my life is hell. It's only for my little Josy, who's 1 year old, that I stay and put up with the insults and blows of the one I must call my husband. I'm afraid he's going to kill me." Rather than advising Suzanne to leave, Ségal described her husband as ill and needing to see a psychologist to figure out what caused his angry outbursts. She urged Suzanne to have the courage and patience to try that approach, insisting that their child, for whom she stayed in the marriage, also suffered from the violence and anger. Ségal put the onus on the abused wife. She emphasized the danger to their child because Suzanne had expressed the need to stay in the marriage for that child's sake. However, after hedging and advising patience and therapy, Ségal emphasized again the need to protect her child. "If this supreme effort fails, you will have the right to get a separation, if only in the interest of your child. The scenes you describe have a harmful and lasting impact on a child's soul. A lawyer will advise you."[42] Ségal opened by encouraging a victim of domestic violence to try and persuade her abuser to get therapy. However, she did not advocate staying at any cost, pointing out Suzanne's right to a legal separation and recommending she get legal counsel to fight for a safer, independent future.

Anne Brunswic, Ségal's great niece, was critical of her response and admitted, "The priest would have ordered Suzanne to endure the ordeal sent by the Savior. The police would have sent the sissy back home." In contrast, "Marcelle brought into play a psychologist and a lawyer, which is more modern," but Brunswic feared "that's not going to save (the writer's) life."[43] In the following years, Ségal occasionally addressed letters from women experiencing violence and abuse. Jacqueline, married with children, wrote that her husband had "a dreadful, crooked, angry, violent character." If Ségal advised her to accept her husband as he was for her children's sake, "what a living hell my life will be." Ségal responded that she clearly had "every right not to accept" his making her life hell. However, she advised Jacqueline to prepare before making a move with such serious consequences. She recommended Jacqueline meet with a lawyer and figure out how she would be able to support herself and her children. Once she had taken those steps she could give her husband an ultimatum: she would leave unless he changed his ways.[44] While letters like this one rarely appeared in her column, Ségal regularly offered to respond directly to correspondents whose alias names may have signaled an abusive situation. For example, Ségal asked Coeur en peine (Heart in Pain) to "write to us directly and send us your address, and don't give up."[45]

According to Brunswic, who found Ségal's unpublished responses to dozens of letters from women in abusive relationships, Ségal's private responses echoed what she had recommended in *Elle,* mentioning the possibility of ending the marriage, but first advocating seeking psychological help for the abuser and consulting a lawyer before considering divorce.[46] However, Ségal's approach shifted over time. In 1960, Ségal responded in *Elle* to a woman suffering from her husband's emotional abuse. He reminded her constantly that she was "living under my roof," and insisted, "This is what a housewife ought to expect." Ségal pointed out, "There's a man who does not mince his words." Since her husband had been up front with her, she could be sure what to expect. Ségal laid out three possible options: she could either continue playing Cinderella, or get a paid job and hire a maid, or "head for the door."[47] To a wife who wrote in 1966 about the pain of knowing her husband regularly slept with other women, Ségal responded that she should stay in the marriage only if she needed her husband's financial support to raise the children, but, she insisted, "not one day more." Her private advice to abused women likely followed that pattern.[48]

In an interview in 1982, Ségal highlighted how attitudes had changed since she started her column. She had always tried "to evolve with the broader customs and moral values that have, after all, changed quite a bit since 1945." She admitted, "If I were to reread my first responses, I have a feeling I would not be proud of them." Early on she might have told a woman whose husband cheated to stay with him. In 1982 she would respond, "It seems to me that this mister is no longer worthy of your trust."[49]

Ségal's early hedging did not challenge the prevalent thinking of the times, although she raised the issue long before it had much public attention. Based on the occasional letters that appeared in *Elle*, Ségal's responses to abused women shifted over time. Even in her early columns, she pointed out the abused woman's right to legal separation and advised consulting with a lawyer. Clearly, Ségal and Auclair shied away from the issue. Their columns were meant not just to guide but to inspire and entertain their readers, which may have made it difficult to take on painful issues of such magnitude. Still, when Ségal occasionally addressed the issue, she did not blame the women who wrote her or recommend that they stay at all costs.

Sexuality: Premarital, Extramarital, and Same Sex

While partner violence came up rarely, topics related to sex and marriage arose frequently. This kind of explicit discussion of sex appeared regularly in both magazines starting in the 1950s, partly triggered by attention to Alfred Kinsey's studies of sexuality. His first book, *Sexual Behavior in the Human Male,* published in 1948, appeared in French that same year. Kinsey's second study, *Sexual Behavior in the Human Female,* appeared in a French translation in 1954. While few people would have read Kinsey's lengthy academic books, references to his work quickly permeated popular books and magazines in the 1950s, heralding more candid discussions about sex.[50]

From younger, unmarried women, who for the most part assumed they would marry, the topic of greatest concern had to do with the issue of premarital sex. Older married women's questions often centered on infidelity, usually of their husbands. In both cases, the responses given by Auclair and Ségal took a practical rather than a judgmental stance. The problem was not that premarital sex was sinful or immoral. In fact, the sense that attitudes toward sex were changing rapidly long pre-dated the sexual revolution that supposedly only started after 1968.[51] Still, for most young women, Ségal and Auclair advised them to resist the pressures for sex they faced from their boyfriends.

By 1951 Ségal was ready to respond at length to a series of questions she had received from her readers about women's sexual liberty, which she described as a "burning question." One correspondent asserted, "my life is my own." The writer complained about both those who resist the "inevitable evolution of morals" and those who "pretend to get ahead of the music."[52] While attitudes toward sex evolved only slowly, change was inevitable.[53] In her 1952 book about being an advice columnist, Ségal dedicated a chapter to the issue of "Sexual Liberty," reporting that she received several letters a week on the topic. She concluded about free sex, "men live it as an adventure, like a fish in the sea, woman like a fish out of water."[54] The young women who wrote her feared getting a bad reputation for having sex outside of marriage, damaging their chances of marriage. But Ségal reported that just as many young women worried about gaining a reputation as a prude because they refused to have sex. Ségal declined to condemn either behavior, reassuring women in both instances that they were their own worst critics.[55] Several years later, Ségal made light of strict attitudes, responding to one "faithful" male reader who asked, "please tell me what you think of a young girl of 14 who has kissed three boys." He signed his letter, "Number One." Ségal responded that, "at her age, I had already kissed more than that. On New Year's Eve alone I kissed fourteen, ha!"[56]

Instead of morality, Ségal focused on the possible consequences of premarital sex, namely pregnancy. In 1955 she counseled a young woman worried that, if she refused her boyfriend's demand to have sex, he might leave her for someone else who would give in to his demands. Ségal agreed, that could happen. But if she went along, Ségal asked, who would take care of the baby? Given the real possibility of pregnancy, Ségal advised the young woman to follow her instincts and refuse her boyfriend's demands.[57]

Marcelle Auclair was particularly critical of young men's attitudes. She met in 1959 with a group of about thirty young men, ages 18–20, to probe their ideas about contemporary young women.[58] To her surprise and chagrin, she reported, the young men insisted that their female counterparts were all playing a game, namely, getting a man to marry them. Young women, they argued, used sex to trap them. "If they let themselves go that easily, it's only so that they can force us to marry them." Given that attitude, Auclair asked the young men directly if they thought it was important to marry a virgin. Several agreed, "We would really like her to be one." Another young man explained, "If she's not a virgin, we would need to know if it was an accident . . . or a regular thing." Auclair pressed them to consider if they should also avoid having sex before marriage. Illuminating the double standard, not one young man responded to Auclair's question. Even more aggravating to Auclair, the young men rejected the idea that they should take responsibility if, as a result of having sex, they got a young woman pregnant. "Girls know what they're doing." "It's their fault if they end up like that!" Barely hiding her indignation,

Auclair responded, "All the same! The boy had something to do with it? No?" Forlornly she concluded, "It seems the answer is no." In retrospect Auclair conceded that much of this was bravado and immaturity. However, to ensure her message got through to her young women readers, she consulted an "adult friend" who worked with young men. He agreed with Auclair's conclusion. "Boys disrespect girls, and it's the girls' fault. Spread the word!"[59]

Auclair complained about the legal double standard on marital infidelity. She attributed the law's lenient penalties for husbands' adultery to the fact that men made the laws.[60] Angry at the double standard that excused or even expected young unmarried men to have sex but vilified young women for the same behavior, Auclair did not deny the reality of sexual desire. She counseled young people to treat sexual appetite like all appetites, as something that can be enjoyed but must be controlled. Clearly shaped by her painful experiences with Prévost, she insisted that young men learn to control their sexual appetites.[61] Again, the advice was couched not in moral but in practical terms. Auclair raised the possibility of pregnancy, but also lamented the continuing assumption that, even as they pressed young women to have sex, young men expected to marry a virgin. Auclair published a letter from a young woman who noted that, if society truly accepted the equality of the sexes, then the notion of female purity as an asset or trump card to a happy marriage was anachronistic. But, the letter concluded, because women faced much higher risks, equality in principle still resulted in an unequal reality.[62] Auclair's readers questioned whether marriage was the only solution for all women and challenged the idea that only marital sex was legitimate. One letter asked why women who never married should not have the right to sexual pleasure.[63]

For heterosexual women, the double standard also levied different judgments on extramarital sex. Ségal noted the frequency of letters about that issue, seven of ten letters, she estimated. Given its prevalence, Ségal advised married women to prepare themselves for the possibility. For too many women, "everything falls apart" when they discover their husband's infidelity. They found themselves obsessed, unable to eat or sleep, and depressed. But, Ségal pointed out, "the bad behavior is common, widespread."[64] Unlike Auclair who criticized men's behavior and dismissed the notion that they could not control themselves, Ségal advised wives to be prepared. Given that warning, Ségal was puzzled about women who were provident and forward looking when it came to illnesses, accidents, and other hardships, but somehow never considered the possibility of their husbands' infidelity. Although Ségal considered women's attitude unrealistic, she insisted that her advice was not intended to encourage husbands to cheat. They hardly needed her encouragement, she noted. Her point was to be prepared and adapt.[65]

In one letter about extramarital sex, an engaged woman, Sidonie, asked for help sorting things out. Her fiancé asked if she would let him have mistresses. "I would be everything for him . . . The others would just be objects, a nice meal eaten without you." He told her that she should agree, to prove that there was more than physical love between them. What they had as a couple was more precious. Sidonie asked Ségal if she should accept this "uncertain happiness." Ségal responded bluntly. "No. Because there's no balance. He ignores the A. B. C.'s of conjugal manners." Ségal chides the fiancé, surprised that he dared call himself French. Most French men were more diplomatic, "tactful"; if they intended to cheat on their wives they did not ask permission. Ségal scolds the fiancé for requesting indulgence in advance, rather than criticizing his expected infidelity. She also complained about the lack of balance since he would not accept that behavior from his fiancée.[66]

Another writer, Babette, referred to herself as "a troubled woman like so many others." She asked her husband to break things off with the other woman, but he refused, explaining that he loved both of them and did not want to lose either one of them. He explained, shamelessly, "you complement each other so well." Asked her opinion, Ségal pointed out that, if she understood Babette's husband correctly, Babette could only make up half of her husband's happiness but he thought he could satisfy that of two women. "Put another way, he is worth four times more than you. Hat's off." Ségal recommended she let go of worshipping him and leave him alone on his summit. Have the courage "to refuse the half-portion." Ségal berated women for taking part in the game by making themselves available for married men. Women should support each other rather than competing for the same man. If women did that, "these misters would only have the choice of one woman or none and so long to the harem, so long to the Pacha." In the meantime, Ségal recognized that some married women with children did not have the resources to survive on their own. In those situations, she recommended only putting up with the cheating husband until their children grew up, but "Not one more day."[67]

Auclair, less jovial about or forgiving of male infidelity, directly took on the double standard that excused men's behavior, imploring men to learn self-control. Not surprising given her marriage to Prévost, she also warned that sexual liberty could become a form of slavery. Auclair also insisted that men who refused to control their sexual behavior had no grounds to expect their wives and daughters to do so.[68]

While it was rare and usually indirect, Auclair and Ségal occasionally touched on the topic of lesbian love. Ségal in 1949 included part of a letter that hinted at same sex attraction. "Miss D" explained to Ségal that she had moved out of her parent's home at age 18, lured to Paris "by a young woman, I... etc..." The letter in *Elle* ended with the ellipses, followed by Ségal's response: "Your letter is not the kind of letter that can be published in a woman's magazine. I'll write to you directly if you send me an address."[69] Auclair's essay in the July 1956 issue of *Marie-Claire* addressed sexual desire, "the most sacrosanct taboo of the era... the love we must have the courage to call physical." The following month Auclair published a letter sent in response to her essay that, in veiled terms, expanded the discussion to include lesbian love.[70]

You Can Handle This

If Auclair and Ségal conveyed one overarching idea to their readers, they reassured the women who wrote them that they could sort things out. Auclair and Ségal viewed themselves as simply helping their readers find their way. As journalist Anne Gallois explained in *Le Monde,* "In four or five lines, [Ségal] lifts your spirits with her secret recipe: the advice of a wise friend, a shot in the arm from a woman of action, the common sense of someone who has lived and suffered, the humor essential to staying healthy... and away we go!"[71] Auclair and Ségal mined their own personal lives and struggles not just for what they had learned but also to emphasize to their readers that they themselves were far from perfect. They too had done things they regretted, behaved badly, made bad choices. They wanted to guide readers but not from a position of superiority. They thereby set a tone that made what they said much more relatable and compelling to readers. Ségal stressed learning from her mistakes. Auclair agreed but also pressed readers to learn to find happiness from within. In her book about her career as an advisor, one message ran through

Ségal's responses over her years of writing the column: learn from my mistakes. To Ségal, to be a good advice columnist, "it's not bad to have done lots of stupid things." The women who wrote to her reminded her of many of the women she knew personally. She even recognized them when she looked in the mirror. "You resemble them, Ségal, do you have what it takes to offer them advice?"[72] It was not that she had all the answers. Rather, she had done many stupid things and wanted to help other women avoid some of them. To her, a good advice columnist "must know the local forest for having gotten lost in it many times, must have skinned her knees, must have stumbled over every stone, must have fallen down, gotten up only to fall down again." In responding to her readers, she relied on what she had learned from her own tumbles. She passed along the "reference points" that had guided her, taking the "the lost person by the hand and telling them: 'Come this way. It might be a longer road but it's not as bad. No, not that one. It leads to a dead end. I've tried it.' "[73]

On a television interview about *Elle*, Ségal advised people to approach life seriously but, "with humor, to laugh, not to make a tragedy out of a problem that's not tragic, to set things straight."[74] Auclair expressed the same idea. "If I hadn't known failures, the trouble every person runs into, if I had not committed follies, not to say foolishness—like so many women, would I understand this world we're living in? Stupid things, we all do them. The essential thing is not to do the same stupid thing twice."[75] Her goal had been to help others avoid "the stupid things I've done."[76]

Having made so many mistakes herself, Ségal explained, she was never tempted to respond harshly or judgmentally to her readers, "What are you doing? Aren't you ashamed of yourself?" S. R. confessed to having cheated on her husband and closed fearfully, "I know you're not easy on adultery, but I beg you, don't come down too hard on me." Ségal responded, "By what right would I come down hard on you? To stone the adulterous woman, you have to be without sin. That is not my case, nor that of your husband."[77] Auclair agreed on that point, "it was not a matter of hectoring anyone."[78] Because everyone makes mistakes, their role was not to judge, particularly because, as they both regularly emphasized, they themselves were not perfect. No matter how dire the situation might seem, Ségal and Auclair reassured their readers that they could work things out. Auclair provided techniques, wanting "to help you find in yourself the source of all good things."[79]

Dealing with Pain

Both Ségal and Auclair recognized that many of the people who wrote them were in pain. Ségal rejected the idea that her job was always to tell the truth regardless of the additional pain it might cause. For example, she saw no point in warning a wife whose husband had abandoned her that he would never return, or advising a person with cancer to give up hope for a cure, or telling a mother that her child was a failure. "Such truths do more harm than good." Rather than adding to the pain, her goal was to "gild the lily" and "turn the thoughts of the 'broken hearted' towards attractive things."[80] She suggested options. She responded to a letter from a depressed 15-year-old boy who was unable to make friends and overwhelmed by his father's constant criticism. He felt all alone, spent all day listening to music, and closed by saying, "I'm afraid you won't understand me." Ségal reassured him, "But of course I understand you." She too had been 15, and "figuring out life can sometimes be painful." Her suggestion, since he liked listening to music, was to take up an instrument, learn to play, join an orchestra or choir, and meet people who shared that interest. She concluded by inviting him to come visit her.[81]

Ségal responded straightforwardly to people who criticized her for telling desperate people to distract themselves. "Deep in my soul and my conscience, I believe I have to say it, that there is no advice that's more effective." She had done it herself hundreds of times, and it had worked hundreds of times.[82]

Auclair agreed in general, although she applied her own spiritual belief system to the topic of dealing with pain. In a lesson titled "Replace . . .," Auclair explained it was not enough to try and stop bad thoughts. "As soon as you uproot a negative thought, it's terribly urgent to replace it with a positive thought." Nature hates a void, she explained, so if you don't substitute good thoughts for bad ones, bad thoughts would pop back up like weeds in a garden. She warned that replacing bad with good thoughts took time. Do it as often as necessary until the bad tendencies give in to new habits. Auclair warned, "fear, criticism, self-doubt, anxiety, etc. . . are extremely tenacious, only little by little will you be able to change your reflexes."[83]

Auclair emphasized the importance of looking forward rather than spending time regretting the past, "the heaviest of burdens." Learn from the past and use the experience to avoid repeating "the stupidity or the harm" committed out of "ignorance or confusion." Rather than dwelling on past mistakes, decide to do better and move on.[84] Ségal agreed, using herself as the example. Not only had she done many stupid things, she explained, four times in her life she had "started over again from zero (absolute zero if I can put it that way)." She was 44 the last time it happened. Having lost it all and started over that many times entitled her, she insisted, to exhort her readers, "Courage, don't despair, you have your whole life ahead of you."[85]

Marcelle Auclair's daughter Françoise pointed out similar ups and downs in her mother's life. In their dual memoir, she noted that Marcelle had "truly ridden the roller coaster . . . Being broke with dad at the start of your marriage, after that your success at

Marcelle Auclair playing with her grandson Jean-Victor Prévost. Photo courtesy of Jean-Victor Auclair Prévost.

Marie-Claire .... Then the war threw everything into the trash and you had to start over again from zero."[86] Still, Auclair retained her approach to life and happiness, which she shared with the world. As she explained, "I believe that you have to take life as it comes, with a lot of philosophy, a lot of good feeling and especially with a certain sense of humor, not take things too seriously, and especially, no drama."[87]

Avoiding Hard News: France's Wars of Decolonization

While the magazines never presented themselves as news sources, the decolonization wars in Indochina and Algeria were significant events in the news cycle with a major impact on French politics yet only appeared occasionally in *Elle* or *Marie-Claire.* In a year-end summary of 1949 for *Elle,* André Maurois included a paragraph about "a final problem, this one serious, the Indochina War." Maurois briefly summarized the situation. Other short references appeared occasionally, but rarely as the topic of an article. Instead, small inserts mentioned a book drive for soldiers in Indochina or a military nurse receiving a medal for her service.[88]

The wars might have appeared more often as a topic in advice columns like Ségal's Letters from the Heart or Auclair's "Your Problems" feature. During World War II, women's magazines in France regularly published letters from wives of French soldiers and POWs asking for advice. The frequency reflected the massive scale of the war effort. In 1939 France mobilized 5 million men ages 20–40. The June 1940 defeat led to the captivity of over 1.58 million French soldiers, 60 percent of whom were married. Some 800,000 POW wives, many of them also mothers, faced alone the extremely difficult conditions of life in wartime France.[89]

Yet compared to World War II, the wars in Indochina and Algeria took place far from Europe and directly impacted far fewer families in France. During the Indochina War, France used career military, colonial troops, and the Foreign Legion rather than mobilizing regular army troops. In Algeria, the strength of the FLN's Algerian liberation movement and France's determination to defeat it led France eventually to mobilize 400,000 troops to serve in what the French government referred to as a "maintenance of order" operation, instead of applying the term war. Although France mobilized a broader percentage of the population than it had during the Indochina War, the number of French soldiers serving in Algeria represented a smaller and younger segment of the population compared to the soldiers of World War II. The vastly different scale of the experience in metropolitan France could explain why so few readers' letters mentioned someone—boyfriend, fiancé or husband—serving in the decolonization wars.[90]

Superstars: Ségal and Auclair on the Small Screen

In addition to their public personas in the print medium, both Ségal and Auclair began to appear on television in the mid-1950s. At that time France's national broadcasting system had just one station. By 1960, only one in four homes in France had a television. These figures rapidly changed. In 1964 national broadcasting started a second station. By 1973, some eighty percent of homes had televisions. Given their celebrity status, both Ségal and Auclair were invited to appear as guests on a variety of shows, featured in some broadcasts, and interviewed in others, particularly Auclair after she published a book. Ségal and Auclair each played with, exaggerating in some ways, the personalities they presented in print.

Ségal's appearances were lighthearted spoofs of herself, someone who took her job seriously but was also ready to make fun of herself and her role. In 1954 Ségal appeared on a show called *Visite à* (*Visit to*), which took viewers every week behind the scenes at a variety of enterprises. For the October 6, 1954 episode they visited "a woman's weekly," taking viewers behind the scenes at *Elle* to watch the editors, photographers, and models put together an issue. The segments included a photo shoot of a model wearing a Dior dress, an editors' meeting where they discussed the week's content, and a discussion with Ségal about her column. She wore a business-like button-down shirt and a skirt and sat at her desk in her office; interviewer Jacques Donot perched himself on her desk to ask questions about the letters she received. To maintain confidentiality, Ségal insisted they move to a different office, which turned out to be the stairwell. Donot questioned her about the typical letter writer. Ségal reported that most writers were young women, but men wrote to her too. At first only about one letter in one hundred came from a man but by 1954, she reported, men sent about one in six or seven letters. The letters asked about everything, from love and family to beauty and how to play the guitar. Ségal explained that she referred writers with serious problems to a support service *Elle* made available to readers in an office on the Champs-Elysées. She and Donot moved back from the stairwell to her office, where Ségal held up a stack of letters. Donot leaned over as if to try and read one of them. Ségal pulled the stack away and scolded him for peeking, insisting that she maintained "absolute discretion."[91]

Jacques Donot interviewing Marcelle Ségal about her column in Elle. "Visite à un hebdomadaire féminin: Elle." Visite à, October 6, 1954. Institut national de l'audiovisuel, France INA 105127817.

Ségal pointed out that, while some letters presented serious issues, many were less than serious. She considered it her job to inject humor into situations, encouraging readers not to make them into a tragedy, getting them to smile or laugh, and helping them "get things back on track." She closed by reading a letter from a young woman whose mother, after seeing her daughter's friend on a scooter, admonished her daughter about the evils of scooters. The mother insisted that her daughter's friend should be ashamed of using a scooter, warning that sooner or later her friend would end up pregnant, threatening "you'll see." Ségal, puzzled responded, "pregnant from a scooter?" She worried more about the scooter causing the friend to break an ankle. Ségal came across as droll, someone who made fun of herself but also took her job very seriously.[92]

Both women appeared, although never together, on a show called *Dim Dam Dom*, first aired in 1965 in conjunction with French broadcasting's expansion to two television channels. *Dim Dam Dom*, which ran until 1971, was linked to *Elle* and produced by the magazine's associate editor-in-chief Daisy de Galard. The show's name indicated its purview: A monthly Sunday broadcast (Dim for Dimanche or Sunday) aimed primarily at a female audience (Dam shorthand for Dames or ladies), and for men (Dom stood for "d'hommes" or men). *Dim Dam Dom* had a modern, sophisticated feel for the era but also took a lighthearted approach. Instead of a regular host, a different well-known woman hosted each episode, including popular singers Françoise Hardy and Sylvie Vartan and actresses Françoise Dorléac (older sister of Catherine Deneuve) and Masha Méril. Something of a variety show, each episode included interviews, skits, guest performers, and a dance troupe, the René Golliard ballet corps. Its illustrious guests included authors Marguerite Duras, Françoise Sagan, and Anaïs Nin; film actress Jeanne Moreau; popular singers Serge

Gainsbourg and Charles Trenet; and artist Salvador Dali. Rock star Jimmy Hendrix and his band played "Hey Joe" on the air.[93] In a recent YouTube post, "George" described avidly watching *Dim Dam Dom* when he was 10. *Dim Dam Dom* "amazed and energized" him. He knew it was special because his mother let him stay up late on a school night to watch it.[94]

Auclair and Ségal each appeared in three different episodes. In 1965, *Dim Dam Dom* produced an episode, "Marcelle Auclair Asks," where she headlined a series of segments and interviews. Given her long interest in physical fitness, in the first segment Auclair discussed new work-out equipment with an expert, while clips demonstrated vibrating belts, weight-lifting equipment, and stationary cycles. The next segment focused on child safety in the home, especially the importance of keeping sharp objects and poisons out of reach. For her final segment, Auclair interviewed a successful businesswoman, the director of personnel for a large department store. The guest reported that she had encountered hostility and resentment from her male colleagues. She struggled to prove herself and admitted to Auclair that the job had taken over her life. She had never married, she told Auclair, and had no private or personal life. Auclair asked if she had any interest in marrying, to which her guest said yes. Auclair advised her of the importance of finding an "open minded" man who would support her ambitions.[95] That had been one trait of her ex-husband, Jean Prévost, that she appreciated both during their marriage and in retrospect. He never expected Marcelle to give up her writing career to become a full-time homemaker.

A few months after that show aired, another episode highlighted the differences between the two Marcelles. *Dim Dam Dom* produced a segment titled "Marcelle Ségal Answers," the name possibly a humorous reference to her rival's segment "Marcelle Auclair Asks." In Ségal's segment, the action plays out as the letter writer, a man, narrates his problem. He confides that he has a serious problem only Ségal can help him solve. On screen appears a dark-haired man dressed in jeans, cowboy boots, and a cowboy hat, riding on the moving handrail of a department store escalator. The cowboy explained that he was 28, "tall, dark, athletic, but deeply shy." Three months earlier he had fallen "crazy in love" with a pretty cashier he saw every day when he shopped. "I've tried everything I can to attract her attention." As he narrates the letter, he poses in his cowboy hat, pointing with a toy gun in each hand, miming a shoot 'em up. "Yesterday," the narrator continues, "she looked at me. It seemed like a good moment but I didn't dare." He asks Ségal for help. The camera shifts to Ségal standing in the cashier's check-out lane. An image of the cashier's left hand appears. Ségal tells the cowboy "but look!"—the cashier was wearing a wedding ring. In what was clearly a spoof, Ségal enjoyed playing with her role.[96]

In contrast, Auclair always presented herself as sober, serious, and elegant. She almost always wore a plain black dress or black blouse accented by a bulky necklace of beads or pearls. Many of her appearances involved someone interviewing her about her most recent book. An interview in 1960 on *Lectures pour Tous* (*Reading for Everyone*) centered on her dialogue with her readers. Like Ségal, Auclair admitted that she never knew for sure if her advice had been helpful, but she pointed out that readers regularly sent letters thanking her.[97]

Empowering Women

For both Ségal and Auclair, the first half of their lives, living as outsiders, struggling with marriage, parenting, and loss gave them insights they drew on, shaped their approach to life, and primed them to pass along what they had learned. By the mid-1950s they had both achieved professional and personal success. Both journalists felt their complicated and at times painful personal experiences prepared them to serve as guides, encouraging and helping women figure out how to solve their own problems. *Marie-Claire* and *Elle* launched Auclair and Ségal's exchanges with their readers. Television appearances involving dialogues with interviewers and fellow guests expanded their audience. In print and on the small screen, Ségal and Auclair urged their readers to resolve problems not by trying to change others but by adjusting their own orientation, trying new activities, changing the focus, dialing back the drama, seeking peace from within, and altering their internal dialogue. They sought to reassure women and give them strategies to manage the problems that came their way.

Bridges to Feminism: Marcelle Auclair, Marcelle Ségal, and Women's Magazines in Twentieth-Century France. Sarah Fishman, Oxford University Press.
DOI: 10.1093/9780197791356.003.0006

6

Parenting, Publishing, Protesting

Life Messages Beyond the Columns

To give you a love of laughter; to watch a zest for life growing, getting bigger and blossoming in you: that's the goal of the little page you read every week called "Letters from the Heart."

MARCELLE SÉGAL, *Mon métier, Le courrier du cœur* (1952)

I believe that you have to take life as it comes, with a lot of philosophy, a lot of good feeling and especially with a certain sense of humor, not take things too seriously, and especially, no drama.[1]

MARCELLE AUCLAIR, *Aujourd'hui Madame*
A2/France 2, 26 June 1975

In spite of their different backgrounds, Marcelle Ségal and Marcelle Auclair approached their work with similar perspectives, crafting messages that resonated with their readers. In addition to their columns in *Marie-Claire* and *Elle*, both Auclair and Ségal penned books that revealed their own personal imperfections and travails in life. For their readers' benefit they elaborated, in writing about their lives, on their stumbles and the lessons they had learned, going well beyond what they could write in limited magazine column space.

Parenting: Father Doesn't Know Best, Being a Single Mother

Ségal's parenting experience followed an unconventional path. As a nearly 50-year-old divorcee by the end of World War II, she embarked on becoming a mother again on her own terms. Shortly after the war, Ségal adopted an 11-year-old orphan, Harold. The following year Harold's closest friend moved in with them. Nine years later, in 1955, Ségal adopted a second boy whose parents had abandoned him. In 1963 she took in one of her younger son's friends. All four of the boys, including her adopted sons, aware that she was not their birth mother, called her Aunt Marcelle rather than mother.[2]

Ségal described her relationship with the boys following a script whereby she became the evil stepmother to her poor orphan sons. They treated her like a sadistic old lady if she dared tell them to wash their hands before dinner or sent them to bed before the end of the television detective show they were watching. At one point, when Harold was deeply unhappy living with her, Ségal proposed sending him to an upscale boarding school and showed him a brochure with appealing photos of tennis courts and playing fields. Harold replied that he had no desire to leave and preferred to stay with her. Puzzled, she told him she thought he was unhappy, to which he replied, "I never said that." Ségal conceded that point, noting that he never said much of anything and instead of responding to questions, he "closed up tight like an oyster." While she found Harold's silence difficult, she had no regrets about any of the boys she adopted or fostered. Her sons' difficult adolescent years were "something that happens along the way." All four boys found good jobs, married, and had children. Ségal, whose biological daughter died at age seven, credits the boys with teaching her everything she knew about adolescence. Raising them had been one of the "great adventures" of her life.[3]

For Auclair, having lost her steady job and needing to support her three adolescents, the immediate postwar years presented significant challenges. Auclair had not married until she was well into her 20s and never gave up her career as a writer/journalist, even after she had three children. She and Jean lived on a tight budget, which they stretched to the limit to pay for household help. Auclair, in discussing the situation with her daughter, explained that she had never been particularly skilled at either housekeeping or cooking. Paying for help made for a tight budget by the end of the month, "but it was better for me to write than to cook and do laundry."[4] Jean supported her decision. Working for wages to pay for household help meant she had never been a full-time parent.

By the end of the war she found herself alone raising 14-, 15- and 16-year-olds, who had been "badly shaken by their father's death." Even without a steady job in the city, Auclair decided to move back to Paris after the war for Michel and Alain's studies. The German army had pillaged her prewar apartment, so she rented a few furnished rooms, "damaged and in ruins," while she worked with an agency to find a new permanent apartment.[5] Her oldest son Michel excelled academically, completed a degree at one of France's elite universities, the Institut des Etudes Politiques (Institute for Political Studies), worked for the United Nation's Educational, Scientific and Cultural Organization (UNESCO), and published a series of young adult novels under the pseudonym Hugues Varnac.[6]

By contrast, Alain's misbehavior got him expelled from several high schools. According to his sister Françoise, Alain spent most of his time just after the war tagging along with American GIs. He even pretended to be a GI, dressed in a uniform he bought from a street peddler so that he could get into movie theaters reserved for American soldiers. With their mother spending most weekends in the countryside, Françoise reported that Alain regularly brought American women back to their Paris apartment. In the end, his American adventures had a positive outcome. Alain mastered English and could speak with either an American or a British accent. Eventually, to get him away from bad influences, Auclair sent Alain to Canada to finish high school. He did so well there that he won a scholarship to attend Princeton University where he completed his degree in 1951.[7] While in the United States, he met and in 1952 married an American woman, Helen Alexander, the daughter of the Under-Secretary of the Army under President Truman.[8]

Several years later, Alain and Helen moved to France and had children. Like his parents, Alain worked as a journalist and author.

Marcelle Auclair with her son Alain Prévost. Photo courtesy of Jean-Victor Auclair Prévost.

He published novels his mother described as "barely disguised autobiographies."[9] In 1971, Alain died unexpectedly of a heart attack, at age 41. In her dual autobiography with her daughter Françoise, Auclair described the day she got the call that Alain had died as one of her most painful memories. "Since then nothing else has brought a tear to my eye." Françoise had not been able to console her mother because she herself had been broken hearted by the loss of a brother she called her best friend and her "accomplice."[10]

Unlike her brothers, Françoise showed little interest in pursuing her education. During the war, she had finished what she called a high school "pre-baccalaureate" and rather than resuming school, she decided to become an actress.[11] In 1946, at age 16, Françoise joined a theater troupe that performed for Allied troops stationed in Germany. Before long she returned to Paris, pregnant. Marcelle took the pregnancy in stride, telling her, "We'll just have one more Prévost." She fought Françoise's plan to marry the baby's father, opposed to the idea of her marrying just to "fix" things. Defying her mother, Françoise married the young man. The pregnancy did not interfere with her acting career.[12] By 1949, Françoise began appearing in films and had the highest public profile of Auclair's three children. By the 1960s, she had gained fame as a leading New Wave film actress. She appeared in some seventy-four films between 1949 and 1985. In addition to numerous French films, she also starred in German, English, American, and Italian films. She played a key role in a 1961 British film, *Payroll*, described by the British Film Institute as a neo-noir "cult classic."[13]

By the time Auclair and Françoise appeared together on a television interview to discuss their joint autobiography, *Mémoires à deux voix* (Memoir in Two Voices), Auclair was the matriarch of a family.[14] Françoise noted that Marcelle referred to her nine

Françoise Prévost in the British film *Payroll*: 1961—UK. Françoise Prévost, Director: Sidney Hayers. Alamy.

grandchildren and great grandchildren as a true United Nations. Her children and grandchildren had married spouses from the United States, Sweden, Ireland, Holland, and Denmark. Auclair had made it clear that she could not be counted on to be the babysitter. "I'm not a grandma but a grandpa" she quipped, because she loved developing her grandchildren's personalities through books and cultural activities.[15] In 1971, she brought her grandson, Alain's son Jean-Victor, with her on a return visit to Chile.[16]

Ségal and Auclair struggled but succeeded as single parents. They both emphasized that as women, they had to assert themselves to get what they wanted. They were financially stable enough to purchase and fix up second homes outside of Paris. In writing about their adventures with buying and renovating properties in the countryside, Auclair and Ségal underscored their struggles to do things the way they wanted.

A House in the Country

Auclair's first country house dated to the 1930s, when she and Jean Prévost were still married. A mutual friend, artist Marie Laurencin offered to sell them her country home in Champrosay, about 25 miles southeast of Paris. They declined because they could not afford it, but Laurencin, without explaining why, wanted them to have the house, furniture and all. She brushed off their concerns about the price and reassured them they could pay her when they could afford it. Auclair loved the house. After her divorce and especially just after the war, she described it as "a providential retreat," the perfect place for writing books.[17] In 1955, she sold it to purchase another country house in Etiolles, a small town down the road from Champrosay. That house was in bad shape but Auclair, without explaining how, managed to "turn this ruin into a bright, beautiful house."[18] When she returned to *Marie-Claire,* she was able to negotiate working from there rather than the magazine's offices. She kept an apartment in Paris, renting out rooms when her children moved out to bring in additional money.[19]

Her counterpart, Marcelle Ségal, provides more detail on her struggles to get what she wanted as she fixed up a country home. By 1947, Ségal, established at *Elle* and having just adopted Harold, decided she wanted a place outside the city to spend time during the summer and holidays. She purchased, "together with friends" she never named, "a charming old shack that we built up and furnished little by little" in the small town of Gouvieux, northeast of Paris.[20] When she first saw the old shack in the middle of a garden surrounded by an old stone wall, it was falling to pieces. Even in its decrepit condition, she knew it was exactly what she wanted. The first time she walked through the shack, a bat startled her. She stepped over broken glass, piles of old newspapers, and empty bottles all over a floor that rolled like "soft clay." Wind blew in through holes in the wall and roof. She emerged covered with spider webs. Her friends nicknamed it the Poverty Castle (Chateau de la Mouise).[21]

Ségal, unable to afford an architect to oversee renovations, drew up her ideas, and marked the walls to show builders where she wanted windows, closets, doors, and a skylight. Over the years it took to finish the work, she got to know the local carpenters, plumbers, electricians, and painters. At times she asked for things that the builders told her could not be done. Ségal stood her ground, and since her ideas worked, the builders stopped fighting her. The repairs took more than ten years by which time the local craftsmen had moved on to work on building the huge suburban low-income housing developments the government began financing in the mid-1950s.[22]

Ségal hosted a celebration at the house the first time she used the fireplace, something she had insisted on installing against the builders' advice. Another celebration took place at the "inauguration of the W.C.!" Banners, speeches, ribbon cutting, and a moment of silence "during which the oldest of the children had the badge of honor of being the first person to pull the chain" marked the occasion.[23] The sound of the toilet flushing elicited bravos and cheers. The terrace she added became the center of the house in the summers, the place where she spent her evenings under the stars, listening to birds, and smoking cigarillos. When the boys were young, they and their friends filled the house, playing ping pong, darts, pétanque, and board games; yelling; and chasing each other. At times she had thirty people at the table or on the lawn, camp cots lined up inside or even in a tent in the yard. Ségal described the years from 1947 to 1967 as "possibly the richest years of my existence," with her advice column, four children, three cats, and a country home.[24]

Ségal particularly grew to love gardening, the "number one pleasure of my summers," ruined only by greedy snails. She was

Marcelle Ségal relaxing with her cat. Photo courtesy of Anne Brunswic.

content sitting in front of the fireplace with a cat on her lap, smoking her cigarillos, and listening to Mozart, Handel, or Bach. Returning to Paris on Mondays always made her sad. She described her country house as the only thing she had ever undertaken that never disappointed her and always filled her with joy. "Thank you, my little shack. I love you."[25] When she retired in 1987, she moved to Gouvieux full time and threw herself into gardening.[26]

Ségal's Memoirs

While *Elle* and *Marie-Claire* were their primary vehicles for communicating to and with their readers, both Ségal and Auclair also published books that bolstered their messages, directly or by personal example. Those books sold extremely well and some of them remain in print.

Ségal published two autobiographical books. Her first, *Mon métier: le Courrier du Coeur* (*My Profession: Letters From the Heart*), published in 1952, answered questions she regularly received about what she did and how she did it. According to Ségal, people asked her the same questions over and over, often in the same order: Are the letters real? Why do people confide their personal problems to someone they don't know? How many letters do you get? Do men write to you? Do people follow your advice? In *Mon métier* Ségal, with her usual dry humor, responded to those questions.

Ségal explained that she had never wanted to become an advice columnist. The job fell on her "like a ton of bricks," but quickly she came to love it.[27] Readers asked her for advice about everything, from help finding a spouse and figuring out if a husband was cheating to choosing a gift. They wrote about their weight, complained about their pimples; they asked for fashion advice. They confided their fears and anxieties about their sex lives. Some parents, knowing that their children read her column, wrote hoping she would be, as she put it, either Santa Claus or the Bogeyman.[28] However, of the thousands of letters she had received since the start of her column, the vast majority, about eighty percent, had to do with love.

Indicating again the two-way nature of the conversation, in a chapter about "the pitfalls" of the profession Ségal described the constant negative feedback the job entailed. No matter what advice she offered, a certain number of readers were sure to disagree or even take offense. They did not hesitate to send her their vehement and even mocking complaints and criticism. Being an advice columnist resembled "walking on a high wire." One second of inattention could result in missing the wire and breaking her neck. Ségal maintained her equilibrium by not responding to the negative feedback. Whatever reaction it might provoke, the advice columnist must "tell the truth, the whole truth and nothing but the truth," and do it all in five lines or less.[29]

While the career required no formal training, Ségal listed what she considered the most important requirement: "an advice columnist must have lived a lot, a long time and badly."[30] She had to have raised children, loved passionately, lost everything, and experienced illness and the death of loved ones. She had to have done many stupid things. Here Ségal lets her readers know that she never considered herself better than the people who wrote to her. Rather than looking down on her correspondents from on high, she presented herself as one of them. In the end, the advice columnist, realistic, prudent, and discreet had to have a thick skin and a writing style with the elegance and precision of a carved inscription.[31]

Another frequently asked question was how she managed to discern her writers' personalities. Ségal pointed out that, in addition to the tone and wording of the letters, the handwriting alone revealed much about the writer's personality. She titled a section of the book: "Handwriting analyst in spite of myself. . . . Even if we sometimes lie, our handwriting never lies."[32] On one page, Ségal set up two columns: the row on the left had facsimiles of actual handwritten words, the row on the right had her verdict across from each handwritten word. In a series of pithy, often one-word descriptions, Ségal indicated each writer's personality based on the handwritten word, for example, "crushed," "slack," "steely," "closed," "bristling with thorns," or "confused." At the bottom of the list appeared the facsimile of a sentence in neat, precise handwriting, "I am a schoolteacher." Ségal's description: "schoolteacher."[33] According to Ségal, while reading her letters, she muttered to herself, "nice handwriting" (or) "good little girl" or "Lord what a mess" or "Could she be English?" Then she closed the chapter with a warning, "Don't believe a word I said. I'm lying."[34]

People also wanted to know whether her correspondents followed her advice. Ségal did not consider that aspect of her role "the most important thing."[35] She pointed out that hardly any letter-writers followed up to tell her what happened. She was also well aware at all times that her messages addressed more than the actual letter-writer. Readers often recognized situations similar to their own, adding to the scope of her influence. She explained, "thousands of readers, men and women, have been kind enough to tell me that reading 'Letters from the Heart' had a beneficial influence on them." Ségal understood that her advice was both personal and relevant to readers in general, not just women. She confirmed that men wrote to her too, though "not often enough."[36] On a regular basis, she closed her response with an invitation, "Would you like to come see me?"[37] While the vast majority never took up that invitation, Ségal, like Auclair, met face-to-face with her readers, mostly women, about two or three times a week. Personal contact reminded her that her letters came from real people with real problems, which helped her understand and better respond to all her readers.[38]

In the final section, Ségal elaborated on what she had learned from reading all the letters. For one thing, Ségal found that at their core, people's emotional needs had not changed much in spite of dramatic changes in social attitudes. She closed the book with an epilogue that set up five scenarios and invited readers to try their hands at responding.[39] Ségal's dry, self-deprecating humor comes through in the text, but she also reveals how seriously she took her role, recognizing her impact on both letter writers and other readers of the column. The book highlights the two-way nature of the dialogue she established and engaged in with her readers over the years. In her books, as in her columns, Ségal's common sense, tendency to downplay drama, and insistence that readers could and should take the needed steps to resolve their problems come through clearly.

Ségal: All the Single Ladies

Although Ségal's first book, a lighthearted but serious presentation of her career as an advice columnist, included personal details about her life, that was not its primary purpose. In her second book, *Moi aussi, j'étais seule (I Was Alone Too)* published in 1971, she focused directly on herself, with an emphasis, as the title indicates, on the fact that she had long been single. By the time Ségal published the memoir she had been living on her own for over forty years. Ségal expressed concern about women who lived only for their husbands or children, really any woman who considered her own life "meaningless in itself!" Her response to the hundreds of letters from women in despair because they did not have a husband was to help them realize "that aside from a man, they had everything: arms, legs, health, sunshine, greenery, home, children, work, sports, books, music, friends, all kinds of great activities. Life, after all." Living for other people might be a sign of the grandeur of women's hearts but it was also the source of many of women's problems. To Ségal, "living only for a man represented the number one cause of women's pain."[40]

Rather than conveying the idea that single women were somehow inferior or lacking, Ségal celebrated them. She challenged single women who considered themselves victims of bad luck. Personally, she explained, after the war she found few men of her age available or desirable. Some widowed men only wanted a second wife to "take over the cash register." She confessed that while living alone, she had "returned to a wild state: eating, sleeping, going out whenever I felt the desire." At one point, she found a man with similar likes, dislikes, and character traits, a soul mate. But she never found out whether their relationship might have lasted because "his brutal death answered the question."[41] She reassures her readers that her personal story was not one of failure, loneliness, and pain. She decided to write about her life, she explains, for all unmarried women. "Let's go single women! Get out of the house! Go for it! Don't be afraid! Adventure awaits!"[42]

Auclair: Biographies

Auclair published at least twenty-five books in France, starting in the 1920s with a novel and a book of poetry. In 1950, she published a major biography of Saint Teresa of Avila, not a devotional saint's life but a deeply researched, carefully footnoted study with a serious bibliography.[43] She had long read and admired Saint Teresa's writings. In fact, when she fled Paris ahead of the German army in 1940, the only book she took was one of Saint Teresa's books on prayer and contemplation.[44] Auclair admired the "beautiful, intelligent, cultured, combative, revolutionary," Teresa, who admitted applicants from all social classes to her order and "had been the first one to include in the order's constitution 'she who wants to eat must work.' "[45] Contemporary reviewers hailed the book as a success. *Le Figaro littéraire* described it as "brilliantly written, solidly documented, as broad, penetrating, alert and picturesque as the subject demands."[46] Auclair tells the story of Saint Teresa, according to Michel Carrouges of *La vie spirituelle,* "with the color and liveliness of a swashbuckling novel but woven on every page with the solid foundation of historical truth," based on contemporary sources. "Here, no concessions to the artificial style of decadent hagiography, but the most human language. And yet, how it leads us with fire to Teresa's trail to the castle of the soul!"[47]

The book sold well, leaving Auclair's finances in better shape than they had been for years. She heard from friends who, while not religious, read her book and came to admire Saint Teresa. In contrast, one supposedly pious acquaintance focused not on Teresa but on the book's commercial success. "Catholic literature pays well! Obviously you'll keep going!" After that comment, as Auclair put it, "I felt myself getting hot under the collar." Annoyed that evening she searched through her bookshelves looking for a new subject and fell upon the work of French socialist Jean Jaurès. Having made money with her biography of Teresa, Auclair decided, "I'm going to allow myself the luxury of spending years writing about a socialist!" Four years later she published her biography of Jaurès. Although it did not sell as well as her previous biography, she took great joy in delving into his life and ideas, finding a number of similarities between Jaurès and Teresa of Avila; "intrepid hearts, they were only at ease in the absolute and pushed the gift of themselves to the death."[48] Auclair's well-known Catholicism and her biography of Saint Teresa left Pierre-Henri Simon of *Le Monde* surprised by her treatment of Jaurès. He pointed out that Auclair wrote about Jaurès "not to slam him but, on the contrary, to raise him up as a hero and martyr to the idea, almost a lay saint."[49] Journalist Robert Coiplet described the subject as "dangerous," yet he praised "this remarkable book" for avoiding the pitfalls and for its "rich painting of the times, and more than the times, of a society."[50]

In addition to another book of poetry, a play, books for children, and several novels, Auclair published a book in 1955 addressed to young women that included short excerpts from a wide variety of writings both literary and philosophical intended to give young women interesting perspectives, both historical and contemporary, on various aspects of life. *Le Monde* approved, concluding "these chosen fragments could be useful for readers other than young women." The reviewer seconded Auclair's complaint that contemporary novels no longer developed compelling young female characters. He included Auclair's citation of Montaigne on young women, "We impose on them nothing other than the face of love, continuously presenting it to them if only to put them off."[51]

Auclair continued to work on translations of Federico Garcia-Lorca's plays and poetry. As his plays began to appear on stages across France, critics applauded Auclair's translations.[52] Robert Kemp, in his review of a production of Garcia Lorca's *Así que pasen cinco años* (*When Five Years Pass*), praised Auclair as "the heroic translator."[53] By the 1960s, she felt ready to tackle Garcia Lorca's biography, starting with a research trip to Spain. She had personally known Garcia Lorca in the 1920s and 30s. In 1928 her friend, poet Saint-Jean Perse, urged her to visit Spain, where she met and was quickly befriended by "this quintessence of the Spanish soul that was Federico Garcia Lorca." According to Auclair, Garcia Lorca had sparked her interest in Saint Teresa, urging her to visit Avila, "the most Castillian city that exists.... Everywhere the shadow of former greatness." Auclair titled her biography *Enfances et mort de Federico Garcia Lorca* (*The Childhoods and Death of Federico Garcia Lorca*). The title came from his explaining to her "my whole life is childhood." Auclair came to understand that Garcia Lorca experienced everything as "an immense first time."[54] In the biography, Auclair focused on his life, his poetry, and his plays. She also explored his homosexuality and how it impacted his relationship with his parents and his career. She had hoped to discover the truth about his death during the Spanish Civil War and searched in vain for information.

She even wrote to the Spanish government asking for information but got no response; this is not surprising since Franco was still in power. Like most of her contemporaries, Auclair knew but could not document that Franco's forces had killed Garcia Lorca.[55] Claude Couffon's review in *Le Monde* lauded Auclair's biography of Garcia Lorca, noting that it was the first biography to appear in the thirty years since Garcia Lorca's death. He describes Auclair's biography as "the book he deserved, in the image of his scintillating work. From now on this book will be the essential complement for anyone wanting to delve into his most intimate details."[56]

Auclair and the Catholic Church

Auclair's reaction to the idea that she intended to make money with biographies of Catholic saints indicates her mixed feelings and troubled relationship with the Catholic Church in France. Catholic mysticism was an integral part of her spiritual outlook, but first she had to overcome the aspects of the Church that repelled her. When she first returned to France in her twenties, the French Catholic Church's formalism, its focus on rules, and its subservience to the wealthy disappointed her. "Private prayer stalls shocked me—one day a lady chased me out of hers."[57] In Chile, she found the widespread superstition amusing; in France, "the collusion between religion and extreme right shocked me."[58] She also chafed at the hypocrisy she saw in a religion that insisted on the sanctity of life when it came to birth control or abortion but supported the death penalty and had also been responsible for the Inquisition and Wars of Religion that killed millions of people.[59] A more personal incident happened when she was in the midst of her divorce. She met "a major Catholic figure" and asked him what he thought about her decision. He told her that he and his wife had separated but had decided not to divorce in order to keep up appearances. From his point of view, divorce between two people as well-known as she and Jean Prévost would be "contrary to the morals of the society we live in." Auclair found that his hypocrisy "sickened me so much that from that moment my decision to divorce became irrevocable."[60] Her dislike of appearance and formalities over faith turned her against Catholic schooling in France, which she considered too focused on the catechism while failing to teach children about "a life of faith."[61] After another unsatisfying interaction in the 1930s with a priest who focused on rules and neglected deeper, spiritual, transcendent values, "I was done with religious practice for twenty-five years."[62]

However, Auclair never lost faith in God and always made time for prayer. She "nourished herself" with the Gospels, only refusing "to present myself at a counter to beg for a certificate of good conduct."[63] As she had in Chile, she supplemented the Gospels with a variety of spiritual texts from different religions; most often she mentions the *Bhagavad Gita*. Eventually, twenty-five years after leaving the Church, she explained, "I returned to practicing Catholicism as easily as I had renounced it."[64] In 1973, Auclair published an autobiographical work centered on her spiritual experiences, *A la grace de Dieu* (*By the Grace of God*). Interviewed on television shortly after the book came out, Auclair discussed the gap between her deep faith and the Catholic Church as an institution.[65]

Her disgust with the French Catholic Church's emphasis on formalities, rules, and its favoring of the wealthy explains her response to the comment about making money from publishing saints' lives and her turn to a socialist. However, having finished her biography of Jaurès, she turned again to a Catholic figure, Saint Bernadette.[66] In spite of the shift from a socialist back to a Catholic saint, the book, published in 1958, attracted the suspicion of a far right-wing Catholic group, the Popular Movement of 13 May linked to Cold War anti-communism. *Le Monde* pointed out that in July 1958 the group published "a tract that attacked Marcelle Auclair's book on Saint Bernadette... This work, which got the Church's nihil obstat [no objection], they label no more no less than crypto-communist."[67] However, the Popular Movement's opprobrium had little impact on Auclair or on her appeal to readers.

Auclair on Happiness

Auclair's most long-lasting and influential work, a series of books on happiness, conveyed her philosophy of life and offered readers lessons on how to manage their internal life to minimize pain and increase serenity. To help others, she shared the meditation and other techniques she and her mother had developed while she was growing up in Chile. Her first book appeared in 1938, *Le bonheur est en vous* (*Happiness is Inside You*). Still in print, the cover touts it as "the cult book of happiness, 500,000 copies sold." A decade after the war she published *Le pratique du bonheur* (*The Practice of Happiness*).[68] A few years later, she published a combination of the two books on happiness with the title *Le livre du bonheur* (*The Book of Happiness*) (1959). A year before she died, coming full circle, she translated and prefaced William Atkinson's *Thought Vibrations*, the book she and her mother had discovered in Chile.[69] Atkinson's book had profoundly shaped her approach to life and given her many of the techniques she developed.

Auclair's series of books on happiness conveyed her philosophy of life and included her personal techniques she shared with others. Her books offered readers an outlook on life, a distillation of her personal spiritual journey, which had been nothing if not eclectic. Auclair admitted "adolescent anxieties" had pushed her to "seek the keys to internal peace, to optimism."[70] She had always believed in God. What she sought had been "a method for managing my internal life."[71] Her books provided ideas, techniques, and ways of thinking about the world to help readers manage their fears and anxieties and find happiness. The books consist of short, one- or two-page chapters that illustrate a particular problem or source of unhappiness, along with a technique for managing it. Each chapter closes with an "application" or exercise for the technique, recommending that readers use the exercises to practice and develop their skills. "You can be happy" was the title of the first section of the *Livre du bonheur* (*The Book of Happiness*). An early chapter about the ways in which thought shapes emotions ended with this application, "notice how many times in a day you deny with your thoughts and words that which you want the most in the world, you'll be surprised to realize that every minute you negate with a massive blow that which you hope for."[72]

As a teenager in Chile, Auclair and her mother met with several yogis. From the *Bhagavad Gita*, she absorbed messages of knowledge and devotion, of multiple paths to spiritual realization including both meditation and action, and of the importance of doing the right thing without expectation of gain. She found the *Gita* prepared her to understand the writings of Saint Teresa of Avila, sixteenth-century mystic and reformer who restored the Carmelites to austerity, contemplation, and labor. Auclair considered Jean Jaurès' ideas a secular version of spirituality. She read Gandhi and incorporated from his teachings what she and her mother had dabbled in back in Chile, listing books by nineteenth-century Indian Hindu mystic Ramakrishna, proponent of the oneness of all existence, unity, and truth of all religions; his disciple Vivekananda; yoga guru and poet Sri Aurobindo; and eleventh-century century Buddhist Tibetan mystic Milarepa.[73] Auclair combined eastern spirituality with ideas of western writers like Saint Teresa and Annie Besant, best known for her political activism for British/English workers and women's rights, but also a follower of theosophy, which drew on Hinduism and Buddhism's teaching that spiritual emancipation was the purpose of life.[74] Auclair justified her eclectic approach, having discovered "you can reach your goal by zigzagging."[75] But her approach had been most deeply impacted by the book she and her mother had read back in Chile, American author William Atkinson's *Thought Vibrations.* Atkinson posited that thoughts, like light and sound, consisted of waves that passed through us, which produced health and happiness. External events only impacted people if they modified or reoriented thoughts. Atkinson's ideas provided a "technique" for managing emotions that accorded well with Auclair's spiritual orientation.[76]

Auclair drew on all of these strands in her books on happiness, a state of being she emphasized was not about love, money, or beauty, but about internal life. With the right outlook, everyone could manage the challenges they faced. She echoed Atkinson's assertion that thoughts and words create reality. Negative self-talk—"I'm ugly," "I'm sick," "I'm going to fail"—only resulted in bringing about negative outcomes. As evidence of the power of words, she pointed out that an angry word to a nice person creates discord, while a friendly word to a difficult person eases tension. Auclair insisted that it was critical to pay attention to words, whether spoken or internal. "Never pronounce a word that you would not want to happen."[77] She also urged her readers to be open to receiving happiness. Being passive, failing actively to seek happiness left a person at the mercy of larger forces. She urged her readers to conjure positive thoughts since passively waiting for them allowed negative thoughts to flourish.[78]

Because accomplishing those goals required practice, Auclair included suggestions about how to practice. She pressed readers to try, even if they might not really believe in it, to start. "The words you say will help you make the change." Becoming happy required exercising the happiness muscle, starting with small efforts. For example, don't slam doors or get angry when there are no empty seats on the bus. She warned that such behavior created waves of anger that would come back and cause worse pain. Small annoyances, she insisted, presented excellent opportunities to practice being happy, or as she put it, to train the happiness muscle.[79] She described happiness as a habit that takes time to develop. Old bad habits can be hard to break, having "dug their paths" into our brains. But every rejection of old, unhappy thought patterns represented a pebble on a pile that eventually would grow to become a wall blocking out negative thoughts. Recognizing the power of thought allowed a person to tap into waves of happiness.[80]

In contrast, Ségal, in her book about being an advice columnist, criticized books on happiness in a chapter titled "Happiness: We Talk Too Much About It," an implicit rebuke of Auclair. Ségal sarcastically reacted to what she called happiness recipes, "a commodity more and more in demand."[81] She noted that "Moralists teach us that Happiness is inside of us: it's in ourselves that we must find it."[82] Ségal thought happiness writers might as well tell people that happiness is on the moon, and all they needed to do was go get it. Instead of vague advice to seek happiness from within, Auclair actually offered specific techniques, prescribed exercises for readers to practice that over time would change thought patterns. In any case, Ségal never mentioned Auclair's name or book titles. She just offered her own approach that, in fact, differed little from what Auclair recommended. Rather than offering lessons and techniques or citing famous authors and poets, Ségal simply told her own story, leaving readers to take away the appropriate lessons.

Rather than seeking "Happiness with a capital H," Ségal recommended "the art of being happy."[83] In the end, her practical advice differed little from Auclair's formula. The point was to learn to live with and learn from unhappiness while suffering as little as possible from "misfortunes" and learning to laugh about them. Ségal corrected herself; she really taught "the art of being unhappy."[84] The letters she had received over the years made clear that most women knew how to protect themselves from physical dangers but found themselves disarmed when dealing with emotional pain. If not managed, unhappiness "festers," which makes the situation worse. "Fretting, there's the problem." Ségal concluded with advice that echoed Auclair. She recommended learning to let go of disappointments and pain. Ségal wanted to help her readers recognize and build up their "joie de vivre." That she concluded, was "the goal of the little page you read every week under the title Letters from the Heart."[85]

Pragmatic and practical rather than judgmental, both Auclair and Ségal saw their role as encouraging their readers not to give in to despair, not to give up, to try new things, and to think in new ways. While they did not directly challenge the fundamental premise about relationships between men and women, or question the assumptions that many women cared about their appearance, wanted to marry, and have children, they also encouraged women to go beyond those boundaries, not to blindly follow the social conventions of gender. Challenging the double standard for unmarried and married women, acknowledging female desire, and rejecting body shaming, Auclair and Ségal took a part in the rethinking of gender that set the stage for the more public acts of feminism of the 1960s. Both Ségal week in and week out in her column and Auclair in *Marie-Claire* and in her books about happiness sought to reassure, guide, and empower women.

Auclair Takes on Women's Reproductive Rights

Ségal and Auclair's empowering voices played a role in reshaping how women thought about themselves more generally. In addition to the committee against the romance press, in the 1950s and 1960s Auclair supported a number of political organizations. She signed appeals in support of various political prisoners.[86] In December 1959, she signed a demand that the French government renounce nuclear testing, and in 1962, she signed a protest against the acquittal of three French military officers accused of torture.

Auclair wrote about and at times gave advice on issues readers raised in their constant stream of letters. Her readers also pushed her beyond writing articles and books to a new level of engagement. Motivated by her readers, Auclair, while not labeling herself a feminist, became ever more vocal in challenging the status quo for women. She personally took up the cause of reproductive rights, fighting for women's ability to control their bodies, an essential element of feminism. She used her renown and wide popularity to try and force a public discussion of the issues despite widespread condemnation by various authority figures and laws that prohibited public discussion of contraception.

The public's linking of Auclair with Catholicism and *Marie-Claire* made her activities surprising, striking, and powerful. Nearly a decade after her death, in a 1990 television broadcast about *Marie-Claire,* host Frédéric Mitterrand (nephew of former president François) described Auclair as "a personality to salute, a totally extraordinary figure." One of his guests, Hélène Mathieu, added to Mitterrand's praise, describing Auclair as having shown "a formidable nerve for the era .... She made huge things happen because she had this iron will. She was a rebel, stirred up by all the injustices women of her era experienced." Another guest, Michelle Marceau, agreed, describing Auclair as "a theologian of liberty" who worked "to liberate women."[87]

After finally gaining the vote in 1945, many postwar feminists focused their primary effort on contraception and abortion rights.[88] However, they usually worked quietly, behind the scenes; their publications were less widely read than a mass-market magazine like *Marie-Claire*. Auclair had already started down the path of disseminating information on contraception in the 1930s. She wrote the preface for a book, *La liberté de la conception* (*The Freedom of Conception*), written by two doctors, which explained in detail the female fertility cycle and its connection to ovulation and pregnancy. The book promoted itself as providing women with information that would help them get pregnant, but that implicitly could be used to avoid pregnancy. They included a calendar for what, at the time, was called the Ogino-Knauss method after the Japanese and Austrian doctors who pioneered the system. The book provided a graph and explained to women how to use a thermometer and calendar to track their cycles. The authors, Dr. A. Marchal and Dr. O. J. De Mero, insisted, in 1935, that Catholic doctrine had no objection to this system, although the Church in France was hardly sanguine about it at that time. In her preface, Auclair opened by proclaiming her love of being a mother and the benefits of having children close together in age. But she stressed that having too many children placed a heavy burden on women's health, not to mention the well-being of the children and the household. The fear of pregnancy, Auclair pointed out, often killed a woman's desire to have sex with her husband, resulting in husbands frequently looking elsewhere for sex. The method in the book only required partial abstinence. As the design on the book's front cover graphic explains, with a wink to contraception, "conception is only possible 65 days of the year. Which ones?"[89]

Published in 1935, the book appeared in the midst of a panic in France about its declining birth rate and fear of being overtaken by rivals like Germany, which resulted in a harsh law passed in 1920 making contraception, abortion, and disseminating information about them illegal. Five years after *La liberté de la conception* appeared, the Vichy government amplified the rhetoric, exhorting women to have lots of babies. Vichy also cracked down on and increased the penalties for abortion, making performing an abortion a crime against the state punishable by death. Under that law, Vichy authorities executed two people for performing abortions. Auclair remained silent about these matters through the four years of Occupation and the Vichy regime but returned to the discussion after the war with a revised preface to a new edition of *La liberté de la conception* in 1954.

Significantly, when Auclair negotiated her return to *Marie-Claire* in 1955, she insisted that for her monthly article she would have "full freedom to write about any topic." According to the magazine's editor-in-chief Marcel Haedrich, "The authority she had, truly *papal,* allowed her to tackle topics that would have raised more than the eyebrows [of the Archbishop]," whose wrath the magazine's director Hervé Mille feared.[90] Auclair explained that from the moment she rejoined *Marie-Claire,* in the letters she received daily from her readers, one of the "thorniest themes . . . was that of contraception." In the early 1930s, after her three children were born, she traveled to England, where she had benefitted from easy access to contraception. Having that experience, she considered the situation in France incomprehensible. The topic had become taboo "to such a point that people did not even dare talk about it."[91] In fact, the 1920 law, to suppress advertising and discourage public discussion, specifically prohibited "propaganda" for birth control. The number of letters Auclair received on the subject and the pain the writers expressed led her to tackle the topic in *Marie-Claire* starting in June 1956 with an article "A Serious Problem: Birth Control."[92]

Auclair's anger at the Catholic Church's response also motivated her. Since the 1930s she had stopped attending mass, frustrated at the Church's formalism, materialism, and links to the far right. The Church's position on contraception further angered her. She pointed out that celibate priests could never understand the pressures women faced. During a discussion with a Catholic Bishop, she pointed out, "You cannot conceive of what it's like to raise a large family." She criticized the church for being "stuck on the idea of prohibiting all birth control." Beyond the clergy, Auclair complained, "I spend my time warning my Catholic colleagues about their good old boy reflexes."[93]

After years of desperate letters from her readers, in 1960, Auclair was ready to use *Marie-Claire* to undertake an even more radical effort. She published a call to readers in the November 1960 issue. Under the banner, "Help me put together the forbidden dossier," she asked readers who had any experience with abortion to send her an un-sanitized, completely honest account. Given the legal risks, Auclair warned anyone responding to her request not to sign their names. She advised people living in small towns to post their letters from a different town. Make sure, she closed, that nothing in your account would allow anyone to identify you or anyone else involved.[94] Jeanne Dodemann, who managed Auclair's correspondence and gathered documentation for her articles, in a 2005 interview, noted that even though Auclair had asked them not to, all the letters were signed. Clearly many of those who wrote Auclair felt strongly and did not want to hide.[95]

In her call for testimony, Auclair lamented that she would not be able to publish an article about the responses in *Marie-Claire* but she promised to bring a report based on the letters to "powerful personalities who determine your fate." She expected to receive about fifty responses. Auclair received 581 letters, propelling her to go beyond her original plan.[96]

In 1962, nearly a decade before the monthly magazine *Le Nouvel Observateur* published "The Manifesto of the 343" credited with signaling the start of the abortion rights campaign in France, Auclair, together with Jeanne Dodemann, published *Le livre noir de l'avortement* (*The Black Book of Abortion*).[97] Auclair wrote the preface, "The Silence of Death," and briefly introduced each chapter, but otherwise Auclair "let women speak for themselves."[98] An overview in the preface broke down the numbers. Of the 581 letters, 440 of the letters came from married women, 81 from single women, 21 from divorced women, 8 from widows, and 31 from men. Only 57 respondents were hostile: 50 women and 7 priests. The 581 letters testified to 2,960 abortions, 2,369 of them clandestine abortions that did not result in medical intervention, meaning they were "neither seen nor known." Some 221 women ended up in the hospital; 82 correspondents wrote Auclair about women who died.[99] Blown away by the magnitude of the suffering, Auclair felt that the only comparable book was Daniel Defoe's *Journal of the Plague Year*.[100]

Each chapter consisted of excerpts from the letters. From a few sentences to several pages, Auclair let women tell their stories, starting with married women, many of whom had children but could not afford or had no space for another. They described alcoholic or abusive husbands, medical conditions that made another pregnancy extremely risky, and caring for children with disabilities. The book proceeded with chapters on widows, then single and divorced women. One chapter she simply titled "What a man can be capable of doing."[101] In a significant number of cases, husbands demanded that their pregnant partner have an abortion. Illustrating the Church's ignorance, Auclair describes a conversation she had with a priest about the anguish and fear women felt, the monthly terror of not knowing if they were pregnant. With contraception illegal, the stress, Auclair pointed out, pushed some women into serious depression. At that the priest shrugged his shoulders and told her that all women were "more or less hysterical!" Infuriated, Auclair wondered how men would respond if they had to live every month in fear of discovering a pregnancy that could overturn their lives.[102]

Another chapter, titled "The Museum of Horrors," included stories about fetuses preserved in a jar in the refrigerator or stuffed into a shoe box.[103] One letter described the sound of blood gurgling as her friend bled to death after a botched abortion, "the blood going glug glug glug."[104] Men's letters got a chapter, as did letters from people in the medical profession.[105] Letters from people who had been convicted under the law made up the final chapter.[106]

Auclair kept her original promise. The Appendix included responses from sixteen of the prominent people to whom she had sent her manuscript, including Guy Mollet (one time Prime Minister and head of the Socialist Party), many prominent medical doctors, film director André Cayatte, journalists, editors, a Catholic canon, and the former female mayor of a small town who called on all women to vote and get involved in politics.[107] In contrast to the generally supportive tone, demographer/pronatalist Alfred Sauvy penned a brief, crabby note objecting to the potential damage to France's birth rate the book's pressure to legalize contraception and abortion might cause. *Marie-Claire's* in-house doctor called on women to fight. "Nothing changes without struggle." It's unclear why she sent her manuscript to

Paul-Emile Victor, Chief of French Polar Expeditions, but his was the final letter. He responded that if he could "lend any weight at all to your initiative, you have my unreserved support."[108]

Historian of French feminism Lisa Greenwald highlights Auclair's book as "the first public statement in defense of abortion rights by a mainstream cultural icon."[109] At the time Auclair expressed frustration that her publisher, Fayard, "did not have the audacity to 'launch' the book." A German publisher, in the process of translating the book, asked Auclair for French press clippings about the book's release. She explained there had been no press releases or published reviews of the book and suggested the German edition launch the book on the theme: "The book the French press did not dare talk about."[110]

Although abortion did not become a major topic of political debate until the 1970s, Auclair's willingness to take on the issue helped open the door, if only a little, to a wider public discussion of a taboo issue. In spite of the publisher's failure to promote the book, in November 1962 Auclair appeared on television to talk about it. In that era, French television developed popular programming centered on books that took on serious intellectual subjects, starting with a program first broadcast in 1953, *Lectures pour Tous* (*Reading for Everyone*), which featured an interview with a different author every week.[111] In 1962, host Pierre Dumayet interviewed Auclair about *Le livre noir de l'avortement*, asking how she came up with the idea. Auclair responded that she had been shocked at the dismissive attitude of many people she spoke with who insisted abortion was neither an important social issue nor a big problem. Incredulous, Auclair decided rather than listening to people who had no personal experiences, she would ask women to tell her about theirs. She told Dumayet she had been "overwhelmed by the anguish" of the responses. Having assembled this "extraordinary human document... I felt I didn't have the right to keep it to myself." She described the letters that poured in as an SOS from women that she could not in good conscience keep to herself. However, she revealed to Dumayet that the first publisher she contacted consulted with a team of lawyers and then rejected it. When she tried to make a copy of her typed manuscript, the copier refused, insisting there was "absolutely no possibility that I copy such a thing." Finally, Fayard agreed to publish the book but, as Auclair pointed out, refused to launch or promote it.[112]

Auclair reassured Dumayet that she had left the letters intact except for excising "the description of the methods used... atrocious methods of an amazing variety, the richness of a desperate woman's imagination reaches a dizzying point." She emphasized the lengths to which women would go to terminate a pregnancy.[113] She deflected Dumayet's question about who was to blame, insisting "both are to blame and no one is to blame." She pointed out that three-fourths of the letters came from married women, many of whom already had three or four children. Often, "a woman who is overwhelmed by daily life, facing a difficult financial situation, living in substandard housing, just cannot handle any more." She described various responses after an abortion, ranging from guilt to relief. Asked if women hesitated before going ahead with an abortion, Auclair pointed out that pregnant women had no time to hesitate or it would be too late. As for the risks involved, Auclair reported that many of her correspondents considered suicide the only other option. In some cases, the husband threatened to leave if his wife had the baby. But as to fear of the procedure itself, or fear of the legal consequences, "zero response to that matter. Only one letter in this mountain of letters testified to that concern." Asked if the women who wrote her shared anything in common, Auclair was clear. "[W]hen a woman has made the decision, nothing can stop her."

When Dumayet asked what had most motivated her to publish the book, Auclair did not hesitate. "Well, it's... what I call the silence of death." To her, silence represented an "abominable wound that spreads out around the world, that currently is an atrocious plague." Here she compared the book to Samuel Pepys' *Diary of the Plague.* No one talked about abortion, "it's through silence that all of this grows and takes on monumental proportions." With most abortions clandestine, she and Dumayet discussed the difficulty of obtaining accurate data on abortion, with estimates ranging from 1.5 million to 500 million abortions. Auclair pointed out, "We really don't know." The interview ended with an image of the plain black cover of the book.[114]

Given her wide popularity and association with *Marie-Claire,* Auclair's book and television appearance helped break the silence. The following year, in 1963, attorney Anne-Marie Dourlen-Rollier published a study, *La verité sur l'avortement* (*The Truth about Abortion*), based on 1,110 dossiers. Journalist Claudine Escoffier-Lambiotte, in her review of Dourlen-Rollier's study in *Le Monde,* mentioned Auclair's book where "you can also find impressive details."[115] A year later, Francine Dumas published an article in the Protestant revue *Réforme* that picked up on Auclair's lament about the deadly silence surrounding the topic, "L'avortement: Il faut en parler" ("Abortion: We Must Talk About It").[116] In 1965, *Le Nouvel Observateur* published Katia D. Kaupp's "L'univers de l'avortement" ("The Abortion Universe"), based on her own investigation.[117] In the end, Marcel Haedrich, *Marie-Claire*'s editor-in-chief, described Auclair's book as "a revolution" that, by opening the topic for discussion, began to limit the Catholic Church's power in France and laid the groundwork for the 1975 Weil law legalizing abortion.[118]

In addition to abortion, Auclair also used *Marie-Claire* to explore and publicize the issue of birth control. Starting in 1956,

Marie-Claire was the first woman's magazine to publish articles about birth control. Marcelle Auclair had the ability to take on the topic because of the full freedom she negotiated to decide on her monthly article. Well in to her 50s, a mother, and a Catholic, Auclair had credibility, and her position at *Marie-Claire* exposed her directly, through readers' mail, to women's personal struggles with pregnancy and childrearing. Some twenty-three percent of the letters she received in 1958 had to do with the topic of birth control. By 1960, she moved beyond responding to letters and published calls for readers to send her letters about contraception.[119]

In the 1963 presidential election, socialist candidate François Mitterrand spoke in favor of the legalization of contraception. Mitterrand did not win the election, but Auclair solicited letters on birth control again in August 1965, asking readers whether they were satisfied with the birth control methods available. Within a month she had received 11,000 responses.[120] Auclair began criticizing the Catholic Church's position. Three months later, *Marie-Claire* reported that Auclair had traveled to the Vatican to present "20,000 confessions" from women who had used birth control at the last session of the Vatican II Council.[121]

In 1966, Auclair appeared on a television interview show called *Face à Face* (*Face-to-Face*), hosted by Robert Barrat. The format was a roundtable with a group of people from various backgrounds focused on a specific topic. Vatican II had just completed its work in December 1965, so the guest of honor was Cardinal Veuillot, Archbishop of Paris. Of the four panelists Auclair was the only woman. It took 34 minutes of the men talking before she managed to break through and ask a question. She described Vatican II's impressive closure, with the Pope blessing various prominent figures, actors, scientists, professors, and a blind man with his guide dog. But, she noted, there had been not a single women—not a mother with her child or even a group of nuns. Unfazed, Veuillot responded, waxing on in patronizing tones about the Catholic Church's deep love and respect for women. Auclair, clearly not impressed, immediately retorted, letting him know that many of her readers expressed an idea that she herself had "caressed." She asked, for her readers' sake, could it be "that the Church is anyway, a little, is it truly . . . misogynist?"[122]

Stunned, Veuillot looked around the table at the other men, threw his hands in the air with the familiar French "bof" gesture, and made no attempt to respond. Auclair, seconded by Barrat, continued to press, prompting Veuillot to complain that so many more women than men attended mass in France that some people labeled Catholicism "a woman's religion." Women, he asserted, were equal members of the community of believers. He insisted that outside liturgical functions, "In the community of believers . . . women have a place completely equal to men." In his closing salvo, Veuillot declared, "you cannot say that the Church overlooks women," ending with what he clearly thought was the coup de grace. "All we need to do is say the name of a certain Virgin Mary." At this Auclair raised an eyebrow, clearly expressing her rejection of Veuillot's sanctimonious platitudes. The discussion continued, with Auclair highlighting general and specific ways the Church excluded women from many Church functions, including, crucially, from the hierarchy. Visibly frustrated, Auclair at times mimed pounding the table with her fists. Then Auclair raised an even thornier issue, one she figured Veuillot must have been expecting, birth control. "That, truly for the majority of women, it's agony for women, they are anguished." Auclair, in her 60s, pointed out that the issue was hardly personal for her. She asked, for her readers, what would Veuillot tell women wanting to know the Church's position on contraception?[123]

Indeed Veuillot was ready for the question. He agreed it was a serious issue that touched millions of women around the world. He assured Auclair that the Church took the issue seriously, "so seriously" that it was taking the time to study it carefully. The Pope, in view of the importance of the issue, had created several committees tasked with examining it. Those committees, Veuillot proudly noted, included married men and women. The study was ongoing. Another member of the panel jumped in to point out that studying the issue was well and good, but couples faced an immediate problem. They had no time to wait for a study; they needed an immediate answer. What, he asked, does the Church instruct priests to say to people in confession who hint at using birth control? Veuillot responded, "for every sin, forgiveness!"[124]

Marcelle Auclair reacts to the Archbishop of Paris as he responds to her question about women in the Catholic Church.
"Monseigneur Veuillot," *Face à Face*, April 18, 1966. Institut National de l'audiovisuel. France/INA CAF 88025841.

Annoyed, Veuillot accused the panelists of suggesting that it was a simple problem. The Church would have its response in several months. Auclair cut in, insisting that women were on the verge of despair, with marriages breaking apart. Veuillot pushed back. The Church, he pontificated, does not invent its doctrine. A response required scrutinizing scripture to uncover what God had to say about the issue. Only then could the Church interpret God's thinking on conjugal life. Auclair and Barrat pressed a bit further, but with time running out, Barrat closed the show by asking Veuillot about a headline that had recently appeared in the *New York Times* and *Time Magazine,* "Is God Dead?" In short, Veuillot said no. The synopsis of the broadcast in *Le Monde* highlighted Auclair's interventions under the subtitles: "Is the Church misogynous?" and "No edicts regarding birth control."[125]

Like the *Black Book,* Auclair's interventions were confrontational, lending her clear support to the fight for birth control and abortion rights. Public opinion in France was shifting by the time she appeared on *Face à face* with the Archbishop, but the open, forceful advocacy by a "mainstream cultural icon" linked to an immensely popular magazine, known for her biographies of saints, contributed to that shift.[126] The Neuwirth Law legalized birth control the next year, 1967, and abortion became legal in 1975. French feminists had continually been working behind the scenes to advance women's reproductive rights. Auclair's very public advocacy began before the more militant feminism following the events of 1968. She had been one of the few prominent women willing to tackle these issues head on. One of the guests in a retrospective about the creation of *Marie-Claire* described Auclair as a "vibrant rebel against injustice towards women."

Throughout the 1950s and 1960s, Auclair and Ségal engaged in an ongoing dialogue with their readers, especially women, through magazines, television, and books. They did not see themselves as sages leading a flock. Instead they responded to the women who wrote them with messages encouraging them not to blindly follow convention or to try and fit themselves, their lives, or their appearances into a standard mold. They promoted change on a personal level that set the stage for feminist movements to come. Auclair, again compelled by the letters she received, threw her efforts not into organizing a movement, but into open advocacy in a variety of media outlets for women's reproductive rights.

Bridges to Feminism: Marcelle Auclair, Marcelle Ségal, and Women's Magazines in Twentieth-Century France. Sarah Fishman, Oxford University Press.
DOI: 10.1093/9780197791356.003.0007

7

Women of a Certain Age

Sixties and Seventies

Auclair and Ségal Together Again... *Femmes*

As they continued their dialogue with readers in *Elle* and *Marie-Claire,* Auclair and Ségal increasingly thought in broader terms about women's place in the world. In 1967, working on the same publication for the first time since they overlapped at *Marie-Claire* in the 1940s, Auclair co-edited and Ségal contributed a chapter to a two-volume collection of essays entitled simply *Femmes* (*Women*). Auclair and co-editor Menie Grégoire, a journalist and advocate for women's rights who had recently launched what became an extremely popular radio call-in show, assembled a number of prominent authors to explore changes underway in women's lives not just in France and the west, but around the world.[1] In spite of its look, an oversized, lavishly illustrated coffee table book, *Femmes* represented a bold and broad approach. The two volumes included essays by some twenty leading intellectuals, artists, journalists, and activists, most of them women and a few men, from France, the United States, Cameroon, and Egypt. The essays tackled a wide array of topics and did not shy away from controversial issues linked to sex and sexuality including contraception, prostitution, and lesbianism. In Volume One, *Le corps et l'âme* (*Body and Soul*), Jean Rostand asked, "Are women truly the stronger sex?" Marie-Andrée Lagroua Weill-Hallé, founder of the French family planning movement, had two essays,

"Liberty, Responsibility, Contraception" and "Being a Mother: Instinct or Social Role?"[2] Monique Berlioux wrote about women's sports, "Conquering the Body: Sports and Liberty." *Elle* editorialist Jean Duché explored "Beauty, Desire and Imagination."[3] The collection took a global perspective. Cameroonian author Thérèse Kuoh Moukouy wrote an essay about African women, "Black Beauty, Hymn to Desire and to Life."[4] Andrée Chedid, a French-Egyptian poet and novelist, contributed, "Beauties of the East, Prisoners and Objects of Dreams," anticipating by a decade Edward Said's notion of orientalism.[5] Jean Kheim wrote about "The Flower Women of the Far East;" journalist and author Paul Mousset contributed "Brown Women and Pacific Mirages."[6] Anthropologist Simone Dreyfus' chapter explored indigenous Araucon, Kayapo, and Kaingang Indians in South America.[7] Marcel Sacotte, an author and scenarist, challenged attitudes toward prostitution in his essay "Is the Prostitute a Victim?"[8] Romi (Robert Miquel), a radio and television personality who "knows everything, understands everything and judges nothing," highlighted the long history of women's same sex love in "A Deviation as Old as Woman." Romi examined artistic representations of same sex love as well as the different legal responses to lesbians and gay men.[9]

Auclair wrote the preface to the first volume. Familiar with Simone de Beauvoir and her writings, Auclair echoes Beauvoir's notion of the second sex, contrasting the many books about "the woman" to the complete absence of books about "the man" because "everything relates to him and is all about him." Only women had to think about the point of their existence. Auclair cited Saint Teresa, "we are not that easy to know." She asserted that, if women did not examine who they were, what they wanted and what they had accomplished, it would be impossible to understand "where they're going and to predict how far they will be able to go."[10] *Femme*'s essays would help women establish "a healthy equilibrium in a world where they and their daughters will no longer have to regret not being born male." Although women had succeeded in exerting themselves, surreptitiously subverting men's attempts to control, bully, and dominate them by manipulating their so-called weakness to gain secret power, "from now on they want to live openly and assert themselves."[11]

The second volume, *La condition féminine* (*The Status of Women*), included an article by American anthropologist Lawrence Wylie, "The American Woman, An Unhappy Goddess." Françoise Dolto, renowned Freudian, described psychoanalysis. In the second volume Marcelle Ségal's essay, "Thirty-six Ways to Wear the Pants," picked up on Auclair's introduction, delving into the various ruses women had used through history to exert power and subvert gender norms. An essay by Auclair examined women's religious orders with a title that could be read as an implicit rebuke to men, "Millions of Women Have Preferred God." Menie Grégoire, who prefaced the second volume with a question, "Is there a Female Condition?" closed with an essay titled, "At Last, Simply Companions to Men." Auclair in the epilogue, "The War of the Sexes Will Not Take Place," a play on the title of Jean Giroudoux's play *The Trojan War Will Not Take Place* (*La guerre de Troi n'aura pas lieu*), encouraged cooperation and harmony between men and women. Instead of competing with each other, in "All Women for One and One for All Women, and All Men" Auclair forcefully promoted female solidarity and attention to the condition of women around the world. "We can only talk about 'women's advancement' when all women around the world are on the way up without oppressors or oppressed, in the free self-fulfillment of women's, and men's, specific gifts." Auclair reassured readers they might not have to wait too long for change to come about. "Things are going so quickly these days that the goal is without a doubt closer than we can imagine."[12] While sales figures are not available, *Femmes* sold enough copies to warrant a new edition in 1977.

May 1968

In a strange way, Auclair's final word about the pace of change foreshadowed what was about to hit France. Not quite a year after *Femmes* appeared, what the French refer to as the "events of May 1968" exploded onto the scene in Paris. That year student demonstrations and youth uprisings took place around the world. In the United States, many student demonstrations began as protests against the Vietnam War. Earlier in the decade, French students had similarly been radicalized in opposition to the Algerian War, which ended in 1962. By 1968, university students in France had grown increasingly frustrated by overcrowded classes and an inflexible, autocratic university system that gave them no voice. In January of 1968, a small group of about twenty-five students started a protest at Nanterre, a new and supposedly progressive university in an industrial suburb of Paris. The harsh police response only fed student anger, and by March the number of student protesters in Nanterre had grown to one thousand students. In a heavy-handed response, the Ministry of Education closed Nanterre. That effort also backfired, shifting student protests from Nanterre to Paris. A similarly brutal overreaction by riot police to student protests in Paris had the same mobilizing effect as in Nanterre. By May, nearly fifty thousand students had taken to the streets of Paris and other cities across France. Then, unexpectedly, France's largest union, the CGT, called for a general strike on May 13 and French workers joined the protests. As many as ten million workers responded with a strike that closed France's economy down. For both students and working people, the crisis brought to the surface their many frustrations and complaints about rigid political, educational, workplace, economic, and social systems in France.[13] The uprising particularly underscored women's frustrations. As the situation developed, student leaders' failure to listen to or include women in leading the movement spurred young women involved in the protests to launch new forms of feminist activism.

The events of May 1968 hardly went unnoticed in Auclair and Ségal's world of women's magazines. Having been unable to publish its usual weekly issue at the end of May, *Elle* published a special issue in June as the events continued, sharing the experiences of several of their journalists and of the group. *Elle* journalist Denise Dubois-Jallais described stepping out onto her balcony with her 5-month-old baby one afternoon in May to enjoy the nice weather. She could not understand what she was seeing: "young people, angry, paving stones in hand, running towards a police car and suddenly, the sound of breaking glass. . . . All of a sudden, it's no longer an ordinary Friday in May. Everything is turned upside down." The rest of her children joined her on the balcony, watching, fascinated. At that point, Dubois-Jallais was sure, "we are all going to be involved. Other than that, I don't know anything."[14]

After missing one week's edition owing to the disruption, Editor-in-Chief Hélène Gordon-Lazareff summoned everyone to the office. "ELLE reassembled. Some arrived on foot, others by hitchhiking or by bicycle." Once there, they worked to sort out what the events of the previous weeks meant for them. "It was a major self-examination. Of our conscience. Of yours. What to tell you? As extraordinary as these events might be, life goes on . . . . We realized, as we gathered, that we had all participated profoundly, in one way or another, in this event. Not as journalists and professional observers, but simply as human beings, like all of you."[15]

Most of that issue of *Elle* focused on events connected to the protests. "Here's the Sorbonne's Day Care" described a temporary nursery set up at the Sorbonne to assist working women since the upheaval had closed schools and day care. Articles covered the shutdown of television broadcasting, as well as the changes underway at universities where students and professors "are learning to work together." However, the last section of the magazine reverted to its more usual fare, starting with an essay titled "Fashion, it's a choice," followed by three pages of fashion shots.[16] After that, a pattern for knitting a "summer sweater" preceded the horoscope and, inside the back cover, the usual crossword puzzle.[17]

Marcelle Ségal enjoying retirement.
Photo courtesy of Anne Brunswic.

The issue encapsulates the "everything's changed/nothing's changed" duality of the events of May 68, while highlighting the shock and incomprehension many adults experienced. Convinced that at her age she had nothing to say to the younger generation, Ségal submitted a letter of resignation. Gordon-Lazareff wisely refused to accept it, well aware of the fervor of Ségal's following and the importance of her Letters from the Heart column to the magazine.[18] Ségal continued to respond to reader's letters for another twenty years, some forty years total, before retiring in 1987 at the age of 90.

Life after 1968

The upheaval of May 1968 in France shook things up for both Auclair and Ségal in terms of both gender and age.

By 1969, Ségal and Auclair were both single, successful professional women with followings of dedicated readers. Although they were cultural icons, the question remained, how should they respond to the latest turn of events and to their own advancing age? Neither retired from the world despite being in their 70s. Both remained active, Ségal continued her column at *Elle* and published a second book, and Auclair continued to research, publish, and speak out. Following her advocacy of contraception and abortion rights, she remained active, weighing in on other hot issues of the day.

Closing a circle, Auclair decided to visit Chile in 1970 and the next year, she returned with her grandson Jean-Victor, Alain's son. She arrived as Chile, under socialist president Salvador Allende, was undergoing serious land reform. Auclair was shocked to discover the dire economic situation created by shortages resulting from poor execution of the reforms and from wealthy landowners' resistance to the changes. Two years after the 1973 coup that overthrew Allende and ushered in a brutal military dictatorship, Auclair published a piece in *Le Monde*, "The Illusions of High Society," expressing her dismay at the response of Chile's upper classes to the regime. Before the coup, from Auclair's point of view, the changes under Allende, while disruptive, were long overdue. Auclair explained that prior to Allende's reforms wealthy landowners in Chile, rather than investing in and modernizing their farms, loved nothing more than to spend their money "parading around Europe." When she visited in 1971, she spoke with Chileans who pointed to the recent military coup in Bolivia, insisting, "That's what we need: a good military dictatorship." They got what they wanted, Auclair observed, repelled by elites celebrating Allende's death.[19] Auclair was clearly dismayed by their support for the coup. Her personal experience and deep knowledge of Chilean society motivated her to speak out on the situation in one of France's leading daily newspapers.

Everybody's Talking about Old Age

In the 1970s, countering the emphasis in May 1968 on youth, both Ségal and Auclair wrote about old age, offering their insights and empowering guidance to the growing number of people reaching their seventies. Having guided generations of their readers through love, marriage, and child rearing, they once again drew on their personal experiences to share their insights about aging with their readers. As Auclair explained, "You're not dead at 60? Don't make it a drama. It's just as dangerous to fall asleep lost in old age as it is to fall asleep out in the snow at 30 below zero. Age, on every level, requires more lucidity, patience, will . . . an optimism better than reasoned: meditated."[20]

In keeping with her series of books on happiness, in 1970 Auclair published *Vers une vieillesse heureuse* (*Towards a Happy Old Age*). The following year, Ségal's book, *Moi aussi, j'étais seule* (*I Was Alone Too*), an autobiography about her life as a single woman, closed with a chapter using a common French expression for old age, "Le troisième age" (The Third Age). Since they both were over 70 by then, there was a logic to the timing. Surprisingly however, at the same moment a third woman, a decade younger than Auclair and Ségal, also published a book on the topic. Simone de Beauvoir's *La Vieillesse* (*Old Age*), an eight hundred-page tome, also appeared in 1970. Why did these three books by three widely read women appear in the first year of the decade? Clearly rising life expectancy meant that a growing number of people could expect to live longer than ever. More people reaching old age increased the significance of the topic. All three women also took up the topic of aging shortly after the events of 1968, which had after all been a youth rebellion. Baby boomers by the late 1960s had come of age, and many of them rejected their parents' generation. To them, the older generation represented rigid barriers to progress and a better world. While 1968 is often considered ground zero of the sexual revolution, the ground had been laid already by the 1950s for questioning older sexual morality, assumptions, and norms by the very parents denigrated in 1968 as behind the times. In fact, the 1950s and early 1960s were rich periods for writing and rethinking sex and sexuality.

If the older generation had in fact been ahead of the Baby Boomers in questions about sex, why not about aging as well? None of the three women took a defensive posture toward youth. Interestingly, each was clearly aware of the other women's preceding book(s). They took three distinct approaches to the topic. Although they differed greatly in tone and approach, Auclair and

Ségal, in stark contrast to Beauvoir, ended up expressing similar positive visions of aging.

Of the three, by far the most well-known in the years since the 1970s, Beauvoir's *La Vieillesse* was the first of the three to hit the shelves.[21] Beauvoir's philosophical book analyzed the social, cultural, political, and economic aspects of aging, starting by defining old age as a transhistorical reality shaped by social context. To understand how the biological and the social aspects of aging interact, Beauvoir adopted a global chronological and geographic scope. Clearly age is a biological fact, but, as she argued in 1949 about gender in *The Second Sex*, it is also culturally bound.[22] However, having made that point, Beauvoir opened by characterizing old age as "irreversible, unfavorable, a decline." So much for culture. She based that view on her examination of the human body as an organism, asserting that from birth to age 20, when physical capacities peak, organic development tends to increase the chances of survival. She then listed negative biological changes that begin as the body ages, based on a variety of studies. Hearing begins to diminish at age 10, raw memory starts weakening at age 12. Citing sex researcher Alfred Kinsey, she claimed that men's sexual power peaks at age 16 and declines after that. Surprisingly for the author of *The Second Sex*, Beauvoir does not describe the trajectory of women's sexual development. She does reassure readers however that after the body's abilities peak, what follows in the years between ages 20 and 30 is involution, not aging. At that point adults can palliate the deficiencies. After 30 the inexorable decline begins.[23]

Having laid out the dismal biological realities, Beauvoir then analyzed the political, social, and economic contexts that created age hierarchies and assigned meaning to declining physical abilities. The book divides the topic of aging into its two manifestations, internal and external realities. Starting with the external aspects of age, she emphasized the critical importance of a person's social circumstances, health, family, and, possibly most significant, social class to an individual's experience of aging. The life of an elderly working-class person had little in common with what Beauvoir described as an "older Onassis," a reference to the Greek billionaire then married to former First Lady Jackie Kennedy.

Beauvoir wrote the book not to denigrate old people but as a pointed critique of the contemporary situation older people faced in France. "The condition of older people today is scandalous."[24] Society, she highlighted, had closed its eyes to the physical and emotional abandonment of older people. The question remained, since every young person would eventually grow old, why did families, and society in general, pay so little attention to the elderly? Here Beauvoir inserted her analysis of aging into a broader critique of capitalism. Children represent the future, adults are productive, but an old person "no longer does anything." Inevitably old age is followed by death, but death hardly represented a goal or project for the elderly. Thus the elderly represent "death on hold." That fact made old people seem like a "foreign species," inspiring "biological repugnance." Because old people "are useless," families park them in retirement homes and "abandon them."[25] Blaming social complicity, lack of solidarity, and dispersal into private homes for older citizens' inability to resist their mistreatment, Beauvoir clearly hoped to shake readers' consciences. The inactivity of older people was not inevitable but a consequence of social choices, which she highlighted by contrasting the situation in France with other places, lauding Scandinavian countries in particular. "Amongst capitalist nations, there are three that consider it imperative to insure every citizen a decent fate: Sweden, Norway and Denmark."[26]

Beauvoir did not write the book to provide guidance to individuals but to analyze the phenomenon of aging, as she had sex, in broader theoretical and sociopolitical–historical terms However, while making valid points about the conditions of aging and the social mistreatment of older people, in this instance, she reinforced negative ideas about aging and older people by referring to aging as an inexorable decline. In contrast, Auclair and Ségal did not approach the topic from an analytical vantage point. Auclair's book, *Towards a Happy Old Age (Vers une vieillesse heureuse)*, like the rest of her series of books on happiness, was meant as a guide. Mental techniques she had developed early in life could also help ensure a happy old age. At the start of the book, Auclair described Beauvoir's book as "the most resounding of the works on aging," which informed the public and public authorities about the "shameful insufficiency of the means of existence accorded to the elderly." But Auclair also labeled Beauvoir's book "nefarious: her personal vision of aging is apt to cause despair" in anyone over age 60. Auclair backed away from a direct challenge, however. "I'll resist the temptation to engage in polemics with Simone de Beauvoir," a person who, Auclair noted, sees the glass as half empty while Auclair preferred to see it as half full.[27] She called on the reader to "get ahold of yourself." Youth is magnificent but brief. Quoting Saint-Jean Perse Auclair said that she wrote her book to help people "achieve in the fullness of our being that part of us that is divine." Like her other books on happiness, *Towards a Happy Old Age* includes personal anecdotes, brief biographical portraits, literature, poetry, and mental techniques.[28]

Auclair opened the book highlighting what she called the "immutable" aspect of personality. Having had the experience of leaving Chili at age 22 and returning 45 years later, she had not watched her friends age slowly over time but could compare the two snapshots of them in time. That experience revealed clearly to her, "we remain exactly what we have been." Dynamic and lively people continued to be dynamic and lively; complainers continued to complain.[29]

Auclair warned her readers against the temptation to blame everything bad or unpleasant on age: loss of strength, memory, concentration, and poor sleep. She characterized complaining about declining abilities as quitting, arguing that complaints speed up, even ensure decline. She urged readers not to take every little sign of aging as a tragedy. Physically "everything can be treated," and mentally "everything can be mastered."[30] Rather than focusing on declining abilities, Auclair recommended trying new things, never using the excuse "I'm too old" to learn a new language or take up an instrument. She described focusing on regret about the past as a tunnel of darkness, best combatted by trying new things, moving to a new home, or changing habits, all acts that can be tonic.[31] Auclair insisted, "we deserve to die young at an advanced age."[32]

Most important, in a chapter titled "No Complaining" Auclair warned against using age to excuse negative behavior. Complaining can motivate a young person to act Auclair conceded, but it had only negative results for an older person. To be happy at an older age, a person must "give up complaining." Auclair explained that complaining did no good, only annoying and driving away friends and family. Besides, she insisted, "everything is transitory."[33] Another warning chapter follows, "The Terrible and Assimilated Elderly," which she introduces with a long quote from the Marquis de Sade: "Old age is rarely pleasant, because it's the time of life when it's no longer possible to hide any flaws." Many old people become troubled souls, but "when a noble life has prepared for old age, it is no longer decadent but the start of immortality."[34] Auclair had noticed that the people who became "difficult" in old age often had been important in their youth, such as statesmen, business executives, and elites who as they aged turned into criers and complainers, warning others of the horrors to come. Finally, Auclair shifted to the positive in Chapter 4, titled "Love." She cites Stendhal's description of old age as "a flower that, having been watered in the morning, changes into a delicious fruit in the evening, when roses are no longer in season."[35] Auclair tells of an old woman who sees again for the first time a man who had been the love of her life when they were teens. The man, on seeing her, announced that she hadn't changed a bit to which she replied, "Put on your glasses. God is so good that when he gives us wrinkles, we must wear glasses to see them."[36]

As in her other books on happiness, Auclair devoted a section near the end, "thought creates," to the ways in which our minds and thoughts shape our reality. She suggested positive affirmation, meditation, prayer, and ways of thinking about death, citing her transcendent experience with her brother after he died. She quotes at length from the Gospels, from her ex-husband Jean Prévost, and from the *Bhagavad Gita*. She includes a passage from gastronome Brillat-Savarin's classic *The Physiology of Taste* about his great aunt's death. He was sitting at her bedside. When she woke up, he recommended a nice glass of wine. She agreed, and he helped her drink a glass of his best wine. After thanking him, she explained that when he reached her age, "you will see that death becomes a necessity, like sleep." Those were her last words. Auclair pointed out that Brillat-Savarin himself did not fight death. At 69, an age when most men were still "strongly attached to life, his last breath was that of a gourmand who had just finished a good dinner."[37]

Auclair closed the book with practical supplements, a chapter on diet and exercise, yoga in particular, with drawn illustrations of the poses. The final chapter included practical information about the Paris Office for the Elderly, created in 1970, with a description of services offered, as well as its address and phone number.[38]

Auclair also spoke about aging on television. In 1975, she appeared on *Aujourd'hui Madame* (*Today Mrs.*) for a special on the theme "Love in Old Age." The show assembled a panel of guests and experts, five men and five women, who sat in a circle. The men included a specialist on sexuality after 50, a psychiatrist, and a gerontologist. Unlike her appearance on the 1967 "Face to Face" panel with Paris Archbishop Veuillot when she waited thirty minutes to get in a question, in this case the host started the show by talking about Auclair. He insisted that Marcelle Auclair, who had recently published *Towards a Happy Old Age*, "needs no introduction." In her opening comments, Auclair focused on the positive aspects of love at older age, more tenderness, and less violence, jealousy, and anguish; "everything is a bit calmer and one discovers tenderness." She had seen couples "evolve towards harmony." One of the other female guests nodded in agreement when Auclair noted that to reach that point of harmony "in your youth you must have lived a very intense, passionate life and have had just about enough of that." Other guests discussed their personal stories of love at a later age. A doctor insisted that there was no age limit on sex. The show's host went back to Auclair at the end of the hour and asked what advice she would give people. She concluded, "We create our own blockages, by dint of thinking about things, we obsess on a theme. I think we must take life as it comes with a lot of philosophy, with much good will and especially with a sense of humor, not take oneself too seriously and most especially, no drama."[39]

In contrast to both Beauvoir and Auclair, Ségal's approach was neither a sociocultural analysis of aging nor an explicit guide to happiness. In her books, unlike columns, Ségal guided readers only indirectly, using her life as an example. She connected her discussion of old age to the theme of the book, being alone or single. Ségal's book recounts her life story emphasizing the fact that, for most of her life, she was alone. Her marriage lasted seven years, her only biological child died, and she never remarried. Ségal emphasized those facts to make her point: being alone did not necessarily mean being lonely. After her husband left her, she took in lodgers. After the war, she adopted two sons and took in two more boys. "I am a single woman who has never lived alone."[40]

Ségal closed her book on single life by addressing loneliness and old age, a theme Auclair had also raised in a chapter titled "A False Friend: Solitude." To clarify, Auclair cited eighteenth-century writer and moralist Luc de Clapiers de Vauvenargues: "Solitude is to the spirit like dieting is to the body: necessary but deadly if it lasts too long." Moments of solitude could be "precious, even indispensable, to take stock in a tête à tête with yourself." But prolonged solitude risked reinforcing egoism. Too shut off in your own comfort zone, "you end up losing interest in everything, except yourself."[41] Ségal's analysis seconded these ideas but developed the theme in greater detail.

Ségal subtitled her chapter "Old Age and Solitude," describing loneliness as "the lot of the elderly. . . . Their parents are dead, their children, married. Friends, little by little, disperse . . . Every year, then every month, a friend disappears. Loneliness gets heavier." Even if the elderly spend time with their families, often they feel apart, too tired to take part in the activities, isolated by hearing loss from joining conversations, quickly leaving gatherings to return home to calm and old habits, feeling happier alone. Ségal continued the negative portrayal, describing the various ailments taking up ever more attention. Family and friends find the complaints of an older relative tiresome and pull away.

spending less time with them, which only causes the person to add complaints about being abandoned to complaints about their ailments. Family and friends don't flee from older people who don't complain, the stoics who never demand pity. Instead they forget about them.[42]

Having set up this no-win situation, Ségal posed a question. Is the loneliness of the elderly inevitable and cruel? Probing her own life as a single woman, she wondered, "Am I alone? Do I suffer from loneliness?"[43] Ségal admitted to sharing some of the traits she had described, tiring more easily, going out less often, and leaving gatherings earlier. But then she challenged her own stereotype. Being alone is not the same as being lonely. In her life, she found balance. She loved her friends but also loved being alone at times. "I need my friends, and I need to be alone."[44] Like Auclair, Ségal warned that being alone all the time could result in egocentrism and hypochondria. Too much being alone could be poisonous. But, typical of Ségal, she also insisted that being alone could be the best thing possible. In her life, being alone gave her time to rest, to reflect, to contemplate, and to work. Ségal criticized something that had become all the rage by then, the insistence on "teamwork." Ségal hated teamwork, finding that she could only get her work done alone. But she pointed out the contradiction of her work: she could not be an advice columnist without other people, the primary sources for the advice columnist. Only listening to and reading what other people had to say made her dialogue with readers possible. Again the paradox: "To do my work, I need other people and I need to be alone."[45]

She concluded that she was not alone. Since she had many friends, she only ended up alone when she wanted to be alone. Solitude was not painful for her, but precious. She loved spending time with friends, but also loved being alone when she wanted.

To Ségal, solitude represented not a prison, but a retreat. She warned that being alone could be dangerous for old people who made no effort to spend time with friends and family, who refused to go for a car ride because of the breeze, to eat out because of their diet, or to go to a show that continued past their bedtime. Or they accepted invitations but spent all their time criticizing everything, retelling stories their companions had heard hundreds of times. Ségal conceded that some older people had been abandoned. Rather than telling her readers what to do, she asked, "what will you do?"[46]

As for how to manage old age, Ségal, like Auclair, recommended not focusing on all the possible negatives, such as possible illnesses. Rather than worrying about and planning for all possible negative eventualities, Ségal explained she had set aside enough money to deal with troubles if and when they happened. She might well fall ill, but if so, she would not have poisoned her life prior to that worrying and complaining about the possibility. If she had to suffer, so be it, but, she insisted, not one day more than necessary. She did not have a moment to lose and insisted on her right to refuse to "suffer any more than I have to, to prefer laughter to tears and, if possible, to laugh even while crying."[47] The cover of her book has a drawn image of a woman in rocking chair, a cat on her lap, a record player to her left, and a bouquet of flowers to her right. Ségal's book, rather than directly advising readers, presented her point of view, inviting readers to learn from her experiences.

Ultimately, the lessons Ségal conveyed with her life story echoed Auclair's advice. While not glossing over or downplaying the difficulties and challenges, neither of them presented a negative vision of old age. Instead they both focused on ways to think about what aging meant and to manage the challenges. As with all of their advice, Auclair and Ségal downplayed the drama and assured women they could handle the situation. They encouraged women to take control of their lives, messages they had conveyed for decades. Those messages continued to resonate long after they retired. Their influence continues to this day.

Bridges to Feminism: Marcelle Auclair, Marcelle Ségal, and Women's Magazines in Twentieth-Century France.
Sarah Fishman, Oxford University Press.
DOI: 10.1093/9780197791356.003.0008

Conclusion

The Enduring Impact of Auclair and Ségal

In 2022, as *Marie-Claire* celebrated its 85th anniversary, journalist Pauline Gallard paid homage to Marcelle Auclair. "*Marie Claire*'s destiny is so deeply linked to that of Marcelle Auclair that you can't talk about one without talking about the other." Auclair, a visionary "on the front lines of women's emancipation," was fundamental to making *Marie-Claire* a magazine that responded to "women's desire for emancipation."[1] The following year, François Forestier, in the newsmagazine *Le Nouvel Obs*, honored her counterpart, Marcelle Ségal, the "grand priestess of 'Letters from the Heart.' " Her columns were "read with passion, detailed with fury, pulled apart with delight by all women (and sometimes men)." Forestier dubbed Ségal a superstar whose fifty years of advice made her "the guardian angel of a well-tempered feminism."[2]

These articles testify to the continuing relevance of Marcelle Ségal and Marcelle Auclair. They had a long-term impact, first through the dialogue they engaged in with their readers. As they responded to readers' questions and comments in advice columns and articles, they built a relationship with their readers and nurtured a sense of community. In her book about early twentieth-century American newspaper advice columns, historian Julie Golia found that the columns fostered exchanges not just between letter writers and columnists but also between readers, who were able to correspond with each other via the columns. Golia concludes that, long before the Internet, American newspaper advice columns created virtual communities that shaped public discourse, transformed the American media landscape, and changed "the very nature of democratic discourse."[3] In France, rather than newspapers, a similar sense of community developed around the strong connections Auclair at *Marie-Claire* and Ségal at *Elle* built with their readers.

Auclair published articles in response to issues readers raised in their letters. She also met with and responded directly to people who wrote to her. She published a series of books on happiness with stories and exercises to help people manage their emotions and minimize pain by changing their inner dialogue. In 1982, a year before she died, Auclair translated and wrote a preface for William Atkinson's book, *Thought Vibrations,* source of many of the techniques she recommended in her books.[4] Ségal, for forty years, responded weekly to readers in her "Letters from the Heart" column, building a deep, long-lasting connection with her readers. She was 91 when she retired in 1987.

Through dialogue, Ségal and Auclair encouraged their readers to "take control of their destinies as modern women."[5] Their ability to connect with readers and the empowering messages they conveyed grew out of early life experiences that broadened their perspectives. Over the first half of the century, their childhoods as outsiders, marriages that did not last, painful losses, and children both biological and adopted deeply shaped their views. Auclair's new age/eastern/Christian spiritual blend had a different tone from Ségal's dry, self-deprecating, Jewish-inflected humor. Nevertheless, they created very similar guideposts for living.

Ségal's platform, the advice column, lives on in France, not just in print media but also in blogs, on websites, and in podcasts. Online personality Dr. Love responds to readers on YouTube under the title "What's my problem?" Tina Karr produces a regular Apple Podcast, using the title Ségal invented, "Letters from the Heart" (*courrier du coeur*). The weekly advice column also continues in *Elle*, where Giulia Foïs responds online to readers' letters in her column "Allo Giulia."[6] Similarly, Auclair's mode of conversation with her readers continues in *Marie-Claire*. Engaging directly with its readers, *Marie-Claire* for example invites them to send their personal stories for a column titled "Me, Reader," which appears in both its print and online editions.[7]

In addition to their dialogue with readers, the enduring impact of Ségal and Auclair includes their shaping of France's most widely read women's magazines. From the start, both *Elle* and *Marie-Claire* communicated ideas about women and gender that pointed to feminism. In the 1950s and 1960s, *Elle* and *Marie-Claire,* in addition to coverage of relationships, fashion, recipes, and domestic life, included stories highlighting professional women, advising young women to learn about educational and career options, and praising women who successfully broke into previously all-male professions. Columnists explored issues of sex and sexuality; they challenged the double standard. By the 1960s women's magazines began advocating for the legalization of birth control.

That aspect of Ségal and Auclair's influence also lives on in the present-day versions of *Marie-Claire* and *Elle.* Both magazines continue to cover not just fashion, culture, lifestyle, and celebrities but also feminist issues. They advocate for women's rights. *Elle* describes itself as "the women's magazine of fashion, beauty, and all current issues for women." *Elle*'s recent articles tackle a variety of contemporary issues critical to women's lives. Late in 2024, *Elle* published an article about Aurore Begé, newly appointed Minister of Female-Male Equality. Another article reported on the move to extend maternity leaves. Lola Gugen's article, "#METOO," addressed the issue of sexual violence against domestic workers. A follow-up piece argued for specialized judges to handle cases of violence against women.[8]

As for Auclair, Gallard's 85th anniversary tribute credited her lasting influence for *Marie-Claire's* continued dedication to "carry on her combat."[9] *Marie-Claire*'s online table of contents includes, along with categories like Fashion, Beauty, and Health, a heading titled "Dedicated Women," about women who are "CEOs, stay-at-home moms, artists … In their own ways all these women are examples of success, and they all have something to teach us."[10] Another section shines the light on women's professional lives, covering "everything you need to know to succeed in your professional life, but also to feel fulfilled at work, or to know when it's time to change careers."[11] In January 2025, Catherine Durand reported on "the struggles of single mothers." Another article spotlighted "Gisèle Pelicot, Taylor Swift, Imane Khelif … 24 women who shaped 2024."[12] Thus, reviewing current content confirms that *Marie-Claire* and *Elle* continue to build on the foundation Auclair and Ségal helped establish.

Shortly after Auclair died in 1983, *Le Monde*'s obituary listed her many hats—journalist, biographer, moralist, pioneer of women's magazines, creator of *Marie-Claire*, novelist, historian—and described her as "an extraordinary woman who always knew how to be as passionate for history as she was for the story of her own times."[13] Ségal celebrated her 100th birthday in 1996 with family and friends by holding a mock wedding ceremony complete with a white gown, veil, flowers, and a young family friend pretending to be the groom. Two years later, after her death, *Le Monde*'s obituary for Ségal described her as the confidante of thousands of readers, mostly women and more than a few men. "In the face of drama, this lady who lived through the century always favored intentional optimism."[14] Rather than holding themselves up as exceptional, Ségal and Auclair aimed to inspire self-confidence and encouraged new ways of thinking and managing problems. Even as they tried to help their readers work through relationships and family life, they urged women to think for themselves and not to leave themselves dependent on others. Their empowering messages supported change on an intimate, personal level reshaping ideas on gender that created a solid and lasting base for feminism.

Epilogue: From Beyond the Grave

Ségal faded more from public view than Auclair after her death. Both of her books rested on her contemporary popularity; once she was no longer in the public eye, her books no longer attracted readers, which is unfortunate because they are humorous, perceptive accounts. Auclair's work continues to be read, in particular her biography of Saint Teresa.[15] A search on the web revealed that her books on happiness continue to generate interest, in print, online, and in blogs. Her techniques combining Atkinson's thought vibrations with Christian mysticism and eastern spirituality still speak to contemporary readers, overlapping with the twenty-first century new age movement.

But references to Auclair also turned up in the media unexpectedly, when I wasn't searching for her. In the summer of 2015, global media covered explosive, newly public information regarding Federico Garcia Lorca, the Spanish poet/playwright whose biography Auclair had published in 1968. Although the regime always denied it, Franco's forces had long been assumed to have executed Garcia Lorca and covered it up after the fact. After nearly eighty years of dead ends and searches that failed to find documentation or even a grave site, in 2015 a Spanish radio station,

Cadena Ser, announced that it had obtained documents and a report on Garcia Lorca's death that confirmed Franco's guilt. Many news outlets picked up the story. Knowing about Auclair's connection to Garcia Lorca, I read the coverage and learned, from the *Guardian*, that the documents found in 2015 "relate to an inquiry into Garcia Lorca's death by French author Marcelle Auclair in the 1960s." Her request for information bounced between several government ministers, as they debated whether to respond. Her request led the Granada police to compile a report on what happened, which they quickly realized they could not let anyone see. But rather than destroying the report, they simply filed it away and never responded to Auclair. Somehow in 2015, Cadena Ser obtained a copy of the report and discovered that it contained the "first admission by Franco-era officials of their involvement in the 1936 death of the Spanish poet and playwright."[16] Lorca's Irish biographer Ian Gibson told the *Irish Times* that the report, tremendously important, "highlights the fact that Lorca was arrested on the orders of the local authorities and that it wasn't just a street murder carried out by anyone."[17]

I shared the fact that I was working on a dual biography of Auclair and Ségal with a family friend in France whom I met during my college study-abroad semester in the late 1970s. In response to my note about my current project, she told me, "It made me smile to hear you talk about Marcelle Auclair et Marcelle Ségal. That was my mother's generation, two intelligent women who contributed, one in *Marie-Claire*, the other in *Elle*, to changing the mentality of the times when these magazines announced and were engaged in what would become feminism."[18]

Bridges to Feminism: Marcelle Auclair, Marcelle Ségal, and Women's Magazines in Twentieth-Century France.
Sarah Fishman, Oxford University Press.
DOI: 10.1093/9780197791356.003.0009

ENDNOTES

Introduction

1. Jacques Dutronc, "Le Courrier du coeur," Side A Track 1 (Disques Vogue, 1968); Antoine Prost, "Public and Private Spheres in France," in Antoine Prost and Gérard Vincent, eds, *A History of Private Life: Riddles of Identity in Modern Times*, vol. 5 (Cambridge: Harvard University Press, 1991), p. 138.

2. *New York Times*, February 21, 2020.

3. Peter Weber, "13 of Dear Abby's best zingers," *The Week*, January 8, 2015, https://theweek.com/articles/468550/13-dear-abbys-best-zingers. Accessed May 26, 2021.

4. Samantha M. Shapiro, "They Lives They Lived: Abigail Van Buren," *The New York Times*, December 21, 2013, https://www.nytimes.com/news/the-lives-they-lived/2013/12/21/abigail-van-buren; Paul O'Neal, "Twin Lovelorn Advisors," *Life*, April 7, 1958, p. 100; Elizabeth Kantor, "The Weekend with the Friedman Twins," *Washington Post*, June 23, 1986, https://www.washingtonpost.com/archive/lifestyle/1986/06/23/the-weekend-with-the-friedman-twins/186b34b3-9322-4899-852f-99edd1e4234c/. Accessed May 25, 2021.

5. Shapiro, "They Lives They Lived."

6. Michel Phelizon, "Du Journal des Dames à Marie-Claire," *Revue de l'action social et des collectivités* (Janvier-Février 1973), p. 75. He reports circulation per issue in 1971 of 664,352 for *Elle* and 805,804 for *Marie-Claire*.

7. Prost, "Public and Private Spheres," p. 138.

8. In France the first telephones were used not for personal contact but to broadcast music and theatre into private homes.

9. Patrice A. Carré, "Uncertain Development. Diffusion of the Telephone in France before 1914," trans. Liz Libbrecht, *Research: Communication-Technologie-Société* 1, no. 2 (Fall 1993), p. 258.

10. Dominque Veillon, "Ésthétique et représentations de la femme à travers la presse féminine (*Marie-Claire et Elle*, 1958–1975)," in *Les années 68: événements, cultures politiques et modes de vie*. Lettre d'information no. 26 (9 June 1997), p. 3.

Chapter 1

1. Michael Marrus and Robert Paxton, *The Politics of Assimilation: A Study of the French Jewish Community at the Time of the Dreyfus Affair* (New York: Oxford University Press, 1981); Michael Marrus, *Les Juifs de France à l'époque de l'affaire Dreyfus* (Paris: Complexe, 1972), p. 181.

2. H. Seton-Watson, "Two Contrasting Policies toward Jews: Russia and Hungary," in B. Vago and G. L. Mosse eds, *Jews and Non-Jews in Eastern Europe, 1918–1945* (New York: Wiley, 1974), pp. 100–107; Mark S. Simpson, "The 'Svyaschonnaya druzhina' and Jewish persecution in Tsarist Russia," *New Zealand Slavonic Journal* no. 2 (1978), pp. 17–26. France, Law of November 13, 1791, "The National Assembly… Revokes all adjournments, reservations, and exceptions inserted into preceding decrees relating to Jewish individuals who take the civic oath…" Paris, November 13, 1791. Coincidentally, Esther and Pauline Freidman's parents left Lithuania during a second wave of pogroms from 1903 to 1906.

3. Marrus and Paxton, *Politics of Assimilation* for more on anti-Semitism in France; see also Paula Hyman, *From Dreyfus to Vichy: The Remaking of French Jewry, 1906–1939* (New York: Columbia University Press, 1979); Pierre Birnbaum and Miriam Kochan, *Anti-Semitism in France: A Political History from Léon Blum to the Present* (Oxford: Blackwell Publishing, 1992); Vicki Caron, "The Antisemitic Revival in France in the 1930s: The Socioeconomic Dimension Reconsidered," *Journal of Modern History* 70, no. 1 (1998), pp. 24–73.

4. Jean-Denis Bredin, *The Affair: The Case of Alfred Dreyfus* (Paris: Braziller, 1986); Zosa Szajkowsi, "The Growth of the Jewish Population of France (Concluded)," *Jewish Social Studies* 8, no. 4 (October 1946), pp. 300, 314.

5. Bredin, *Affair.*

6. Michael Aronson, *Troubled Waters: The Origins of the 1881 Anti-Jewish Pogroms in Russia* (Pittsburgh: University of Pittsburgh Press, 1990). Aronson's

book includes a map of pogroms showing that in 1881 they all took place south of present-day Lithuania, p. 109; see also John Doyle Klier, *Russian Jews and the Pogroms of 1881–1882* (Cambridge: Cambridge University Press, 2011).

7. Marcelle Ségal, *Moi aussi, j'étais seule* (Paris: Centurion/Grasset, 1971), p. 40.

8. Ségal, *Moi aussi*, p. 9.

9. Ségal, *Moi aussi*, p. 11.

10. Ségal, *Moi aussi*, p. 10.

11. Ségal, *Moi aussi*, p. 12.

12. Ségal, *Moi aussi*, p. 12.

13. Ernest Lavisse, *Histoire de France: cours élémentaire* (Paris: Librairie Armand Colin, 1913), p. 1.

14. Ségal, *Moi aussi*, p. 13.

15. Ségal, *Moi aussi*, p. 14.

16. Ségal, *Moi aussi*, pp. 19–20.

17. James E. Connolly, *The Experience of Occupation in the Nord, 1914–18* (Manchester: Manchester University Press, 2018), p. 20.

18. Ségal, *Moi aussi*, pp. 23–24.

19. Ségal, *Moi aussi*, pp. 24–25.

20. Ségal, *Moi aussi*, p. 25.

21. *Il y a 140 ans naissait Victor Auclair (1866–1928)* (Commentry: Espace Culturelle de la Pléade, 2006).

22. Marcelle Auclair, *A la grâce de Dieu* (Paris: Seuil, 1973), pp. 14–15.

23. *Il y a 140 ans naissait Victor Auclair.*

24. Gladys Hansen and Emmet Condon, *Denial of Disaster* (Petaluma, CA: Cameron and Company, 1989); The USGS estimated three thousand deaths, "Casualties and damage after the 1906 Earthquake," USGS, Earthquake Hazards Program, https://earthquake.usgs.gov/earthquakes/events/1906calif/18april/casualties.php. Denis Smith, *San Francisco Is Burning: The Untold Story of the 1906 Earthquake and Fires* (New York: Viking, 2005).

25. Almost all of the buildings in the newest neighborhood, the Almendral, "collapsed in the quake or burned in the fires that followed." Samuel Martland, "Reconstructing the City, Constructing the State: Government in Valparaiso after the Earthquake of 1906," *Hispanic American Historical Review* 87, no. 2 (2006), p. 235.

26. Curtiss reported, "nearly all of Santiago slept out of doors that night, in spite of the rain." The quake was followed by four hours of nearly continuous aftershocks. Curtiss counted over one hundred aftershocks by August 20. W. W. Campbell, "Note on the Chile Earthquake of August 16th," *Publications of the Astronomical Society of the Pacific* 18, no. 111 (December 1906), pp. 313–314.

27. Francine Perrin, "La fondatrice de 'Marie-Claire' a grandi au Chili," *Le petit journal-Santiago* (June 23, 2008, mis à jour le novembre 13, 2012), https://lepetitjournal.com/santiago/communaute/edition-la-fondatrice-de-marie-claire-grandi-au-chili-8961. Accessed March 6, 2024.

28. Loren B. Valderrama, "Seismic Forces and State Power: The Creation of the Chilean Seismological Service at the Beginning of the Twentieth Century," *Historical Social Research.* 40, no. 2 (January 2015), pp. 91–92, https://doi.org.10.12.754/hsr.40.2015.2.81–104. Accessed April 25, 2019; Valderrama, "Seismic Forces," p. 91.

29. Valderrama, "Seismic Forces," pp. 91–92.

30. Perrin, "La Fondatrice de 'Marie-Claire.'"

31. Victor Auclair published a booklet in Spanish describing the techniques he developed while in Santiago, *Concreta armada, Sistema Victor Auclair (Santiago: Editorial Zig Zag, 1921).*

32. Francine Perrin, " L'apport de Victor Auclair dans la construction en béton armé au Chili," https://www.villes-developpement.org/france-chili-reseau-franco-chilien-du-patrimoine-red-franco-chileno-del-patrimonio/.

33. Auclair, *A la grâce,* p. 21.

34. Auclair, *A la grâce,* pp. 23–24.

35. Auclair, *A la grâce,* p. 27.

36. Auclair, *A la grâce,* p. 32.

37. Auclair, *A la grâce,* pp. 35–37.

38. William Walker Atkinson, *Thought Vibration or The Law of Attraction in the Thought World* (Chicago: The Library Shelf, 1908).

39. Auclair, *A la grâce,* pp. 35–40.

40. Auclair, *A la grâce,* pp. 40–41.

41. Perrin, "La fondatrice de 'Marie-Claire.'"

42. Marcelle Auclair and Françoise Prévost, *Mémoires à deux voix* (Paris: Seuil, 1978), pp. 38, 62.

43. In her discussion with her daughter, she described her presentation of the paper on Maria de Heredia as a "delirious success," Auclair and Prévost, *Mémoires à deux voix*, pp. 98, 104; Perrin, "La fondatrice de 'Marie-Claire.'" *El Mercurio* named Auclair its Paris correspondent when she returned to France.

44. Perrin, "La fondatrice de 'Marie-Claire'"; Auclair, *A la grâce*, pp. 43, 49; Auclair and Prévost, *Mémoires à deux voix*, p. 104.

45. Auclair, *A la grâce*, pp. 46–47.

46. Auclair, *A la grâce*, p. 53.

47. Auclair, *A la grâce*, pp. 67–68.

48. Auclair, *A la grâce*, p. 51.

49. Auclair, *A la grâce*, p. 52.

50. Auclair, *A la grâce*, p. 55.

51. Auclair, *A la grâce*, pp. 56–57.

Chapter 2

1. Ségal, *Moi aussi*, p. 31.

2. Ségal, *Moi aussi*, p. 32.

3. Her brother created the French army's meteorology service during World War I and retired as Chief Engineer of Mines. Information from *Les Annales des Mines*, https://www.annales.org/archives/x/schereschewsky.html. Ségal, *Moi aussi*, pp. 32–34, her daughter's middle name was after her father, Benjamin.

4. Ségal, *Moi aussi*, p. 34.

5. Ségal, *Moi aussi*, p. 35.

6. Paris, 12e arrondissement: Actes d'état civil, Acte 2699 recorded June 25, 1927, p. 350, Registre d'état civil, p. 350. https://archives.paris.fr/s/4/etat-civil-actes/resultats/.

7. Developed at first for communication between business offices, users dropped a stamped note on official stationery into a specific slot that sent the message into a series of pneumatic tubes. Messages arrived at the postal service that sorted and delivered the messages to the addressee. J. D. Hayhurst, *The Pneumatic Post of Paris* (London: France & Colonies Philatelic Society of Great Britain, 1974), digital format by Mark Hayhurst, https://www.coppoweb.com/pneuma/book3.html. Accessed March 3, 2024.

8. Ségal, *Moi aussi*, p. 35.

9. Auclair, *A la grâce*, p. 61. She recounts this also in *Mémoires à deux voix*, p. 107.

10. Auclair, *A la grâce*, p. 56.

11. Some American women, many of them graduates of Seven Sisters women's colleges, played important roles in interwar France, including Chloe Owings, a major force behind juvenile justice reforms in France and Margaret Curtis, pioneer of the case study social work method. Beach, whose family lived in France before the war, returned to Paris after 1918. Shari Benstock, *Women of the Left Bank* (Austin: University of Texas Press, 1987), pp. 202–223.

12. Laure Murat, *Passage de l'Odéon: Sylvia Beach, Adrienne Monnier et la vie littéraire à Paris dans l'entre-deux-guerres* (Paris: Gallimard, 2005), p. 147.

13. Murat, *Passage de l'Odéon*, p. 13.

14. Murat, *Passage de l'Odéon*, p. 291, Marcelle Auclair and Françoise Prévost, *Mémoires à deux voix* (Paris: Seuil, 1978), p. 134.

15. *Le Navire d'Argent* (July 1925), p. 177.

16. Benstock, *Women of the Left Bank*, p. 197.

17. Murat, *Passage de l'Odéon*, p. 80.

18. Benstock, *Women of the Left Bank*, p. 208.

19. Eventually Monnier found the workload of running the journal overwhelming and passed it along to another publisher. Benstock, *Women of the Left Bank*, p. 226.

20. According to Murat, Prévost wrote two erotic short stories for Beach and Monnier, *Passage de l'Odéon*, p. 358.

21. *Le Navire d'argent* (January 1, 1916).

22. Valery Larbaud, "Shakespeare and Company," *Le Navire d'argent* (May 1, 1926). Monnier and Beach should have appeared in the Woody Allen's film *Midnight in Paris.* Shari Benstock, *Women of the Left Bank* has a chapter on Beach and Monnier, pp. 201–229.

23. Murat, *Passage de l'Odéon*, p. 8.

24. Auclair, *A la grâce*, p. 63.

25. Valery Larbaud, *Lettres à Adrienne Monnier et à Sylvia Beach 1919–1933, correspondance établie et annotée par Maurice Saillet* (Paris: IMEC, 2004), p. 205.

26. She published translations and poems in *Le Navire d'argent.*

27. Auclair, *A la grâce*, p. 65.

28. Noel Riley Fitch, *Sylvia Beach and the Lost Generation: A History of Literary Paris in the Twenties & Thirties* (New York: W. W. Norton, 1985), pp. 188–189.

29. Jérôme Garcin, *Pour Jean Prévost* (Paris: Gallimard, 1994), pp. 61–65, 70. According to Garcin Prévost rejected only tennis and skiing which he considered too posh. Prévost wrote about his love of sports in *Plaisirs des sports: Essais sur le corps humain* (Paris: Editions de la Nouvelle revue française, 1925).

30. Fitch, *Sylvia Beach*, p. 189. Hemingway introduced Beach and Monnier to boxing, took them to a boxing match at Menilmontant and to a bicycle race at the Vel d'Hiv.

31. Fitch, *Sylvia Beach*, p. 190.

32. *Le Navire d'argent* (February 1926), p. 194. As Murat put it, Hemingway "broke a thumb on Prévost's thick head," *Passage de l'Odéon*, p. 144.

33. Auclair and Prévost, *Mémoires à deux voix*, pp. 159–160.

34. Auclair and Prévost, *Mémoires à deux voix*, p. 161. Ramon Fernandez, literary critic, Marxist in the 1920s shifted to the far right and collaborated with the Nazis during the Occupation, Alice Kaplan, "Ghostly Demarcations: On Ramon Fernandez," *The Nation* (15 February 2010). https://www.thenation.com/article/archive/ghostly-demarcations-ramon-fernandez/. Accessed March 9, 2024.

35. Auclair and Prévost, *Mémoires à deux voix*, p. 163.

36. Ségal, *Moi aussi*, p. 37. She explained without providing details that the first time she called the police was after a suicide, the second time after a kidnapping.

37. Ségal, *Moi aussi*, pp. 37–38.

38. Ségal, *Moi aussi*, p. 39.

39. Ségal, *Moi aussi*, p. 39.

40. While searching for a job, Schereschewsky came to recognize another of her traits. Her sharp, somewhat sarcastic humor eventually served her well as a columnist but her cheeky responses to questions proved less helpful in her job applications. She responded "Adam and Eve" to a question about her ancestry and "full-blown insanity" to a question about hereditary illnesses. She eventually learned to hold her tongue. Ségal, *Moi aussi*, p. 43.

41. Ségal, *Moi aussi*, p. 44.

42. Ségal, *Moi aussi*, p. 51.

43. Ségal, *Moi aussi*, p. 52.

44. Ségal, *Moi aussi*, p. 65.

45. Ségal, *Moi aussi*, p. 71.

46. Ségal, *Moi aussi*, p. 76.

47. Married to author Alfred Machard, Raymonde after World War II became the Director of the Théatre du Grand Guignol in Paris.

48. Marcelle Ségal, "Repas à la chaine," *Journal de la femme* (March 7, 1936), p. 8.

49. Ségal, *Moi aussi*, p. 77.

50. "Ceux de la Terre Promise: La halte des errants," *Journal de la femme* (May 1936), p. 1.

51. On the cover, "Un Joyeux reportage: Au Pays de la Reine, une essai de paix dans l'Europe" (A Joyful Report: In the Land of the Queen, A Test of Peace in Europe); Ségal, "Images de Hollande," *Journal de la femme* (August 1936), pp. 1, 8.

52. Ségal, *Moi aussi*, p. 79.

53. Ségal, *Moi aussi*, p. 83. She also published occasional short stories, "Ma vie était inutile" *Marie-Claire* (October 6, 1939); "A votre aise, ma fille," *Marie-Claire* (January 26, 1940), p. 24.

54. Auclair and Prévost, *Mémoires à deux voix*, p. 164.

55. Auclair and Prévost, *Mémoires à deux voix*, p. 165.

56. Auclair and Prévost, *Mémoires à deux voix*, p. 163.

57. Auclair and Prévost, *Mémoires à deux voix*, p. 165.

58. Auclair and Prévost, *Mémoires à deux voix*, p. 167.

59. Auclair and Prévost, *Mémoires à deux voix*, p. 168.

60. Auclair and Prévost, *Mémoires à deux voix*, p. 168.

61. Clotis was married to André Malraux. Vincent Soulier, *Presse féminine: La puissance frivole* (Paris: Editions Archipel, 2008), p. 93.

62. Auclair and Prévost, *Mémoires à deux voix*, p. 287.

63. Marc Capelle, *Jean Prouvost: Un patron du Nord, l'empereur de la presse Parisienne* (Paris: Vuibert, 2010); see also Adam Stanley, *Modernizing Tradition: Gender and Consumerism in Interwar France and Germany* (Baton Rouge: LSU Press, 2008), p. 179 on *Paris-Soir*; Philippe Bernard and Henri Dubief list *Paris-Soir*'s daily circulation as 1.75 million, compared to *Le Petit Parisien* at 1 million and *Le Temps* at 70,000, Philippe Bernard and Henri

Dubief, *The Decline of the Third Republic,* trans. Anthony Forster (New York: Cambridge University Press, 1985), p. 263.

64. Auclair, *A la grâce,* p. 70.

65. Auclair and Prévost, *Mémoires à deux voix,* p. 291.

66. Marie-Claire Servan-Schreiber became an anti-colonial activist and married eventual Prime Minister Pierre Mendès-France, Vincent Soulier, *Presse féminine,* p. 92. Soulier, senior lecturer at top journalism school (CELSA Paris-Sorbonne), directed Marie-Claire Group marketing from 2000 to 2007.

67. Catherine Mallaval, "Marie-Claire un demi-siècle engagé," *Libération,* September 17, 2004. https://www.liberation.fr/medias/2004/09/17/marie-claire-un-demi-siecle-engage_492770. Accessed March 8, 2019. Octave Mirabeau prefaced the novel and nominated it for the Prix Goncourt. Audoux's book won the Prix Femina, an award determined by an all-female jury created to protest the Goncourt prize's all-male jury. The first woman to win the Goncourt was Elsa Triolet in 1944 for her novel *Le Premier accroc coute 200 francs.*

68. Marguerite Audoux, *Marie-Claire* (Paris: Editions Fasquelle, 1910).

69. Marcelle Auclair, "Ce que Marie-Claire vous apporte," *Marie-Claire* 1 (March 3, 1937), p. 1. See also Soulier, *Presse féminine,* p. 94.

70. Soulier, *Presse féminine,* p. 93.

71. Capelle, *Jean Prouvost,* p. 161.

72. Auclair and Prévost, *Mémoires à deux voix,* p. 305.

73. According to Jérôme Garcin, it was poet Saint-Jean Perse (Alexis Léger), Garcin, *Pour Jean Prévost,* p. 70.

74. Auclair and Prévost, *Mémoires à deux voix,* p. 231.

75. Garcin, *Pour Jean Prévost,* p. 62.

76. Auclair and Prévost, *Mémoires à deux voix,* p. 229.

77. Auclair and Prévost, *Mémoires à deux voix,* p. 229.

78. Marcelle Auclair, *Le mauvais cœur* (Paris: Seuil, 1957), p. 37.

79. Auclair and Prévost, *Mémoires à deux voix,* pp. 230–231.

80. Auclair and Prévost, *Mémoires à deux voix,* p. 235.

81. BNF Manuscripts: Fonds Jean Prévost, NAF 26186 Cahiers, carnets, journal et agenda LXXI October 26, 1936—March 29, 1939. NAF 26206 Corréspondance de Jean Prévost, Letters.

82. Divorce was not common in the 1930s. There were about five divorces per 10,000 people in the 1930s, five times lower than the present-day rate. See Sandra Brée, "Did the War Break Couples?: Marriage and Divorce in France During and After WWI," Sandra Brée and Saskia Hin, eds., *The Impact of World War I on Marriages, Divorces, and Gender Relations in Europe* (Routledge, 2020), p. 183; https://www.ined.fr/en/everything_about_population/data/france/marriages-divorces-pacs/divorces/.

Chapter 3

1. Ségal, *Moi aussi*, p. 87.

2. "Prenez vos précautions," *Marie-Claire* (September 8, 1939), p. 7; *Marie-Claire* (September 15, 1939); (September 22, 1939), pp. 12–13, 24–25.

3. *Marie-Claire* (December 15, 1939), p. 1.

4. Auclair, "Le bon coté des choses," *Marie-Claire* (March 29, 1940), p. 1.

5. Auclair, "Je les ai vus la-bas," *Marie-Claire* (December 8, 1939), pp. 4–5.

6. "Jeunes femmes d'aujourd'hui, Colette vous parle," *Marie-Claire* (May 24, 1942), p. 2.

7. Marcelle Auclair, "L'Elan de l'espoir," *Marie-Claire* (May 31, 1940), p. 1.

8. Pierre Lazareff, *Deadline The Behind-the-Scenes Story of the Last Decade in France* (New York: Random House, 1942), p. 310.

9. https://www.upi.com/Archives/1940/06/03/German-bombers-hit-Paris/4413583280132/The bombers, in five waves of twenty-five each plus one wave of thirty planes, were forced by French fighters to stay at a high altitude—around 30,000 feet—unable to aim bombs accurately at military objectives from that height.

10. Lazareff, *Deadline*, pp. 328–330.

11. Auclair and Prévost, *Mémoires à deux voix*, p. 332.

12. Auclair, *A la grâce de Dieu*, p. 90; Auclair and Prévost, *Mémoires à deux voix*, p. 337.

13. For an excellent account of the Exodus, see Hannah Diamond, *Fleeing Hitler: France 1940* (New York: Oxford University Press, 2007).

14. See Fabien Théofilakis, *Les prisonniers de guerre français en 40* (Paris: Fayard, 2022).

15. Ségal, *Moi aussi*, p. 87.

16. Ségal, *Moi aussi*, p. 88.

17. Ségal, *Moi aussi*, pp. 88, 90–91.

18. Denis Broussolle, "L'Elaboration du Statut des juifs de 1940," *Le Genre humain* (January 30–31, 1996), p. 113. Vichy's law defined as Jewish any person descended from three Jewish grandparents, and, broader than Germany's Nuremburg Laws, anyone with two Jewish grandparents and a Jewish spouse. The October 1940 law was the first step in a series of increasingly harsh restrictions and property seizures, easing the task for the Nazis when they targeted Jews in France starting in the summer of 1942.

19. She never named the person who fired her, most likely Prouvost, Ségal, *Moi aussi*, p. 91.

20. Ségal, *Moi aussi*, p. 92.

21. Robert Paxton, *Vichy France: Old Guard and New Order* (New York: W. W. Norton, 1972) explored the Vichy government's origins, motives, and policies. See also Jean-Pierre Azema, *From Munich to the Liberation 1938–1944* (Cambridge: Cambridge University Press, 1985); Jean-Pierre Azéma, Yves Durand, Denis Peschanski, and Dominique Veillon, *Collaboration and Resistance: Images of Life in Vichy France 1940–1944* (New York: Harry N. Abrams, 2000).

22. André Gide, *Journal 1939–1942* (Paris: Gallimard, 1946), p. 44. Several days later Gide reconsidered his rejection of Vichy, unsure where he stood.

23. Gide, *Journal*, p. 45.

24. Kenneth Mouré, *Marché Noir: The Economy of Survival in Second World War France* (New York: Cambridge University Press, 2023).

25. Garcin, *Pour Jean Prévost* (Paris: Gallimard, 1994), p. 136.

26. Ségal, *Moi aussi*, p. 92.

27. Ségal, *Moi aussi*, p. 93. In 1940, Camus worked for *Paris-Soir* and also took part in the Exodus. In 1943 he moved back to Paris. Many thanks to Robert Zaretsky for his insights on Camus.

28. Ségal, *Moi aussi*, pp. 93–95.

29. After November 11, 1942 Germany occupied all of France, but still maintained the Demarcation Line as a border between what became the Northern and Southern zones in France.

30. Ségal, *Moi aussi*, p. 97.

31. Ségal, *Moi aussi*, pp. 97–98.

32. Philippe Burrin, *France under the Germans: Collaboration and Compromise*, trans. Janet Lloyd (New York: The New Press, 1998).

33. Michel Prévost, *Retrouver Jean Prévost: Romancier, critique, essayiste et journaliste* (Grenoble: Presses Universitaires de Grenoble, 2002), p. 110.

34. Jean Prévost, *La création chez Stendhal: Essai sur le métier d'écrire et la psychologie de l'écrivain* (Marseille: Editions du Sagittaire, 1942).

35. Prévost, *Retrouver Jean Prévost*, p. 110.

36. Marcel Haedrich, *Citizen Prouvost: Le portrait incontournable d'un grand patron de la presse française* (Paris: Filipacchi, 1995), p. 87.

37. The actual crime involved Antoine Berthet, low born, self-educated social climber who tutored children for wealthy families. He was fired for having an affair with the wife in one family, hired by another family that later fired him when they found out about his earlier affair. Berthet attempted to murder his first mistress; she survived; he was convicted and executed. *Marie-Claire*'s wartime issues included pieces by other well-known authors.

38. Louis Aragon, another notable member of the French Resistance, had also published during the war. Michel used these examples to argue against the blanket condemnation of publishing per se during the Occupation.

39. Prévost, *Retrouver Jean Prévost*, pp. 109–110.

40. Prévost, *Retrouver Jean Prévost*, p. 111.

41. "Le Courrier de *Marie-Claire*," *Marie-Claire* (November 16, 1940), p. 1.

42. *Marie-Claire* (November 16, 1940), p. 3.

43. See for example "Bon cœur," *Marie-Claire* (August 9, 1941).

44. Auclair, "Ne renoncez jamais," *Marie-Claire* (November 23, 1940), p. 2.

45. *Marie-Claire* (December 14, 1940), p. 2.

46. *Marie-Claire* (December 14, 1940), pp. 3–4.

47. *Marie-Claire* (September 6, 1941), p. 2.

48. "Je vous aime, Monsieur le Maréchal!...écrivent les petits enfants de France," *Marie-Claire* (February 22, 1941), pp. 13–14. One of the photos shows a young boy holding up a letter that says, "I love you Mister Marshal." The rest of the feature included facsimiles of various children's letters to Pétain and children's drawings. Clearly amused, the editors also included this letter: "I asked dear Jesus that you livetobeold." (vivréyvieux)

49. "Trop peu d'enfants, voilà une des causes de notre défaite," *Marie-Claire* (July 26, 1941).

50. Marie-Thérèse Chabord, "Les Archives des Chantiers de la jeunesse," *La Gazette des archives* 81 (1973), p. 85. doi: https://doi.org/10.3406/gazar.1973.2300; https://www.persee.fr/doc/gazar_0016-5522_1973_num_81_1_2300.

51. *Marie-Claire* (August 2, 1941).

52. *Marie-Claire* (August 2, 1941), pp. 4–5. In the accompanying photo, a Companion, bare-chested, wore a beret above the caption "the handsome kind of young man that develops in the Companions movement."

53. *Marie-Claire* (November 16, 1940), p. 23. The article exhorted readers to be both "thrifty and clever." *Marie-Claire* (November 30, 1940); "L'Art de conserver de A jusqua'à Z," *Marie-Claire* (December 7, 1940) and (December 14, 1940). Two issues later, *Marie-Claire* promised to continue the series of recipes adapted for the food that was available, *Marie-Claire* (December 21, 1940), pp. 21–22. The issue included an illustrated feature on how to get around town with photos of people riding bicycles, driving horse carts, riding in bicycle-driven jitneys. "Any way you can is good." "Good tips for your home" appeared on December 28, 1940, p. 10.

54. "Fidèlement à vous," *Marie-Claire* (December 1, 1943), p. 2.

55. *Marie-Claire* (June 1, 1944). While *Marie-Claire* continued to cover the completely unattainable world of Paris high fashion, many articles suggested ways women could remain fashionable by reusing the previous years' clothing, refashioning what they had to conform to the new styles. In May 1943, a somewhat surprising title appeared, "Knit your dog," pointing out poodle fur could be sheared and woven like wool.

56. "Professeur de Latin, capitaine d'équipe, Cécile Agnel championne de ski," *Marie-Claire* (January 4, 1941), pp. 4–5; The French national downhill team, "whenever we have one again," would be chosen from that group. See also *Marie-Claire* (September 10, 1943).

57. *Marie-Claire* (December 10, 1943).

58. "Parlons en amies," *Marie-Claire* (March 1, 1941), p. 1. The piece is unsigned, but the ideas match closely Ségal's description of her job search between the wars and it appeared while she was still at the magazine; *Marie-Claire* (January 4, 1941), pp. 4–5.

59. Jérome and Jean Tharaud, "L'Heure est à l'enthusiasme," *Marie-Claire* (February 2, 1942), p. 2.

60. Léon-Paul Fargue, "Femmes 43," *Marie-Claire* (January 10, 1943), p. 2.

61. *Marie-Claire* (January 20, 1943); For more of this kind of advice, see June 20, 1943 and January 15, 1944; November 20, 1942, May 20, 1942, March 10, 1943, June 10, 1943, April 10, 1943, July 10, 1943, October 20, 1943, November 1, 1943, and August 1, 1944.

62. "Noël sans lui," *Marie-Claire* (December 20, 1942).

63. *Marie-Claire* (February 10, 1943), p. 2. These messages echo ideas she espoused during the Phony War, " Le Bon Coté," and " Un Coeur ne se trompe jamais," *Marie-Claire* (March 15, 1940).

64. *Marie-Claire* (January 20, 1943), pp. 8–9.

65. Auclair, "Le Chapeau, l'amour et l'architecte," *Marie-Claire* (May 15, 1944).

66. Auclair explained to her daughter that after the divorce she resumed intimate relations with Jean, but had no intention of remarrying him, Auclair and Prévost, *Mémoires à deux voix*, p. 238.

67. "Ni peur ni haine," Prévost, *Retrouver Jean Prévost*, pp. 105–107.

68. Garcin, *Pour Jean Prévost*, p. 118.

69. Garcin, *Pour Jean Prévost*, p. 118.

70. Gisèle Sapiro, *The French Writers' War, 1940–1953*, trans. Vanessa Doriott Anderson and Dorrit Cohn (Durham: Duke University Press, 2014), see especially Chapter 7, "The Sense of Subversion: The Comité national des écrivains," pp. 362–436.

71. Garcin, *Pour Jean Prévost*, p. 128; Jean Prévost, *La Création chez Stendhal*

72. Jean Prévost's only open complaint about a German soldier followed an incident on a train from Lyon to Paris. Prévost watched a German soldier in his compartment take out bread, slowly spread butter on the bread, and devour his snack with obvious pleasure under the hungry eyes of a young French boy sitting next to him, never offering the boy a bite. After the train pulled into a station and the German soldier went off to take a break, Jean pilfered the food from the German soldier's suitcase and distributed it to the other passengers in the compartment. Prévost, *Retrouver Jean Prévost*, p. 114.

73. Prévost, *Retrouver Jean Prévost*, p. 145.

74. Garcin, *Pour Jean Prévost*, pp. 152–153.

75. Garcin, *Pour Jean Prévost*, pp. 152–153.

76. Garcin, *Pour Jean Prévost*, p. 152.

77. Garcin, *Pour Jean Prévost*, p. 156.

78. Detained as a foreign national, Beach spent six months in a women's internment camp at Vittel. After that Beach lived illegally in a student hostel at 93 Boulevard Saint Michel, around the corner from Monnier's bookstore, which, in addition to its regular stock, sold books under the table by Editions de Minuit, the publishing arm of the Resistance. "Mapping Expatriate Paris," (*Mapping Expatriate Paris: The Shakespeare and Company Lending Library Project* (MEP), a digital humanities project, sponsored by the Center for Digital Humanities (CDH) at Princeton University, examines the Lost Generation using the Sylvia Beach Papers in the Department of Rare Books and Special Collections at Princeton's Firestone Library. Accessed April 5, 2024.

79. From Laure Murat, *Passage de l'Odéon*, p. 146. Hemingway embedded as a journalist with the army. https://shakespeareandco.princeton.edu/analysis/. Accessed April 5, 2024.

Chapter 4

1. Ségal, *Moi aussi*, p. 101.

2. Stéphane Simmonet, *Les Poches de l'Atlantique: Les batailles oubliées de la Libération janvier 1944-mai 1945* (Paris: Tallandier, 2019).

3. For more on the aftermath of wartime choices, see Megan Koreman, *The Expectation of Justice: France, 1944–1946* (Duke University Press, 2000).

4. Fabrice Virgili, *Shorn Women: Gender and Punishment in Liberation France*, trans. John Flower (New York: Berg, 2002).

5. Alice Kaplan, *The Collaborator: The Trial and Execution of Robert Brasillach* (Chicago: University of Chicago Press, 2000).

6. Ségal, *Moi aussi*, p. 102; For a fascinating history of the black market see Kenneth Mouré, *Marché Noir: The Economy of Survival in Second World War France* (New York: Cambridge University Press, 2023).

7. Ségal, *Moi aussi*, p. 103. « nous étions follement heureux » p. 102.

8. Sarah Fishman, *We Will Wait: Wives of French Prisoners of War 1940–1945* (New Haven: Yale University Press, 1992), p. 152.

9. Haedrich, *Citizen Prouvost*, p. 56.

10. Ségal, *Moi aussi*, p. 106.

11. Denise Dubois-Jallais, *La Tzarine: Hélène Lazareff et l'aventure de "Elle"* (Paris: Robert Laffont, 1984), pp. 73–78. Hélène Gordon-Lazareff, born in

Russia in 1909, escaped to France with her family during the Russian Revolution. She married in 1930, had a daughter Michele, divorced two years later. In 1939 she married Pierre Lazareff and had a second daughter, Nina, with Pierre.

12. Dubois-Jallais, *La Tzarine*, pp. 88–89, 93, 97; Haedrich, *Citizen Prouvost*, p. 9. Hélène Gordon-Lazareff, "Marie-Claire in America," *Marie-Claire* (July 21, 1939).

13. Gordon-Lazareff, "Marie-Claire in America."

14. Lazareff, *Deadline*, p. 79.

15. Lazareff, *Deadline*, p. 340.

16. Haedrich, *Citizen Prouvost*, p. 135.

17. Marcelle Ségal, *Mon métier, le courrier du cœur* (Paris: Horay, 1952), pp. 105–106.

18. *Elle* (February 13, 1946), p. 8. The translated story's by-line, "adapted from English by Marcelle Ségal" did not include original authors, see "A 14 ans on comprend déja, nouvelle adapté de l'anglais par MS." *Elle* (May 7, 1946); Marcelle Ségal, "Tsimta tatata …" *Elle* (December 17, 1946), p. 17, one of her few signed stories.

19. Given the continuing material difficulties of the postwar, for the many families still without housing, dealing with rationed food and the difficult burden of daily chores, the luxe of *Elle* may have not been appealing.

20. Ségal, *Mon métier*, pp. 17–18.

21. *Elle* (July 23, 1946), p. 8.

22. Ségal, *Mon métier*, p. 22.

23. *Elle* (December 17, 1946), p. 39; *Elle* (December 24, 1946), p. 23.

24. Ségal, *Mon métier*, pp. 22–23.

25. Anne Gallois, "La dame de coeur," *Le Monde*, August 16, 1982. https://www.lemonde.fr/archives/article/1982/08/16/la-dame-de-c-ur_2908508_1819218.html.

26. Gallois, "La dame de coeur." Ségal also refused to respond to letters pretending they were writing on behalf of a friend. Recognizing it as a ruse, she wanted writers to come clean before she would respond. *Mon métier*, pp. 23–24. In *Elle* (September 19, 1949), p. 5; Ségal instructed readers if they included a self-addressed envelope in their letters, she would respond.

27. "Courrier du cœur," *Elle* (April 8, 1947), p. 10; (February 25, 1947), p. 23; (March 15, 1949), p. 4.

28. "Courrier du cœur," *Elle* (April 8, 1947), p. 10.

29. "Courrier du cœur," *Elle* (June 27, 1949), pp. 8–9.

30. "Courrier du cœur," *Elle* (April 8, 1947), p. 14.

31. "Courrier du cœur," *Elle* (April 8, 1947); Ségal, *Mon métier*, p. 63.

32. Anne Brunswic, *Crown Letter*, November 2–9, 2022, https://crownproject.art/?s=marcelle+s%C3%A9gal.

33. Interview with Anne Brunswic, July 13, 2021. Perhaps Marcelle chose the pseudonym Christian to de-emphasize her own Jewishness. Interestingly, her great niece explained that the boy's Jewish parents, who died in the camps, had protected him during the war by sending him to live with another family that raised him as a Christian.

34. Ségal, "Comment j'ai adopté un enfant," *Elle* (April 4, 1949), pp. 16–17.

35. Ségal, "Comment j'ai adopté un enfant," pp. 16–17.

36. Ségal, "Comment j'ai adopté un enfant," pp. 16–17.

37. According to Anne Brunswic, she adopted another older boy after Harold left for his military service; November 2–9, 2022, Crown Letter, https://crownproject.art/?s=marcelle+s%C3%A9gal.

38. Ségal, *Moi aussi*, pp. 118–129.

39. Haedrich, *Citizen Prouvost*, p. 114.

40. Haedrich, *Citizen Prouvost*, p. 88.

41. Haedrich, *Citizen Prouvost*, pp. 87–88, 113.

42. Haedrich, *Citizen Prouvost*, p. 106.

43. Haedrich, *Citizen Prouvost*, pp. 114, 106, 107, 124.

44. It is not clear where the funding came from, if she had the backing of a press group.

45. The directors listed were Andrée Braive, who had published on social security and children, Jeanne E. Durand and Marcelle Magdinier, who published a novel about a Berber woman.

46. *Marie-France* started a new series in 1956 that lasted until 1972.

47. Isabelle Antonutti, *Cino Del Duca: De Tarzan à Nous Deux, itinéraire d'un patron de presse* (Rennes: Presses Universitaires de Rennes, 2012), p. 96.

48. Jean-Pierre Arthur Bernard, *Paris rouge: 1944–1964: Les communistes français dans la capitale* (Seyssel: Champ Vallon, 1991), p. 120.

49. Antonutti, *Cino Del Duca*, p. 120.

50. *Vrai Visage de la presse du coeur* (no. 1, June 1953), p. 2.

51. *Vrai Visage* (no. 2, 1953), p. 3.

52. *Vrai Visage* (no. 2, 1953), p. 3.

53. *Vrai Visage* (no. 1, June 1953), p. 2.

54. *Vrai Visage* (no. 1, June 1953), p. 2.

55. *Vrai Visage* (no. 3, November–December 1953), p. 6.

56. Antonutti, *Cino Del Duca*, pp. 14–16, 19–20.

57. Antonutti, *Cino Del Duca*, pp. 26, 32.

58. Antonutti, *Cino Del Duca*, p. 35.

59. Antonutti, *Cino Del Duca*, p. 36.

60. Antonutti, *Cino Del Duca*, pp. 64–65, 68, 71, 74–75.

61. In any case, *Nous Deux* was a big success and continues to the present. According to its website, "A century-old weekly magazine with an optimistic and friendly tone, this magazine has established itself as an essential women's interest magazine. Every week, you'll find photo essays, historical and romantic news, and a moment for daydreaming and feeling." https://www.unipresse.com/subscription/nous-deux/.

62. *Vrai Visage*, Auclair translated many Garcia Lorca works. She met him on her trip to Spain in the early 1930s to research the life of Saint Teresa of Ávila. Thirty years later she published a biography, *Enfances et mort de Garcia Lorca* (Paris: Éditions du Seuil, 1968).

63. *Vrai Visage* 3 (November–December 1953); Bernard, *Paris rouge*, pp. 120–121.

64. Antonutti, *Cino Del Duca*, p. 121.

65. The Loi Moustier of August 2, 1954 updated the Law of September 30, 1944 on the "dissolution de titres paru sous l'occupation." (termination of titles that appeared during the Occupation).

66. See Patrick Eveno, "La presse en France depuis la Libération," *La presse à la Une, Exposition* (April 11–July 15, 2012) Bibliothèque Nationale de France, http://expositions.bnf.fr/presse/arret/05.htm.

67. Haedrich, *Citizen Prouvost*, p. 143.

68. Haedrich, *Citizen Prouvost*, p. 144.

69. Haedrich, *Citizen Prouvost*, p. 144.

Chapter 5

1. "Ma femme mariée s'appellera Charlotte et aura un amant, dit Jean-Luc Godard," *France-Soir*, June 16, 1964, p. 9; Richard Brody, *Everything is Cinema: The Working Life of Jean-Luc Godard* (New York: Henry Hold, 2008), pp. 189–190. Ségal's great-niece Anne Brunswic found Godard's letter of June 19, 1964 and included it on her Crown Project page: From "Marcelle Ségal (8), une femme mariée," Crown project, February 22 to March 1, http://crownproject.art/anne-brunswic/. Brunscwic points out that Godard's film ended not with Ségal's letter but a quote from Racine.

2. Ségal, *Moi aussi*, back cover.

3. Pierre Desgroupes, "Ínterview, Marcelle Auclair, *Connaissance de l'amour*," Lecture pour Tous, 1ere chaine, October 12, 1960.

4. Vincent Soulier, *Presse féminine*, location 1938 of 3967.

5. Jean Fourastié, *Les trente glorieuses: Ou la révolution invisible de 1946 à 1975* (Paris: Fayard, 1979).

6. For more on the Indochina war, see Christopher Goscha, *The Road to Dien Bien Phu: A History of the First War for Vietnam* (Princeton: Princeton University Press, 2022).

7. https://fr.wikipedia.org/wiki/Constellation_(revue); Michel Jamet, "L'Express, du Journal d'opinion au News-Magazine," *Communication et Langages* no. 56 (1983), p. 95; Imogen Long, "A Powerful Political Platform: Françoise Giroud and *L'Express* in a Cold War Climate," *French History* 30, no. 2 (June 2016), pp. 241–258. *France Observateur*, weekly newsmagazine and precursor of *Le Nouvel Obs*, had a circulation of 100,000 in 1954. https://fr.wikipedia.org/wiki/Le_Nouvel_Obs; An American equivalent, *Ladies Home Journal*, sold about 4.6 million copies a month in 1955, in a total US population of 166 million (2.7%). With France's population at the time 44 million, *Marie Claire*'s circulation in France of 1.1 million per 44 million represented an equivalent, if slightly lower, proportion (2.4%).

8. Examples include an article on the juvenile justice system's treatment of two 13-year-old girls removed from their families, *Elle* 488 (March 30, 1959), pp. 100–125; in 1959, a feature with photos took readers inside De Gaulle's first presidential reception, *Elle* 485 (March 9, 1959), pp. 57–59.

9. Veillon, "Ésthétique et représentations", p. 3.

10. "Si, nous sommes féministes!" *Elle*, 217 (January 23, 1950), p. 26.

11. Sian Reynolds' work on French feminism disputes the notion of a "trough between the two waves of French feminism, lasting from the end of the Second World War to the events of May 1968." See Sian Reynolds, "Before *Les femmes s'entêtent*: The Bermuda Triangle of French Feminism?," in Margaret Atack et al., eds, *Making Waves: French Feminisms and Their Legacies 1975–2015* (Liverpool: Liverpool University Press, 2019), pp. 21, 19.

12. Karen Offen, *European Feminisms 1700–1950: A Political History* (Stanford: Stanford University Press, 2000), p. 385. Political parties energized their efforts to mobilize women's support within the parties.

13. See Soulier, *Presse féminine*; Bibia Pavard, "Contraception et avortement dans *Marie-Claire (1955–1975)*: de la méthode des températures à la méthode Karman," *Le Temps des médias* 12, no. 1 (2009), pp. 100–113; Marie Hazan, "Le Fonctionnement de l'implicite dans les discours des magazines féminins. Analyse d'un exemple: la campagne pour le contrôle des naissances dans *Elle* et *Marie-Claire*," *Langage et société* no. 48 (1989), pp. 59–78; journalist Nicole Vulser pointed to Marie-Claire as "one of the first (monthlies) to give voice to those whose voices were rarely heard; Nicole Vulser, "*Marie-Claire*: une histoire de famille," *Le Monde*, February 14, 2001. According to Vulser, *Marie-Claire* made it a "point d'honneur" to adopt a global vision of social problems. https://www.lemonde.fr/archives/article/2001/02/15/marie-claire-une-histoire-de-famille_4184095_1819218.html.

14. Frédéric Orvan, "Avec milles excuses aux ministres en exercice, *Elle* constitue Le ministère de femmes," *Elle* 254 (October 9, 1950), pp. 36–37, 45.

15. Paul Guérin, "Une enquête sociale de 'Elle' à travers la France," *Elle* 557 (April 9, 1956), p. 34.

16. Jean Duché, *Elle* 689 (March 9, 1959), p. 5.

17. Jean Duché, *Elle* 841 (February 9, 1962), p. 17.

18. Veillon, "Ésthétique et representations," p. 5.

19. See *Marie-Claire* (January 1957), p. 181.

20. Desgroupes, "Ínterview, Marcelle Auclair."

21. *Marie-Claire* listed Auclair's personal address and instructed readers to write her directly to schedule a meeting. *Marie-Claire* (May 1956), p. 8

22. Ségal, *Mon métier*, p. 77.

23. Desgroupes, "Ínterview, Marcelle Auclair."

24. Gallois, "La dame de coeur," *Le Monde*, August 16, 1982.

25. Marcelle Auclair, *Le livre du bonheur* (Paris: Seuil, 1959), p. 148

26. Auclair, *Le livre du bonheur*, pp. 148–149.

27. About 5′8″ and 5′11″ Ségal, "Courrier du Cœur," *Elle* (August 14, 1964), p. 4.

28. Ségal, "Courrier du Cœur," *Elle* (December 29, 1961), p. 8.

29. Ségal, "Courrier du Cœur," *Elle* (March 29, 1954), p. 3.

30. Ségal, "Courrier du Cœur," *Elle* (August 14, 1964), p. 4.

31. Ségal, *Mon métier*, pp. 186–187.

32. Ségal, *Moi aussi*, p. 72.

33. Ségal, "La Femme et l'amour," in *La Française d'aujourd'hui* (Paris: Juillard, 1961), pp. 46–47.

34. Ségal, "Courrier du Cœur," *Elle* (March 15, 1954), p. 5.

35. Ségal, "Courrier du Cœur," *Elle* (October 14, 1965), p. 3.

36. Ségal, "Courrier du Cœur," *Elle* (November 5, 1951), p. 3.

37. Ségal, "Courrier du Coeur," *Elle* (April 1, 1957), p. 4.

38. Marcelle Auclair and Jeanne Dodemann, *Qui épousez-vous?* Paris: Bloud et Gay, 1961, p. 100; Brunswic January 11th to January 17th Marcelle (5), Courrier du Cœur 1948 in Crown Project http://crownproject.art/anne-brunswic/.

39. Auclair, "Depuis 20 ans que vous me faites confidence," *Marie-Claire* 29 (March 1957), p. 63.

40. Auclair, "Le courrier des lectrices de Marie-Claire," *Marie-Claire* 76 (February 1961), p. 17.

41. Ségal, *Elle*, 75, April 22, 1947, p. 14.

42. Ségal, *Elle*, 120, March 9, 1948, p. 8.

43. Brunswic January 11th to January 17th Marcelle (5), Courrier du Cœur 1948 in Crown Project http://crownproject.art/anne-brunswic/.

44. *Elle* 537 (April 9, 1956), p. 5.

45. Ségal, "Courrier du Cœur," *Elle* 154, November 9, 1948; "Courrier du Coeur," *Elle* 310 (November 5, 1951), p. 3.

46. Anne Brunswic, Crown Letter January 11–17, 2022, https://crownproject.art/?s=marcelle+s%C3%A9gal.

47. Ségal, "Courrier du Coeur," *Elle* 741 (March 4, 1960), p. 46.

48. Unfortunately, I can only rely on the few letters in *Elle* and excerpts her great niece included on her web page since I have not located files with actual copies of her correspondence with readers. She claimed she regularly destroyed the letters. Her great niece Anne Brunswic, an artist, included material from Ségal in her entries to *The Crown Letter*, an online participatory project for women artists. http://crownproject.art/anne-brunswic//.

49. Gallois, "La dame de coeur," *Le Monde*, August 16, 1982.

50. Alfred Kinsey, *Sexual Behavior in the Human Female* (Philadelphia: W. B. Sanders, 1953), translated and published in French in 1954); for the public reception of Kinsey's reports in France, see Sarah Fishman, *From Vichy to the Sexual Revolution: Gender and Family Life in Postwar France* (New York: Oxford University Press, 2017), pp. 32, 52–54. Historian Judith Coffin labeled the wide interest in and discussion of sex across the media, films, magazines, and books "mid-century sex." Judith Coffin, *Sex, Love, and Letters: Writing Simone de Beauvoir* (Ithaca: Cornell University Press, 2020), p. 15.

51. See Sarah Fishman, "Sex Before '68: Adolescence and the *Presse feminine*," in Nina Kushner and Andrew Israel Ross, eds, *Histories of French Sexuality* (Lincoln: University of Nebraska Press, 2023), pp. 267–279.

52. Ségal, "Courrier du Coeur," *Elle* (November 12, 1951), p. 3.

53. Ségal, "Courier du Coeur," *Elle* (November 12, 1951), p. 3.

54. Ségal, *Mon métier*, p. 191, the title of chapter 18 is "La liberté sexuelle"

55. Ségal, *Mon métier*, pp. 195, 197. On boys wanting sex see, *Elle* (March 15, 1954).

56. Ségal, "Courrier du Coeur," *Elle* 425 (February 1, 1954), p. 3.

57. Ségal, "Courrier du Coeur," *Elle* (April 18, 1955), p. 5.

58. Marcelle Auclair, "Ce que les garçons pensent des filles: confidences recueillis par Marcelle Auclair," *Marie-Claire* (April 1959), p. 54.

59. Auclair, "Ce que les garçons," pp. 55–58.

60. Auclair, "Pourquoi les femmes sont-elles moins libre que les hommes?" *Marie-Claire* (January 1957), p. 66.

61. Auclair, "Pourquoi les femmes," p. 55.

62. Fishman, *From Vichy to the Sexual Revolution*, p. 101.

63. Auclair, "Pourqoui les femmes," pp. 69, 55; Fishman, *From Vichy to the Sexual Revolution*, p. 101.

64. Ségal, "Courier du Coeur," *Elle* (March 29, 1954), p. 3.

65. Ségal, "Ce qu'enseigne le courrier du coeur," *La Francaise d'aujourd'hui: La femme et l'amour,* 8, no. 5 (January–March 1961), pp. 48–49; Anne Brunswic, her great niece, described Ségal as cynical, viewing men as deeply flawed and not to be trusted.

66. Ségal, "Courrier du Coeur," *Elle* (April 28, 1966), pp. 5–6.

67. Ségal, "Courrier du Coeur," *Elle* (April 28, 1966), pp. 5–6.

68. Auclair, "Pourquoi les femmes," p. 66.

69. Ségal, "Courrier du Cœur," *Elle* (July 11, 1949), p. 3.

70. *Marie-Claire* (July 1956), pp. 46–49; *Marie-Claire*(August 1956), p. 43; Soulier, in *Presse féminine,* loc 2871 mentions an article by Giroud in *Elle* in 1953 discussing the Kinsey report that also raised the issue of lesbian love. I was not able to find that article. I did find full page coverage of the Kinsey report volume on women, "Cable de New York: Les femmes ont tout avoué au Professeur Kinsey," *Elle* (August 31, 1953), pp. 6–7.

71. Gallois, "La dame de coeur," *Le Monde,* August 16, 1982.

72. Ségal, *Mon métier,* pp. 74–75.

73. Ségal, *Mon métier,* p. 74.

74. Jacaques Donot, "Visite à un Hébdomadaire féminin: Elle," *Visite à,* 1ere chaine, October 6, 1954.

75. Auclair and Prévost, *Mémoires à deux voix,* pp. 13–14.

76. Pierre Desgroupes, "Interview, Marcelle Auclair."

77. Ségal, "Courrier du Coeur," *Elle* (February 15, 1954), p. 3.

78. Jacques Garat, "L'Amour au troisième age," *Aujourd'hui Madame,* A2, June 26, 1975.

79. Auclair, *Le livre du bonheur,* p. 10.

80. Ségal, *Mon métier,* p. 53.

81. Ségal, "Courrier du Coeur," *Elle* (November 5, 1951), p. 52.

82. Ségal, *Mon métier,* p. 53.

83. Auclair, "Remplacer," *Le livre du bonheur,* pp. 202–203, 240.

84. Auclair, *Le livre du bonheur,* pp. 35–36.

85. Ségal, *Mon métier,* pp. 74–75.

86. Auclair and Prévost, *Mémoires*, pp. 370–371.

87. Garat, "L'Amour au troisième age."

88. *Elle* (December 26, 1949), p. 5. There was a letter from a young man in love with young woman already engaged to marry a soldier in Indochina. *Elle* (March 16, 1948), p. 10; a letter from a young woman in love with a man about to leave for Indochina whose parents forbid her from writing to him (August 15, 1949), p. 3; a few other similar letters, January 4, 1954 and January 17, 1954. A short insert, "Cette semaine elle félicite" covered a nurse receiving a military medal, *Elle* (October 9, 1950), p. 12; an article on Indochina passed along information to readers to impress husbands, "Apprenez ceci et vous étonnerez vos maris," *Elle* (August 20, 1946), p. 5; a search for "Indochine" in digitized issues of *Elle* turned up 7 brief mentions in 1949, 12 in 1950, 13 in 1951, 14 in 1952 and 16 in 1953. I was not able to do a similar search of *Marie-Claire*, which only restarted in 1954, since the postwar issues are not digitized. However, my random sampling did not turn up anything on Algeria.

89. Fishman, *We Will Wait*, p. xv; Hugh Schofield, "The WW2 Soldiers France has forgotten," BBC News, Paris, June 4, 2015, https://www.bbc.com/news/magazine-32956736. Accessed February 14, 2024.

90. For more on decolonization, see Todd Shepard, *The Invention of Decolonization: The Algerian War and the Remaking of France* (Ithaca: Cornell 2006); James McDougal, "The Impossible Republic: The Reconquest of Algeria and the Decolonization of France, 1945–1962," *The Journal of Modern History* 89, no. 4 (2017), pp. 772–811; A. J. Johnston, James D. Le Sueur, and Tyler Stovall, eds, *France Overseas: Studies in Empire and Decolonization* (Lincoln: University of Nebraska Press, 2017).

91. Donot, "Visite à un Hébdomadaire féminin: Elle."

92. Donot, "Visite à un Hébdomadaire féminin: Elle."

93. https://www.youtube.com/watch?v=JUrvbg3-nlM&list=PLsnV8xAP_cNit4cFhoSu_90vpjjgWhhnW&index=548. Accessed August 2, 2021.

94. Comment by George, posted on YouTube, March 2021, https://www.youtube.com/watch?v=tk-49n2jRdI. Accessed August 2, 2021.

95. "Marcelle Auclair Intérroge," *Dim Dam Dom*, 2e chaine, March 23, 1965.

96. "Marcelle Ségal répond," *Dim Dam Dom*, 2e chaine, July 28, 1965.

97. Desgroupes, "Ínterview, Marcelle Auclair," She explained that she received many thank-you notes without a return address, which she took to indicate that the writer did not expect her to reply.

Chapter 6

1. Ségal, *Mon métier*, p. 246; Armand Jammot, "L'amour au troisième age," *Aujourd'hui Madame*, A2/France 2, June 26, 1975.

2. Ségal, *Moi aussi*, pp. 120–121.

3. Ségal, *Moi aussi*, pp. 121–122, 125; Aside from the 1949 article about adopting "Christian" Ségal provided no personal information about her sons, protecting their privacy. A local town newsletter reported that she spent summers with them at her country home in Gouvieux, north of Paris, "Gens d'ici: Marcelle Ségal, le monument du magazine Elle," *Contact Gouvieux: Le mensuel de la ville de Gouvieux*, no. 240 (December 2016), p. 8.

4. Auclair and Prévost, *Mémoires à deux voix*, p. 167. Auclair's daughter Françoise pointed out the class differences in expectations. For working-class wives, "staying home represents... a social promotion." Marcelle had friends whose husbands prevented them working outside or developing a career.

5. Auclair, *A la grâce de Dieu*, p. 109.

6. Auclair and Prévost, *Mémoires à deux voix*, pp. 365, 372. His books for children included '*Passage Nord-Ouest* and *L'ile fantome*.' See also his obituary, "Michel Prévost," *Le Monde*, January 31, 1998; https://www.lemonde.fr/archives/article/1998/01/31/michel-prevost_3656677_1819218.html?random=1226828293. He also published novels under his own name, *Dierdre des chagrins* (Paris: Belfond, 1992), *Au dela du pont* (Paris: Robert Laffont, 1965), and translations of Federico Garcia-Lorca plays.

7. Auclair and Prévost, *Mémoires à deux voix*, pp. 364–365.

8. Given the bride's prominent family, the *New York Times* announced Alain and Helen's marriage, which took place on September 11, 1952. Archibald Alexander's sister-in-law married Henry Cabot Lodge Jr, clearly a well-connected family. *The New York Times*, June 27, 1952. In addition to their marriage on September 11, there are other coincidental date convergences in Auclair's family: Marcelle Auclair was born on November 11, twenty years earlier than the Armistice, and died on a final significant anniversary, June 6, D-Day, all coincidental but they jumped out to this historian of twentieth-century France!

9. Auclair and Prévost, *Mémoires à deux voix*, p. 377. Alain's novels include, *Le pont des absents, Le Chemin de vie, Le peuple impopulaire,* and *Bonne chance quand même!*

10. Auclair and Prévost, *Mémoires à deux voix*, pp. 373–374.

11. Auclair and Prévost, *Mémoires à deux voix*, p. 364. She hung out in the bars of St Germain-des-Près and saw performers like Juliette Greco and Boris Vian before they became famous.

12. Auclair and Prévost, *Mémoires à deux voix*, p. 375.

13. Adam Scovell, "Watch a cult classic # 9: Payroll," *British Film Institute* (January 14, 2021). In 1961, she also appeared in *Paris nous appartient* (*Paris Belongs to Us)* directed by Jacques Rivette, https://www.bfi.org.uk/features/watch-cult-classic-9-payroll. Accessed March 25, 2024.

14. They wrote the book as a series of dialogues, discussing key episodes in each of their lives, each one asking questions of the other. They used incidents from their lives to explain their personal development.

15. Auclair and Prévost, *Mémoires à deux voix*, p. 377.

16. Interview with Jean Victor Auclair Prevost (June 20, 2015).

17. Auclair and Prévost, *Mémoires à deux voix*, pp. 243–244, 236.

18. Auclair and Prevost, *Mémoires à deux voix*, p. 380. Etiolles is 27 km (17 miles) southeast of Paris.

19. Marcelle Auclair, *Vers une vieillesse heureuse* (Paris: Seuil, 1970), p. 11. Her mother moved into the Etiolles home and oversaw all things domestic becoming the house's "lion heart." Auclair and Prévost, *Mémoires à deux voix*, p. 424. There is also a Marcelle Auclair street in Montluçon, where she was born.

20. 38 km/24 miles northeast of Paris, near Chantilly.

21. Ségal, *Moi aussi*, pp. 131–134.

22. Ségal, *Moi aussi*, pp. 131–134.

23. Ségal, *Moi aussi*, pp. 131–134.

24. Ségal, *Moi aussi*, p. 117.

25. Ségal, *Moi aussi*, p. 137.

26. The town of Gouvieux included her in its 2016 newsletter, "Gens d'ici: Marcelle Ségal," *Contact Gouvieux* (December 2016), p. 8.

27. Ségal, *Mon métier*, p. 17. In a chapter titled "How I work" she explained that she works "in the most perfect disorder," p. 31.

28. Ségal, *Mon métier*, p. 45.

29. Ségal, *Mon métier*, pp. 51–52.

30. Ségal, *Mon métier*, p. 69.

31. Ségal, *Mon métier*, pp. 75–76.

32. Ségal, *Mon métier*, p. 89.

33. Ségal, *Mon métier*, p. 91.

34. Ségal, *Mon métier*, p. 93.

35. Ségal, *Mon métier*, p. 127.

36. Ségal, *Mon métier*, p. 132.

37. Ségal, "Courrier du Coeur," *Elle* (November 5, 1951), p. 52.

38. Ségal, *Mon métier*, pp. 159, 169.

39. Ségal, *Mon métier*, pp. 250–252.

40. Ségal, *Mon métier*, pp. 182–184.

41. Ségal, *Moi aussi*, pp. 111–112. About a decade after publishing this book, according to her great niece, Ségal developed a close relationship with the sculptor Philippe Asselin, Anne Brunswic, *Crown Letter* November 2–9, 2022; https://crownproject.art/?s=marcelle+s%C3%A9gal.

42. Ségal, *Moi aussi*, p. 149.

43. Marcelle Auclair, *La vie de Sainte Thérèse d'Avila: La dame errante de Dieu* (Paris: Seuil, 1950); A 2013 edition of the book is still available on Amazon. Auclair received a rarely granted permission to enter Carmelite cloisters in Spain to gather material.

44. Auclair, *A la grâce de Dieu*, p. 107.

45. Auclair, *A la grâce*, p. 152.

46. From the French Amazon page, attributed to *Le Figaro littéraire*, https://www.amazon.com/sainte-Th%C3%A9r%C3%A8se-dAvila-RELIGION-French-ebook/; On the English Amazon, book is "the most vivid existing biography of this great saint," https://www.amazon.com/Saint-Teresa-Avila-Marcelle-Auclair.

47. All three reviews are included on the Amazon page for the book. Of 26 ratings on Amazon, 84 percent are 5 stars. One of the comments from March 18, 2023: "Other than the saint's own writings, this book is the best novel I've read on St Teresa. I find it hard to put down;" https://www.amazon.com/gp/product/B00R35M8JG/ref=dbs_a_def_rwt_hsch_vapi_tkin_p1_i2.

48. Auclair and Prevost, *Mémoires à deux voix*, p. 152; Marcelle Auclair, *La vie de Jean Jaurès, ou, la France d'avant 1914* (Paris: Éditions du Seuil, 1954).

49. Simon described Auclair's Jaurès biography as a wager she took "and she won!" Pierre-Henri Simon, "Destin et philosophie de Jaurès, *Le Monde*, November 10, 1954, https://www.lemonde.fr/archives/article/1954/11/10/destin-et-philosophie-de-jaures_2027550_1819218.html.

50. Robert Coiplet, "*La vie de Jaurès* de Mme Marcelle Auclair," *Le Monde*, May 28, 1955, https://www.lemonde.fr/archives/article/1955/05/28/la-vie-de-jaures-de-mme-marcelle-auclair_1955478_1819218.html; A few years later in "Essais sur Jaurès de M. Georges Tétart," Coiplet described Auclair's biography, compared to Tétard's essays, as providing readers with "a living Jaurès." Coiplet, "Essais sur Jaurès de M. Georges Tétart," *Le Monde*, September 26, 1959, https://www.lemonde.fr/archives/article/1959/09/26/essais-sur-jaures-de-m-georges-tetard_2142798_1819218.html. That year, the 45th anniversary of Jaurès' death, a Society of Jaurassienes Studies was founded and Auclair's name was first on the non-alphabetical list of luminaries who were members. "Constitution d'une Société d'études Jauressiennes," *Le Monde*, July 7, 1959, https://www.lemonde.fr/archives/article/1959/07/07/constitution-d-une-societe-d-etudes-jauressiennes_2153367_1819218.html.

51. Marcelle Auclair, *Pour une jeune fille* (Paris: Amiot-Dumont, 1956); *Le Monde*, May 5, 1956, https://www.lemonde.fr/archives/article/1956/05/05/lectures-pour-une-jeune-fille_2255555_1819218.html.

52. Robert Kemp, "Les noces de sang," *Le Monde*, December 5, 1951, https://www.lemonde.fr/archives/article/1951/12/05/les-noces-de-sang_2070909_1819218.html, and April 20, 1963 Robert Kemp, "Dona Rosita. *Le Monde*, December 4, 1952, https://www.lemonde.fr/archives/article/1952/12/04/dona-rosita_2008041_1819218.html.

53. Robert Kemp, "Lorsque 5 ans seront passé de F.-G. Lorca, *Le Monde*, December 24, 1958, https://www.lemonde.fr/recherche/?search_keywords=Robert+Kemp&start_at=24%2F12%2F1958&end_at=25%2F12%2F1958&search_sort=date_asc. Pierre Drouin in a review of a radio 1951 broadcast of Garcia Lorca's play "Lorsque cinq ans seront passes" called Auclair's translation a "righteous adaptation." *Le Monde*, May 15, 1951, https://www.lemonde.fr/archives/article/1951/05/15/lorsque-cinq-ans-seront-passes-de-federico-garcia-lorca_2079819_1819218.html.

54. Claude Couderc and Thierry Nolin interview Marcelle Auclair, "Federico Garcia Lorca," *La vie est là*, RTF/ORTF 1ère Chaine, November 29, 1973.

55. She published the biography of Garcia Lorca in 1968. The following year, 1969, Paris Theatre put on Garcia Lorca's *Noces de Sang* (Blood Wedding) Auclair was interviewed on television about the play. Lise Elina, Max Favalelli, Paul-Louis Mignon, "Interview Marcelle Auclair et extraits de 'Noces de sang,'" *Les trois coups*, RTF/ORTF 1ère Chaine, March 22, 1969; In another interview about Garcia Lorca from 1973, Auclair described the circle she formed with a group of artists and authors including Bunuel, Dali, Neruda, a

"new Golden Age" in Spain that ended with Franco. Claude Couderc and Thierry Nolin interview Marcelle Auclair, "Federico Garcia Lorca."

56. Claude Couffon, "Revue: un poète secret et lumineux 'Enfances et Mort de Garcia Lorca," *Le Monde* (April 13, 1968), https://www.lemonde.fr/archives/article/1968/04/13/un-poete-secret-et-lumineux-enfances-et-mort-de-garcia-lorca_3066608_1819218.html; "Garcia Lorca quarante-cinq ans après," *Le Monde*, December 2, 1981. In a tribute to Garcia Lorca forty-five years after his death, Couffon referred readers to Auclair's book, "a moving and very complete autobiography... Everything has been said, in exactly the right words." https://www.lemonde.fr/archives/article/1981/12/02/garcia-lorca-quarante-cinq-ans-apres_2724452_1819218.html.

57. Auclair, *A la grâce*, p. 73.

58. Auclair, *A la grâce*, p. 74.

59. Auclair and Prévost, *Mémoires à deux voix*, pp. 240, 387.

60. Auclair and Prévost, *Mémoires à deux voix*, p. 240.

61. "A la grâce de Dieu," *Magazine du Dimanche*, RTF/ORTF1ère chaine, May 12, 1974.

62. Auclair, *A la grâce*, p. 75.

63. Auclair, *A la grâce*, p. 76.

64. Auclair, *A la grâce*, p. 153.

65. "A la grâce de Dieu," *Magazine du Dimanche*.

66. Marcelle Auclair, *Bernadette* (Paris: Desclee, 1958).

67. The group supported the May 13, 1958 attempted coup in Algeria. *Le Monde* accused the group of conducting witch hunts when it insisted that 80 percent of philosophy professors were communists, which *Le Monde* called 'the height of fantasy," "'L'esprit du 13 mai et la chasse aux sorcières," *Le Monde*, July 7, 1958, https://www.lemonde.fr/archives/article/1958/07/07/l-esprit-du-13-mai-et-la-chasse-aux-sorcieres_2295018_1819218.html.

68. Marcelle Auclair, *Le bonheur est en vous* (Paris: Seuil, 1938), most recent edition 2014; *Le pratique du bonheur* (Paris: Seuil 1956); *Le livre du bonheur* (Paris: Seuil 1959); most recent edition 2015. It still sells on Amazon and gets lots of reader comments, 74 percent of 164 ratings gave it 5 stars.

69. William W. Atkinson, *Vibration de la pensée: la loi d'attraction dans le monde de la pensée*, trans. Marcelle Auclair (Paris: Astra, 1984).

70. Auclair and Prévost, *Mémoires à deux voix*, p. 13.

71. Auclair, *A la grâce*, pp. 36–37, 38, 39, 40.

72. Auclair, *Le livre du bonheur*, p. 11.

73. Auclair, *A la grâce*, pp. 46–47.

74. Auclair, *A la grâce*, pp. 81–85.

75. Auclair, *A la grâce*, p. 40.

76. Auclair *A la grâce*, pp. 38–39.

77. Auclair, *Le livre du bonheur*, p. 28.

78. Auclair, *Le livre du bonheur*, pp. 34, 202.

79. Auclair, *Le livre du bonheur*, p. 87.

80. Auclair, *Le livre du bonheur*, pp. 52–53. See also pp. 43–44, 55, 88, 90–91.

81. Ségal, *Mon métier*, p. 235.

82. Ségal, *Mon métier*, p. 236.

83. Ségal, *Mon métier*, p. 237.

84. Ségal, *Mon métier*, p. 237.

85. Ségal, *Mon métier*, p. 246.

86. "Des intellectuels français s'élèvent contre les exécutions de Téhéran," *Le Monde*, October 27, 1954; "Un Appel au Roi de Grèce en faveur de Manolis Glezos," *Le Monde*, July 14, 1960; Manolis Glezos, a Greek intellectual and wartime Resistance hero, worked as a journalist, was arrested by the authorities, sentenced to death, and then imprisoned for life. He was released in 1962 owing to international protests and pressure, "Manolis Glezos obituary". *The Times*, April 21, 2020, https://www.thetimes.co.uk/article/manolis-glezos-obituary-d7r3qq8m6. Retrieved March 25, 2024; Auclair also took part in antinuclear activities, *Le Monde*, December 2, 1959; a march to the Mémorial Juif on the occasion of the Eichmann trial, "Manifestation à Paris le 23 avril devant le Mémorial Juif," *Le Monde*, April 19, 1961; and a protest against officers accused of torture, "La Protestation contre l'acquittement de trois officiers accusés de tortures," *Le Monde*, February 9, 1962.

87. Frédéric Mitterrand, "Magazine Marie-Claire," *Du côté de chez Fred*, Antenne 2, May 3, 1990; one guest, *Marie-Claire*'s editor-in-chief Hélène Mathieu noted that in 1961 Auclair "dared to write about clandestine abortions . . . something incredible in those days."

88. Greenwald describes it as a 'quiet activism that resulted in significant material changes for women in the two arenas where their lives were specifically affected because of their gender: the Civil Code and laws governing

access to reproductive freedom," in Lisa Greenwald, *Daughters of 1968: Redefining French Feminism and the Women's Liberation Movement* (Lincoln: University of Nebraska Press, 2018), p. 57.

89. Dr. A. Marchal and O. J. De Mero, *La liberté de la conception* (Lille: Medicis, 1935), pp. 1–14.

90. Haedrich, *Citizen Prouvost*, p. 144.

91. Auclair and Prévost, *Mémoires à deux voix*, pp. 381–382.

92. Marcelle Auclair, "Un grave problème: le contrôle des naissances," *Marie-Claire* (June 1956), p. 38.

93. Auclair and Prévost, *Mémoires à deux voix*, p. 383.

94. *Marie-Claire* (November 1960).

95. François Choyé, "Les Années Marie-Claire," Documentary, France 2, March 9, 2006.

96. Marcelle Auclair and Jeanne Dodemann, *Le livre noir de l'avortement* (Paris: Fayard, 1962), p. 13.

97. "Le Manifeste des 343," *Le Nouvelle Observateur* (April 5, 1971). Jeanne Dodemann, coauthor, had been Auclair's office manager, she collected and sorted the correspondence. See Haedrich, *Citizen Prouvost*, p. 145 on Dodemann's work with Auclair. Dodemann also wrote for *Marie-Claire*, co-authored *Qui est votre femme* with Auclair, and published a book on law for handicapped children. In the early '60s, she worked with the anti-racist group MRAP (movement contre le racism et pour l'amitiés des peoples). Catherine Lloyd's book *Discourses of Antiracism in France* (New York, Ashgate, 1998) has several pages on Dodemann, the MRAP and specifics on the abortion Manifesto of 343.

98. Isabelle Tournier and Danièle Voldman, eds., *La Bataille de l'avortement* (La Documentation française, 1986), p. 31.

99. Auclair and Dodemann, *Le livre noir de l'avortement*, pp. 13–15.

100. Auclair and Dodemann, *Le livre noir de l'avortement*, p. 14.

101. Auclair and Dodemann, *Le livre noir de l'avortement*, p. 80.

102. Auclair and Dodemann, *Le livre noir de l'avortement*, pp. 80–81.

103. Auclair and Dodemann, *Le livre noir de l'avortement*, p. 109.

104. Auclair and Dodemann, *Le livre noir de l'avortement*, p. 113.

105. Auclair and Dodemann, *Le livre noir de l'avortement*, pp. 180–186, 187–201.

106. Auclair and Dodemann, *Le livre noir de l'avortement*, pp. 202–208.

107. Auclair and Dodemann, *Le livre noir de l'avortement*, pp. 213–240.

108. Auclair and Dodemann, *Le livre noir de l'avortement*, pp. 238, 239, 240.

109. Greenwald argues that the book galvanized public opinion, *Daughters of 1968*, pp. 80–81; Tournier and Voldman on the other hand argued that Auclair's Livre noir had little impact, ending up in the pulp mill. Tournier and Voldman, *La Bataille*, p. 31.

110. Tournier and Voldman, *La Bataille*, p. 35.

111. The show continued until 1964, a precursor to Bernard Pivot's extremely popular book show *Apostrophes* that ran from 1975 to 1990.

112. Pierre Dumayet, Lectures pour tous, 1ere chaine, November 7, 1962.

113. Dumayet, Lectures pour tous.

114. Dumayet, Lectures pour tous.

115. Anne-Marie Dourlen-Rollier, *La verité sur l'avortement: Deux enquêtes inédites* (Paris: Librarie Malouine, 1963); review of *La verité sur l'avortement* in Escoffier-Lambiotte, "Pour une prophylaxis de l'avortement, *Le Monde*, May 10, 1963, https://www.lemonde.fr/archives/article/1963/05/10/ii-pour-une-prophylaxie-de-l-avortement_2213135_1819218.html.

116. Greenwald, *Daughters of 1968*, p. 81.

117. Katia D. Kaupp. "L'univers de l'avortement." *Le Nouvel Observateur*, April 22, 1965. https://www.nouvelobs.com/culture/20050422.OBS4812/l-univers-de-l-avortement.html. Accessed April 10, 2024; Tournier and Voldman, *Bataille*, pp. 31–32.

118. Haedrich, *Citizen Prouvost*, pp. 145–146.

119. Historian Bibia Pavard describes Auclair as the "instigator" "Contraception et avortement dans *Marie-Claire* (1955–1975): De la méthode des températures à la méthode Karman," *Le temps des médias* 12, no. 1 (2009), pp. 100–113, 104. "Marcelle Auclair pense qu'il faut en parler: le controle des naissances," *Marie-Claire* (August 1960); See also "Marcelle Auclair ouvre le dossier interdit," *Marie-Claire* (October 1961); issues of November 1960 and October 1961.

120. Pavard, "Contraception et avortement," pp. 100–113, 104.

121. "Controle des naissances: Marcelle Auclair lance le referendum de la derniere chance," Marcelle Auclair, "Les 20,000 confessions que j'emporte à Rome," *Marie-Claire* (October 1965); Pavard, "Contraception et avortement," p. 102; Catherine Durand wrote about the *Marie-Claire's* role in the struggle for

abortion rights, "Dans les archives de 'Marie Claire': soixante ans d'engagement en faveur de l'IVG," *Marie-Claire* (November 2022) online October 2022, https://www.marieclaire.fr/ivg-avortement-engagement-marie-claire,1434544.asp. See also Marie Hazan, "Le Fonctionnement de l'implicite dans les discours des magazines féminins. Analyse d'un exemple: la campagne pour le contrôle des naissances dans *Elle* et *Marie-Claire*," *Langage et société* no. 48 (1989), pp. 59–78.

122. Robert Barrat, "Monseigneur Veuillot," *Face à Face*, 1ère chaine, April 18, 1966.

123. Barrat, "Monseigneur Veuillot."

124. Barrat, "Monseigneur Veuillot."

125. Barrat, "Monseigneur Veuillot"; "Les declarations de l'archevêque coadjuteur," *Le Monde*, April 20, 1966, https://www.lemonde.fr/archives/article/1966/04/20/les-declarations-de-l-archeveque-coadjuteur_2696134_1819218.html.

126. Mitterrand, "Magazine Marie-Claire."

Chapter 7

1. Marcelle Auclair and Menie Grégoire, eds. *Femmes*, 2 vols. (Paris: Plon, 1967).

2. Jean Rostand, "Le Féminin est-il vraiment le sexe fort?," Grégoire and Auclair, *Femmes* I, pp. 18–29; Marie-Andrée Lagroua Weill-Hallé, "Liberté, responsabilité, contraception," and "Être mère: Un instinct ou un rôle social?" Grégoire and Auclair, *Femmes* I, pp. 68–75, 262–269.

3. Monique Berlioux, "Conquête du corps: sports et liberté"; Grégoire and Auclair, *Femmes* I, pp. 76–107; Jean Duché, "La beauté, le désir et l'imagination," Grégoire and Auclair, *Femmes* I, pp. 108–147.

4. Thérèse Kuoh Moukouy, "Beauté noir, hymne au désir et à la vie," Grégoire and Auclair, *Femmes* I, pp. 168–175.

5. Edward W. Said, *Orientalism* (New York: Vintage, 1979).

6. Andrée Chedid, "Beautés d'Orient, prisonnières et rêvées," Grégoire and Auclair, *Femmes* I, pp. 148–155; Jean Kheim, "Les femmes fleurs d'extrême orient," Grégoire and Auclair, *Femmes* I, pp. 156–167; Paul Mousset "Femmes brunes et mirages du pacifique," Grégoire and Auclair, *Femmes* I, pp. 176–183.

7. Simone Dreyfus, "Le mariage, la famille et les sociétés," Grégoire and Auclair, *Femmes* I, pp. 242–261.

8. Marcel Sacotte, "La prostituée est-elle une victime?," Grégoire and Auclair, *Femmes* I, pp. 312–325.

9. Romi, "Une deviation vieille comme la femme," Grégoire and Auclair, *Femmes* I, pp. 304–312.

10. Auclair, "Pleins feux sur les femmes," Grégoire and Auclair, *Femmes* I, p. 14.

11. Auclair, "Pleins feux," p. 15.

12. Lawrence Wylie, "L'Américaine, une déesse malheureuse"; Grégoire and Auclair, *Femmes* II, pp. 56–65; Ségal, "Trent-six façons de porter la culotte" Grégoire and Auclair, *Femmes* II, pp. 232–247; Auclair, "Des millions de femmes ont préférée Dieu," Grégoire and Auclair, eds. *Femmes* II, pp. 298–309.

13. Mark Kurlansky, in his book about 1968, explained the uprising in May '68 not as an attempted revolution, but as "an explosion against a suffocatingly stagnant society," Kurlansky, *1968: The Year that Rocked the World* (New York: Ballantine Books, 2004), pp. 228, 213–215.

14. Denise Dubois-Jallais, "Sous le balcon d'Albertine, cinq mois, une révolution éclate." *Elle Spéciale* (June 17, 1968), p. 10.

15. Hélène Gordon-Lazareff, *Elle Spéciale*, p. 6.

16. "Voici la crèche de la Sorbonne;" "La mode, c'est un choix," *Elle Spéciale*, pp. 22–25.

17. "Un pull d'été' à tricoter en côtes alternées," *Elle Spéciale*, p. 26.

18. "Le magazine féminin *Elle* fête cette année ses 70 ans," *La minute conso*, France Bleu, September 28, 2015; see "Gens d'ici: Marcelle Ségal, le monument du magazine *Elle*," *Contact Gouvieux* no. 240 (December 2016), np.

19. Auclair, "Les illusions de la haute société," *Le Monde*, October 4, 197[illegible].

20. Auclair, *Vers une vieillesse heureuse*, p. 11.

21. Simone de Beauvoir, *La vieillesse* (Paris: Gallimard, 1970).

22. Beauvoir, *La vieillesse*, p. 23.

23. Beauvoir, *La vieillesse*, p. 20.

24. Beauvoir, *La vieillesse*, p. 306.

25. Beauvoir, *La vieillesse*, pp. 301, 310.

26. Beauvoir, *La vieillesse*, p. 318.

27. Auclair, *Vers une vieillesse heureuse*, pp. 22–23.

28. Auclair, *Vers une vieillesse heureuse*, p. 26.

29. Auclair, *Vers une vieillesse heureuse*, p. 27.

30. Auclair, *Vers une vieillesse heureuse*, p. 35.

31. Auclair, *Vers une vieillesse heureuse*, p. 49.

32. Auclair, *Vers une vieillesse heureuse*, p. 35.

33. Auclair, *Vers une vieillesse heureuse*, pp. 38–39.

34. Auclair, *Vers une vieillesse heureuse*, p. 58.

35. Auclair, *Vers une vieillesse heureuse*, p. 71.

36. Auclair, *Vers une vieillesse heureuse*, p. 76.

37. Auclair, *Vers une vieillesse heureuse*, pp. 195–196, one of the first of its kind, his book on gastronomy became a classic, Jean-Anselm Brillat-Savarin, *Physiologie du gout, ou meditation de gastronomie transcendante; ouvrage theorique, historique et a l'ordre du jour, dedie aux gastronomie parisiens* (Paris: Sautelet, 1826).

38. Auclair, *Vers une vieillesse heureuse*, pp. 260–261.

39. Armand Jammot, "L'amour au troisième age," *Aujourd'hui Madame*, France 2, June 26, 1975.

40. Ségal, *Moi aussi*, p. 37.

41. Auclair, *Vers une vieillesse heureuse*, pp. 43–44.

42. Ségal, *Moi aussi*, p. 143.

43. Ségal, *Moi aussi*, p. 144.

44. Ségal, *Moi aussi*, p. 145.

45. Ségal, *Moi aussi*, p. 146.

46. Ségal, *Moi aussi*, p. 146.

47. Ségal, *Moi aussi*, pp. 149, 155.

Conclusion

1. Pauline Gallard, "Marcelle Auclair: au bonheur des dames," *Marie Claire*, 2022. The article uses the title of Emile Zola's novel *Au Bonheur des dames* (The Ladies' Paradise), https://www.marieclaire.fr/marcelle-auclair-journaliste,1435180.asp.

2. François Fourrier, "Quand Marcelle Ségal, grande prêtresse du « Courrier du cœur », réparait les âmes," *Le Nouvel obs* (March 17, 2023), https://www.nouvelobs.com/bibliobs/20230317.OBS70982/quand-marcelle-segal-grande-pretresse-du-courrier-du-c-ur-reparait-les-ames.html.

3. Julie Golia, *Newspaper Confessions: A History of Advice Columns in a Pre-Internet Age* (New York: Oxford University Press, 2021), p. 2.

4. William Walker Atkinson, *Vibration de la pensée: la loi d'attraction dans le monde de la pensée,* trans. Marcelle Auclair (Paris: Astra, 1934).

5. Samra-Martine Bonvoisin and Michèle Magnien, *La Presse Féminine* (Paris Presses Universitaires de France, 1980), p. 20.

6. "C'est quoi mon probleme?" https://www.youtube.com/watch?v=adiAf HAlPPA; ARTE radio's advice feature in 2018 was called "Elodie Font et Klaire fait Grr (Mycose the night) répond à vos questions;" "Allo Giulia," *Elle*, https://www.elle.fr/pages/La-redaction/Giulia-Fois.

7. "Moi, Lectrice: tous les témoignages des lectrices Marie Claire," *Marie Claire,* https://www.marieclaire.fr/recherche?q=moi+lectrice.

8. "Ministre de L'égalité femmes-hommes;" Lola Uguen, "#METOO. Enquête sur les violences sexualles chez les aides à domiicles," *Elle,* https://www.elle.fr/Societe/News/Aurore-Berge-de-nouveau-ministre-de-l-Egalite-femmes-hommes-qu-attendent-les-assos-feministes-et-LGBT-4295750; " La Cour des comptes recommande d'allonger le congé maternité d'un mois," *Elle*, https://www.elle.fr/Societe/News/La-Cour-des-comptes-recommande-d-allonger-le-conge-maternite-d-un-mois-4294407; « "Violences faites aux femmes : Il faut des juges spécialisés" réclame Anne-Cécile Mailfert," *Elle* (November 25, 2024), https://www.elle.fr/Societe/Interviews/Violences-faites-aux-femmes-Il-faut-des-juges-specialises-reclame-Anne-Cecile-Mailfert-4288348.

9. Gallard, "Marcelle Auclair."

10. Femmes engagés, *Marie Claire,* https://www.marieclaire.fr/,femmes-engagees,2610407.htm.

11. Vie Pro, *Marie Claire,* https://www.marieclaire.fr/vie-professionnelle-au-feminin,2615883.asp2.

12. "Gisèle Pelicot, Taylor Swift, Imane Khelif…24 femmes qui ont marqué 2024é 2024," *Marie Claire,* https://www.marieclaire.fr/femmes-qui-ont-marque-2024,1486395.asp; https://www.marieclaire.fr/ivg-avortement-contraception-etats-unis-risque-election-donald-trump,1485475.asp; Catherine Durand, "Reportage à Monpellier: le combat des mères solos," *Marie Claire,* November 8, 2024, https://www.marieclaire.fr/reportage-a-montpellier-le-combat-des-meres-solos,1483838.asp; https://www.marieclaire.fr/marie-claire-85-ans-engagement-nft-associations,1439294.asp.

13. In French the word *histoire* means both "story" and "history." NZ, "Mort de Marcelle Auclair, journaliste, biographe, moraliste," *Le Monde,* June 8, 1983 https://www.lemonde.fr/archives/article/1983/06/08/mort-de-marcelle-auclair-journaliste-biographe-moraliste_2827821_1819218.html.

14. Allain Salles, "Marcelle Ségal," *Le Monde*, December 30, 1998. https://www.lemonde.fr/archives/article/1998/12/30/marcelle-Ségal_3687782_1819218.html.

15. In March 2023, Paula gave it 5 stars on Amazon, calling it "A great read on an exceptional saint." https://www.amazon.com/Saint-Teresa-Avila-Marcelle-Auclair/dp/0932506674.

16. Ashifa Kassam, "Federico Garcia Lorca was killed on official orders, say 1960s police files," *The Guardian*, April 23, 2015, www.theguardian.com/culture/2015/apr/23/federico-garcia-lorca.

17. Guy Hedgecoe, "Lorca executed by Francoists at start of civil war, Poet was killed in 1936 on orders of troops loyal to Franco, police papers confirm," *Irish Times*, April 24, 2015. *Irish Times* mentioned Auclair's request as having led to the report. https://www.irishtimes.com/news/world/europe/lorca-executed-by-francoists-at-start-of-civil-war-1.2186941.

18. Laurence Doubinsky, Email to author, January 22, 2021.

BIBLIOGRAPHY

PRIMARY SOURCES

Atkinson, William Walker. *Thought Vibration or The Law of Attraction in the Thought World.* Chicago: The Library Shelf, 1908.

Atkinson, William Walker. *Vibration de la pensée: la loi d'attraction dans le monde de la pensée.* Trans. *Marcelle Auclair.* Paris: Astra, 1984.

Auclair, Marcelle. *L'Amour—notes et maxims.* Paris: Hachette, 1963.

Auclair, Marcelle. *Bernadette.* Paris: Bloud et Gay, 1957.

Auclair, Marcelle. *Le bonheur est en vous.* Paris: Seuil, 1938.

Auclair, Marcelle. *Connaissance de l'amour.* Paris: Plon, 1960.

Auclair, Marcelle. *Enfances et mort de Garcia Lorca.* Paris: Éditions du Seuil, 1968.

Auclair, Marcelle. *A la grâce de Dieu.* Paris: Seuil, 1973.

Auclair, Marcelle. *Le livre du bonheur.* Paris: Seuil, 1959.

Auclair, Marcelle. *Le mauvais cœur.* Paris: Seuil, 1957.

Auclair, Marcelle. *La novel adel amor doliente.* Santiago: Imprenta Universitaria, 1923.

Auclair, Marcelle. *Pour une jeune fille.* Paris: Amiot-Dumont, 1956.

Auclair, Marcelle. *Le pratique du bonheur.* Paris: Seuil, 1956.

Auclair, Marcelle. *Transparence.* Santiago de Chile: Imprenta Universitaria, 1919.

Auclair, Marcelle. *Vers une vieillesse heureuse.* Paris: Seuil, 1970.

Auclair, Marcelle. *La vie de Jean Jaurès, ou, la France d'avant 1914.* Paris: Seuil, 1954.

Auclair, Marcelle. *La vie de Sainte Thérèse d'Avila: La dame errante de Dieu.* Paris: Seuil, 1950.

Auclair, Marcelle and Françoise Prévost. *Mémoires à deux voix.* Paris: Seuil, 1978.

Auclair, Marcelle and Jeanne Dodemann. *Le livre noir de l'avortement.* Paris: Fayard, 1962.

Audoux, Marguerite. *Marie-Claire.* Paris: Editions Fasquelle, 1910.

Beauvoir, Simone de. *La Vieillesse*. Paris: Gallimard, 1970.

Bertin, Célia. *Le temps des femmes*. Paris: Hachette, 1959.

BNF Manuscripts Fonds Jean Prévost, NAF 26186.

Campbell, W. W. "Note on the Chile Earthquake of August 16th." *Publications of the Astronomical Society of the Pacific* 18, no. 111 (December 1906) pp. 313–314.

Dourlen-Rollier, Anne-Marie. *La vérité sur l'avortement: Deux enquêtes inédites.* Paris: Librairie Malouine, 1963.

Dutronc, Jacques. "Le Courrier du coeur." Side A Track 1. Disques Vogue, 1968.

Escoffier-Lambiotte. "Pour une prophylaxis de l'avortement." *Le Monde*, May 10, 1963. https://www.lemonde.fr/archives/article/1963/05/10/ii-pour-une-prophylaxie-de-l-avortement_2213135_1819218.html

Grégoire, Menie and Marcelle Auclair, eds. *Femmes*. 2 vols. Paris: Plon, 1967.

Kinsey, Alfred. *Sexual Behavior in the Human Female*. Philadelphia: W. B. Saunders, 1953.

Larbaud, Valery. *Lettres à Adrienne Monnier et à Sylvia Beach 1919–1933, correspondance établie et annotée par Maurice Saillet*. Paris: IMEC, 2004.

Larbaud, Valery. "Shakespeare and Company." *Le Navire d'argent*, May 1, 1925.

Lavisse, Ernest. *Histoire de France: cours élémentaire*. Paris: Armand Colin, 1913.

Lazareff, Pierre. *Deadline: The Behind-the-Scenes Story of the Last Decade in France*. New York: Random House, 1942.

Marchal, A. and O. J. De Mero. *La liberté de la conception*. Lille: Medicis, 193[illegible].

O'Neal, Paul. "Twin Lovelorn Advisors." *Life Magazine*. April 7, 1958, p. 100.

Prévost, Jean. *La création chez Stendhal: essai sur le métier d'écrire et le psychologie de l'écrivain*. Marseilles: Editions du Sagittaire, 1942.

Prévost, Jean. *Plaisirs des sports: essais sur le corps humain*. Paris: Editions de la Nouvelle revue française, 1925.

Ségal, Marcelle. *Moi aussi, j'étais seule*. Paris: Centurion/Grasset, 1971.

Ségal, Marcelle. *Mon métier, le courrier du cœur*. Paris: Horay, 1952.

Szajkowsi, Zosa. "The Growth of the Jewish Population of France (Concluded)." *Jewish Social Studies* 8, no. 4 (October 1946), pp. 300–314.

PERIODICALS/NEWSPAPERS

Elle

Femmes françaises

France-Soir

Journal de la femme

Marie-Claire

Le Monde
Navire d'Argent
New York Times
Nouvelle Observateur
Vrai visage

SECONDARY WORKS

Anderson, Margaret Cook. *Regeneration through Empire: French Pronatalists and Colonial Settlement in the Third Republic*. Lincoln: University of Nebraska Press, 2015.

Antonutti, Isabelle. *Cino Del Duca: De Tarzan à Nous Deux, itinéraire d'un patron de presse*. Rennes: Presses Universitaires de Rennes, 2012.

Aronson, Michael. *Troubled Waters: The Origins of the 1881 Anti-Jewish Pogroms in Russia*. Pittsburgh: University of Pittsburgh Press, 1990.

Atack, Margetet, Alison S. Fell, Diana Holmes, and Imogen Long, eds. *Making Waves: French Feminisms and Their Legacies 1975–2025*. Liverpool: Liverpool University Press, 2019.

Azéma, Jean-Pierre, Yves Durand, Denis Peschanski, and Dominique Veillon. Collaboration and Resistance: Images of Life in Vichy France 1940–1944. New York: Harry N. Abrams, 2000.

Bantigny, Ludivine. *1968: de grands soirs en petits matins*. Paris: Seuil, 2018.

Bauer, Nancy. *Simone de Beauvoir, Philosophy, and Feminism*. New York: Columbia University Press, 2001.

Beauvoir, Simone de. *La Vieillesse*. Paris: Gallimard, 1970.

Benstock, Shari. *Women of the Left Bank*. Austin: University of Texas Press, 1987.

Bernard, Jean-Pierre Arthur. *Paris rouge: 1944–1964: les communistes français dans la capitale*. Seyssel: Champ Vallon, 1991.

Bernard, Philippe and Henri Dubief. *The Decline of the Third Republic*. Trans. Anthony Forster. New York: Cambridge University Press, 1985.

Betts, Raymond F. *France and Decolonization: The Making of the Twentieth Century*. London: Red Globe Press, 1991.

Birnbaum, Pierre and Miriam Kochan. *Anti-Semitism in France: A Political History from Léon Blum to the Present*. Oxford: Blackwell Publishing, 1992.

Boittin, Jennifer Anne. *Colonial Metropolis: The Urban Grounds of Anti-imperialism and Feminism in Interwar Paris*. Lincoln: University of Nebraska Press, 2010.

Bonvoisin, Samra-Martine and Michèle Magnien. *La presse féminine*. Paris: Presses Universitaires de France, 1980.

Bredin, Jean-Denis. *The Affair: The Case of Alfred Dreyfus*. Paris: Brasiller, 1986.

Brée, Sandra, "Did the War Break Couples?: Marriage and Divorce in France During and After WWI." Sandra Brée and Saskia Hin, eds. *The Impact of World War I on Marriages, Divorces, and Gender Relations in Europe*. New York: Routledge, 2020, pp. 155–190.

Brody, Richard. *Everything is Cinema: The Working Life of Jean-Luc Godard*. New York: Henry Holt, 2008.

Brunswic, Anne. *Crown Letter*, November 2–9, 2022. https://crownproject.art/?s=marcelle+s%C3%A9gal

Brunswic, Anne. Godard's letter of 19 June 1964, From "Marcelle Ségal (8), une femme mariée." Crown Letter, February 22 to March 1, 2022. http://crownproject.art/anne-brunswic/

Brunswic, Anne. Marcelle (5), Courrier du Cœur 1948 in Crown Letter, January 11 to January 17, 2022. http://crownproject.art/anne-brunswic/

Brunswic, Anne. *Voyages avec l'absente*. Arles: Actes Sud, 2014.

Burch, Noël and Geneviève Sellier. *The Battle of the Sexes in French Cinema 1930–1956*. Trans. Peter Graham. Durham: Duke University Press, 2014.

Burrin, Philippe. *France under the Germans: Collaboration and Compromise*. Trans. Janet Lloyd. New York: The New Press, 1998

Cahill Ann, J. and Jennifer L. Hansen, eds. *French Feminists: Critical Evaluations in Cultural Theory*. New York: Routledge, 2008.

Capelle, Marc. *Jean Prouvost: Un patron du Nord, l'empereur de la presse Parisienne*. Paris: Vuibert, 2010.

Caron, Vicki. "The Antisemitic Revival in France in the 1930s The Socioeconomic Dimension Reconsidered." *Journal of Modern History* 70, no. 1 (1998), pp. 24–73.

Carré, Patrice A. "Uncertain Development. Diffusion of the Telephone in France before 1914." Trans. Liz Libbrecht, *Research: Communication-Technologie-Société* 1, no. 2 (Fall 1993), pp. 245–260.

Chabord, Marie-Thérèse. "Les archives des Chantiers de la jeunesse." *La Gazette des archives* 81 (1973), p. 85. doi:https://doi.org/10.3406/gazar.1973.2300. https://www.persee.fr/doc/gazar_0016-5522_1973_num_81_1_2300

Chafer, Tony. *The End of Empire in French West Africa: France's Successful Decolonization?* Oxford: Berg, 2002.

Choi, Sung-Eun. *Decolonization and the French of Algeria: Bringing the Settler Colony Home*. London: Palgrave MacMillan, 2015.

Coffin, Judith. *Sex, Love, and Letters: Writing Simone de Beauvoir*. Ithaca, NY: Cornell University Press, 2020.

Connolly, James E. *The Experience of Occupation in the Nord, 1914–18*. Manchester: Manchester University Press, 2018.

Cooper, Frederick. *Colonization and African Society: The Labor Question in French and British Africa*. New York: Cambridge University Press, 1996.

Delphy, Christine. "The Invention of French Feminism: An Essential Move." *Yale French Studies* No. 97, 50 Years of Yale French Studies: A Commemorative Anthology. Part 2: 1980–1998 (2000), pp. 166–197.

Denis, Broussolle. "L'Elaboration du Statut des juifs de 1940." *Le Genre Humain* 1, no. 30–31, (1996), pp. 115–139.

Diamond, Hannah. *Fleeing Hitler: France 1940*. New York: Oxford University Press, 2007.

Dubois-Jallais, Denise. *La Tzarine: Hélène Lazareff et l'aventure de "Elle."* Paris: Robert Laffont, 1984.

Duchen, Claire. *Feminism in France: From May '68 to Mitterrand*. Boston: Routledge & Kegan Paul, 1986.

Durand, Catherine. "Dans les archives de 'Marie Claire': soixante ans d'engagement en faveur de l'IVG." *Marie-Claire,* no. 842 (November 2022), online October 2022. https://www.marieclaire.fr/ivg-avortement-engagement-marie-claire,1434544.asp

Eveno, Patrick. "La presse en France depuis la Libération." *Le presse à la une, exposition,* April 11–July 15, 2012 at the BNF. http://expositions.bnf.fr/presse/arret/05.htm

Fishman, Sarah. *From Vichy to the Sexual Revolution: Gender and Family Life in Postwar France*. New York: Oxford University Press, 2017.

Fishman, Sarah. *We Will Wait: Wives of French Prisoners of War 1940–1945*. New Haven: Yale University Press, 1991.

Fitch, Noel Riley. *Sylvia Beach and the Lost Generation: A History of Literary Paris in the Twenties & Thirties*. New York: W. W. Norton, 1985.

Forestier, François. "Quand Marcelle Ségal, grande prêtresse du 'Courrier du cœur', réparait les âmes." *Le Nouvel Obs,* March 17, 2023. https://www.nouvelobs.com/bibliobs/20230317.OBS70982/quand-marcelle-segal-grande-pretresse-du-courrier-du-c-ur-reparait-les-ames.html

Fourastié, Jean. *Les trente glorieuses: ou la révolution invisible de 1946 à 1975*. Paris: Fayard, 1979.

Gallard, Pauline. "Marcelle Auclair : au bonheur des dames." *Marie Claire > Société > Femmes Engagées,* 2022.

Gallois, Anne. "La dame de coeur." *Le Monde.* August 16, 1982.

Garcin, Jérôme. *Pour Jean Prévost.* Paris: Gallimard, 1994.

"Gens d'ici: Marcelle Ségal, le monument du magazine Elle." *Contact Gouvieux: Le mensuel de la ville de Gouvieux* 6, no. 240 (December 2016), p. 8.

Gide, André. *Journal 1939–1942.* Paris: Gallimard, 1946.

Golia, Julie. *Newspaper Confessions: A History of Advice Columns in a Pre-Internet Age.* New York: Oxford University Press, 2021.

Goscha, Christopher. *The Road to Dien Bien Phu: A History of the First War for Vietnam.* Princeton: Princeton University Press, 2022.

Greenwald, Lisa. *Daughters of 1968: Redefining French Feminism and the Women's Liberation Movement.* Lincoln: University of Nebraska Press, 2018.

Guilhaumou, Jacques. "Mémoires d'un étudiant en mai 1968: le flux des manifestations et le protagoniste de l'évènement." *Le mouvement social* 233, no. 1 (May 2010), pp. 165–181.

Haedrich, Marcel. *Citizen Prouvost: Le portrait incontournable d'un grand patron de la presse française.* Paris: Filipacchi, 1995.

Hansen, Gladys and Emmet Condon. *Denial of Disaster.* Petaluma, CA: Cameron and Co, 1989.

Hayhurst, J. D. *The Pneumatic Post of Paris.* C. S. Holder, ed. Digital format Mark Hayhurst, Copyright © 1974. The France & Colonies Philatelic Society of Great Britain. https://www.cix.co.uk/~mhayhurst/jdhayhurst/pneumatic/book2.html. Accessed August 21, 2019.

Hazan, Marie. "Le fonctionnement de l'implicite dans les discours des magazines féminins. Analyse d'un exemple: la campagne pour le contrôle des naissances dans *Elle* et *Marie-Claire.*" *Langage et société*, no. 48 (1989), pp. 59–78.

Hedgecoe, Guy. "Lorca Executed by Francoists at Start of Civil War, Poet was Killed in 1936 on Orders of Troops Loyal to Franco, Police Papers Confirm." *Irish Times,* April 24, 2015. https://www.irishtimes.com/news/world/europe/lorca-executed-by-francoists-at-start-of-civil-war-1.2186941. Accessed August 22, 2021.

Hendrickson, Burleigh. *Decolonizing 1968: Transnational Student Activism in Tunis, Paris, and Dakar.* Ithaca: Cornell University Press, 2022.

Hyman, Paula. *From Dreyfus to Vichy: The Remaking of French Jewry, 1906–1939.* New York: Columbia University Press, 1979.

"Il y a 140 ans naissait Victor Auclair (1866–1928)" *Commentry.* Espace Culturelle de la Pléade, 2006.

Jobs, Richard. *Riding the New Wave: Youth and the Rejuvenation of France after the Second World War.* Stanford: Stanford University Press, 2007.

Jobs, Richard. "Tarzan Under Attack: Youth, Comics, and Cultural Reconstruction in Postwar France." *French Historical Studies* 26, no. 4 (Fall 2003), pp. 687–725.

Johnston, A. J., James D. Le Sueur, and Tyler Stovall, eds. *France Overseas: Studies in Empire and Decolonization*. Lincoln: University of Nebraska Press, 2017.

Joseph-Gabriel, Annette K. *Reimagining Liberation: How Black Women Transformed Citizenship in the French Empire*. Urbana: University of Illinois Press, 2020.

Kantor, Elizabeth. "The Weekend with the Friedman Twins" *Washington Post*, June 23, 1986. https://www.washingtonpost.com/archive/lifestyle/1986/06/23/the-weekend-with-the-friedman-twins/186b34b3-9322-4899-852f-99edd1e4234c/. Accessed May 25, 2021.

Kaplan, Alice. *The Collaborator: The Trial and Execution of Robert Brasillach*. Chicago: University of Chicago Press, 2000.

Kaplan, Alice. "Ghostly Demarcations: On Ramon Fernandez." *The Nation*, February 15, 2010. https://www.thenation.com/article/archive/ghostly-demarcations-ramon-fernandez/. Accessed March 9, 2024.

Kassam, Ashifa. "Federico Garcia Lorca was Killed on Official Orders, Say 1960s Police Files." *The Guardian*, April 23, 2015. www.theguardian.com/culture/2015/apr/23/federico-garcia-lorca. Accessed June 8, 2015.

Klier, John Doyle. *Russian Jews and the Pogroms of 1881–1882*. Cambridge: Cambridge University Press, 2011.

Koreman, Megan. *The Expectation of Justice: France, 1944–1946*. Durham: Duke University Press, 2000.

Kurlansky, Mark. *1968: The Year That Rocked the World*. New York: Random House, 2005.

Lloyd, Catherine. *Discourses of Antiracism in France*. New York: Ashgate, 1998.

Long, Imogen. *"A Powerful Political Platform: Françoise Giroud and L'Express in a Cold War Climate."* French History 30, no. 2 (June 2016), pp. 241–258.

Lorcin, Patricia M. E. and Todd Shepard, eds. *French Mediterraneans: Transnational and Imperial Histories*. Lincoln: University of Nebraska Press, 2016.

Mallaval, Catherine. "Marie-Claire un demi-siècle engagé." *Libération*, September 17, 2004. https://www.liberation.fr/medias/2004/09/17/marie-claire-un-demi-siecle-engage_492770. Accessed March 8, 2019.

Mapping Expatriate Paris: The Shakespeare and Company Lending Library Project (MEP). https://mep.princeton.edu/shakespeare-and-company

Marrus, Michael. *Les juifs de France à l'époque de l'affaire Dreyfus*. Paris: Complexe, 1972.

Marrus, Michael and Robert Paxton. *The Politics of Assimilation: A Study of the French Jewish Community at the Time of the Dreyfus Affair*. New York: Oxford University Press, 1981.

Martland, Samual. "Reconstructing the City, Constructing the State: Government in Valparaiso after the Earthquake of 1906." *Hispanic American Historical Review* 87, no. 2 (2006), pp. 221–254.

McDougal, James. "The Impossible Republic: The Reconquest of Algeria and the Decolonization of France, 1945–1962." *The Journal of Modern History* 89, no. 4 (2017), pp. 772–781.

Mouré, Kenneth. *Marché Noir: The Economy of Survival in Second World War France*. New York: Cambridge University Press, 2023.

Muel-Dreyfus, Francine. *Vichy and the Eternal Feminine*. Trans. Kathleen A. Johnson. Durham: Duke University Press, 2001.

Murat, Laure. *Passage de l'Odéon: Sylvia Beach, Adrienne Monnier et la vie littéraire à Paris dans l'entre-deux-guerres*. Paris: Gallimard, 2005.

Naylor, Phillip C. *France and Algeria: A History of Decolonization and Transformation*. Gainesville: University Press of Florida, 2000.

Offen, Karen. *European Feminisms, 1700–1950: A Political History*. Stanford: Stanford University Press, 2000.

Pagis, Julie. *May '68: Shaping Political Generations*. Amsterdam: Amsterdam University Press, 2018.

Pavard, Bibia. "Contraception et avortement dans *Marie-Claire (1955–1975)*: de la méthode des températures à la méthode Karman." *Le temps des médias*, 1, no. 12 (2009), pp. 100–113.

Paxton, Robert. *Vichy France: Old Guard and New Order*. New York: W. W. Norton, 1972.

Perrin, Francine. "El concreto armado en Santiago." blog post, September 15, 2008. http://1.bp.blogspot.com/_-TJK2XwO0ns/SM7M-OoQXel/AAAAAAAAAoA/NDONLYktsUQ/s1600-h/L1020498

Perrin, Francine. "La fondatrice de 'Marie-Claire' a grandi au Chili." *Le petit journal-Santiago*. June 23, 2008.

Phelizon, Michel. "Du Journal des Dames à Marie-Claire." in *Revue de l'action social et des collectivités* (January–February 1973).

Pollard, Miranda. *Reign of Virtue: Mobilizing Gender in Vichy France, 1940–1944*. Chicago: University of Chicago Press, 1998.

Prévost, Michel. *Retrouver Jean Prévost: romancier, critique, essayiste et journaliste*. Grenoble: Presses Universitaires de Grenoble, 2002.

Prost, Antoine. "Public and Private Spheres in France." *A History of Private Life, Volume V: Riddles of Identity in Modern Times*. Antoine Prost, Gérard Vincent, and Arthur Goldhammer, eds. Cambridge: Belknap Press of Harvard University Press, pp. 1–143.

Reynolds, Sian. "Before *Les Femmes s'entêtent*: The 'Bermuda Triangle' of French Feminism?" *Making Waves: French Feminisms and Their Legacies 1975–2025*. Margeret Atack et al., eds. Liverpool: Liverpool University Press, 2019.

Said, Edward W. *Orientalism*. New York: Vintage, 1979.

Sapiro, Gisèle. *The French Writers' War, 1940–1953*. Trans. Vanessa Doriott Anderson and Dorrit Cohn. Durham: Duke University Press, 2014.

Scheck, Raffael. *Literature, Ethics, and Decolonization in Postwar France: The Politics of Disengagement*. New York: Cambridge University Press, 2015.

Schrier, Joshua. *Arabs of the Jewish Faith: The Civilizing Mission in Colonial Algeria*. New Brunswick: Rutgers University Press, 2010.

Seidman, Michael. *The Imaginary Revolution: Parisian Students and Workers in 1968*. New York: Berghahn, 2004.

Seton-Watson, H. "Two Contrasting Policies toward Jews: Russia and Hungary." *Jews and Non-Jews in Eastern Europe, 1918–1945*. B. Vago and G. L. Mosse, eds. New York: Wiley, 1974, pp. 99–112.

Shapiro, Samantha M. "They Lives They Lived: Abigail Van Buren." *The New York Times*, December 21, 2013. https://www.nytimes.com/news/the-lives-they-lived/2013/12/21/abigail-van-buren

Shepard, Todd. *The Invention of Decolonization: The Algerian War and the Remaking of France*. Ithaca: Cornell University Press, 2006.

Simmonet, Stéphane. *Les poches de l'Atlantique: Les batailles oubliées de la Libération janvier 1944-mai 1945*. Paris: Tallandier, 2019.

Simpson, Mark S. "The 'Svyaschonnaya druzhina' and Jewish Persecution in Tsarist Russia." *New Zealand Slavonic Journal*, no. 2 (1978), pp. 17–26.

Smith, Andrew W. M. and Chris Jeppesen, eds. *Britain, France and the Decolonization of Africa: Future Imperfect?* London: UCL Press, 2017.

Smith, Denis. *San Francisco Is Burning: The Untold Story of the 1906 Earthquake and Fires*. New York: Viking, 2005.

Soulier, Vincent. *Presse féminine: La puissance frivole*. Paris: Editions Archipel, 2008.

Stanley, Adam. *Modernizing Tradition: Gender and Consumerism in Interwar France and Germany*. Baton Rouge: LSU Press, 2008.

Sweatman, Jennifer L. *The Risky Business of French Feminism: Publishing, Politics, and Artistry*. Lanham, MD: Lexington Books, 2014.

Théofilakis, Fabien, ed. *Les prisonniers de guerre français en 40*. Paris: Fayard, 2022.

Tournier, Isabelle and Danièle Voldman. *La bataille de l'avortement*. Paris: La documentation française, 1986.

USGS. "Casualties and damage after the 1906 Earthquake." Earthquake Hazards Program. https://earthquake.usgs.gov/earthquakes/events/1906calif/18april/casualties.php

Valderrama, Loren B. "Seismic Forces and State Power: The Creation of the Chilean Seismological Service at the Beginning of the Twentieth Centrey." *Historical Social Research*, 40, no. 2 (January 2015), pp. 81–104.

Veillon, Dominque. "Ésthétique et representations de la femme à travers la presse féminine (*Marie-Claire et Elle*, 1958–1975)." *Les années 68: événements, cultures, politiques et modes de vie*. Lettre d'information, no. 2[illegible] (June 9, 1997), p. 3.

Vince, Natalya. *Our Fighting Sisters: Nation, Memory and Gender in Algeria 1954–2012*. Manchester: Manchester University Press, 2015.

Virgili, Fabrice. *Shorn Women: Gender and Punishment in Liberation France*. Trans. John Flower. New York: Berg, 2002.

Vulser, Nicole. "*Marie-Claire*: Une histoire de famille." *Le Monde*, February 1[illegible], 2001.

Weber, Peter. "13 of Dear Abby's Best Zingers." *The Week*, January 8, 2015. https://theweek.com/articles/468550/13-dear-abbys-best-zingers. Accessed May 26, 2021.

TELEVISION BROADCASTS

Barrat, Robert, "Monseigneur Veuillot." *Face à Face*, April 18, 1966 1ère chaine.

Choyé, François, Director. *Les Années Marie-Claire*, March 9, 2006. France 2.

Couderc, Claude and Thierry Nolin, "Interview, Marcelle Auclair, Federico Garcia Lorca." *La vie est là*, November 29, 1973. 1ère Chaine.

Desgraupes, Pierre. "Connaissance de l'Amour." *Lectures pour Tous*, October [illegible], 1960. 1ère chaine.

Donot, Jacques "Visite à un Hébdomadaire féminin: Elle." *Visite à*, October 5, 1954. 1ère chaine.

Dumayet, Pierre, "Marcelle Auclair: Le livre noir de l'avortement." *Lectures pour tous*, November 7, 1962. 1ère chaine.

Jammot, Armand. "L'amour au troisième age." *Aujourd'hui Madame*, June [illegible], 1975 2e chaine.

Hendrix, Jimi. *Dim Dam Dom,* 2e chaine, October 10, 1967. https://www.youtube.com/watch?v=JUrvbg3-nlM&list=PLsnV8kAP_cNit4cFhoSu_90vpjjgWhhnW&index=548

"Marcelle Auclair, A la Grace de Dieu." *Magazine du Dimanche,* May 12, 1974. 1ère chaine.

"Marcelle Auclair interroge." *Dim Dam Dom,* March 28, 1965. 2e chaine.

"Marcelle Auclair répond." *Dim Dam Dom,* April 30, 1965. 2e chaine.

"Marcelle Ségal répond." *Dim Dam Dom,* September 24, 1965. 2e chaine.

Mitterrand, Frédéric. "Magazine Marie-Claire." *Du côté de chez Fred,* May 3, 1990. Antenne 2.

Schofield, Hugh. "The WW2 Soldiers France has forgotten." *BBC News,* Paris, June 4, 2015. https://www.bbc.com/news/magazine-32956736. Consulted February 14, 2024

INDEX

Note: Figures are indicated by an italic *f*.

For the benefit of digital users, indexed terms that span two pages (e.g., 52–53) may, on occasion, appear on only one of those pages.